HEROES OF FLIGHT

WHO CHANGED THE WORLD

First edition for the United States and Canada published in 2019
by B.E.S. Publishing Co.

All inquiries should be addressed to:
B.E.S. Publishing Co.
250 Wireless Boulevard
Hauppauge, NY 11788
www.bes-publishing.com

ISBN: 978-1-4380-1198-1

Library of Congress Control No.: 2018959956

Conceived, designed, and produced by The Bright Press,
an imprint of The Quarto Group.
The Old Brewery, 6 Blundell Street,
London, N7 9BH, United Kingdom
T (0) 20 7700 6700 F (0) 20 7700 8066
www.QuartoKnows.com

Publisher: Mark Searle
Creative Director: James Evans
Managing Editor: Jacqui Sayers
Editor: Judith Chamberlain
Project Editor: Natalia Price-Cabrera
Art Director: Katherine Radcliffe
Design: Lyndsey Harwood and Geoff Borin

Date of Manufacture: December 2018
Manufactured by: Hung Hing Printing, Shenzhen, China

Printed in China

9 8 7 6 5 4 3 2 1

HEROES OF FLIGHT

WHO CHANGED THE WORLD

ILLUSTRATED BY JADE SARSON

CONSULTANT EDITOR DAN GREEN

B.E.S.
PUBLISHING

CONTENTS

GEORGE CAYLEY
British (1773–1857)

Meet George Cayley, the gentleman scientist who kicked off the story of flying machines. Often called the "Father of Aviation," Cayley figured out the physical forces that move a wing in flight and how heavier-than-air planes could fly. This clever experimenter also made the first unpowered, manned flight.

OTTO LILIENTHAL
German (1848–1896)

This German flying ace was known as the "Glider King." Inspired by watching birds, Otto and his brother built gliders made of lightweight wood and canvas, and launched them from the top of a steep hill. Like an early YouTuber, Lilienthal captured many of his 2,000 flights on film.

WILBUR & ORVILLE WRIGHT
American (1867–1912; 1871–1948)

The world's most famous duo of flying heroes, Wilbur and Orville Wright were the first to achieve the dream of powered flight. These bicycle-mad brothers built the first airplane and got it off the ground at Kitty Hawk, North Carolina, in 1903.

ALBERTO SANTOS–DUMONT
Brazilian (1873–1932)

This balloon-building Brazilian spent years in Paris making lighter-than-air aircraft and dreaming of his own powered, heavier-than-air machine. In 1906, when he eventually achieved that goal, it was widely thought that he had made the world's first manned, powered flight in the world. Sadly for him, the Wright brothers had beaten him to it.

LOUIS BLÉRIOT
French (1872–1936)

After many failed attempts making aircraft with flapping wings, French adventurer and inventor Louis Blériot hand-built his own fixed-wing airplanes and entered competitions. He achieved instant celebrity status when he became the first person to fly across the English Channel in 1909.

AMELIA EARHART
American (1897–1937; disappeared)

Amelia Earhart was hooked on flying from an early age and set many new records, including becoming the first woman to fly across the Atlantic Ocean. With her career soaring, Earhart was determined to fly solo around the world. However, this adventure-loving aviation pioneer never returned from her attempt to do so in 1937.

IGOR SIKORSKY
Russian–American (1889–1972)

Igor Sikorsky is an important person in the story of the conquest of the skies. This Russian whiz kid built planes and later designed mass-produced aircraft. His big breakthrough was solving the tricky problem of making a working helicopter. His designs have been replicated and now helicopters rescue thousands of people all around the world.

FRANK WHITTLE
British (1907–1996)

Meet Frank Whittle, the pint-sized dreamer with a vision for a powerful new engine. While studying and training as a pilot, the British airman invented the turbojet engine. Whittle's invention allowed airplanes to fly long distances at high altitudes, where air resistance is lower.

CHUCK YEAGER
American (1923–present)

Be thrilled by the daredevil exploits of this American flying ace. Chuck Yeager was a "top gun" fighter pilot during World War II who went on to test the U.S. Air Force's experimental airplanes. He became the first person to travel faster than the speed of sound in an aircraft. Yeager certainly loved things to go fast!

GEORGE CAYLEY
(1773–1857)
THE FATHER OF AVIATION

AS A SCHOOLBOY, GEORGE TRIED TO UNDERSTAND THE PRINCIPLES OF FLIGHT. AT AGE 26, GEORGE FIGURED OUT THE PHYSICS BEHIND FLYING A HEAVIER-THAN-AIR FLIGHT.

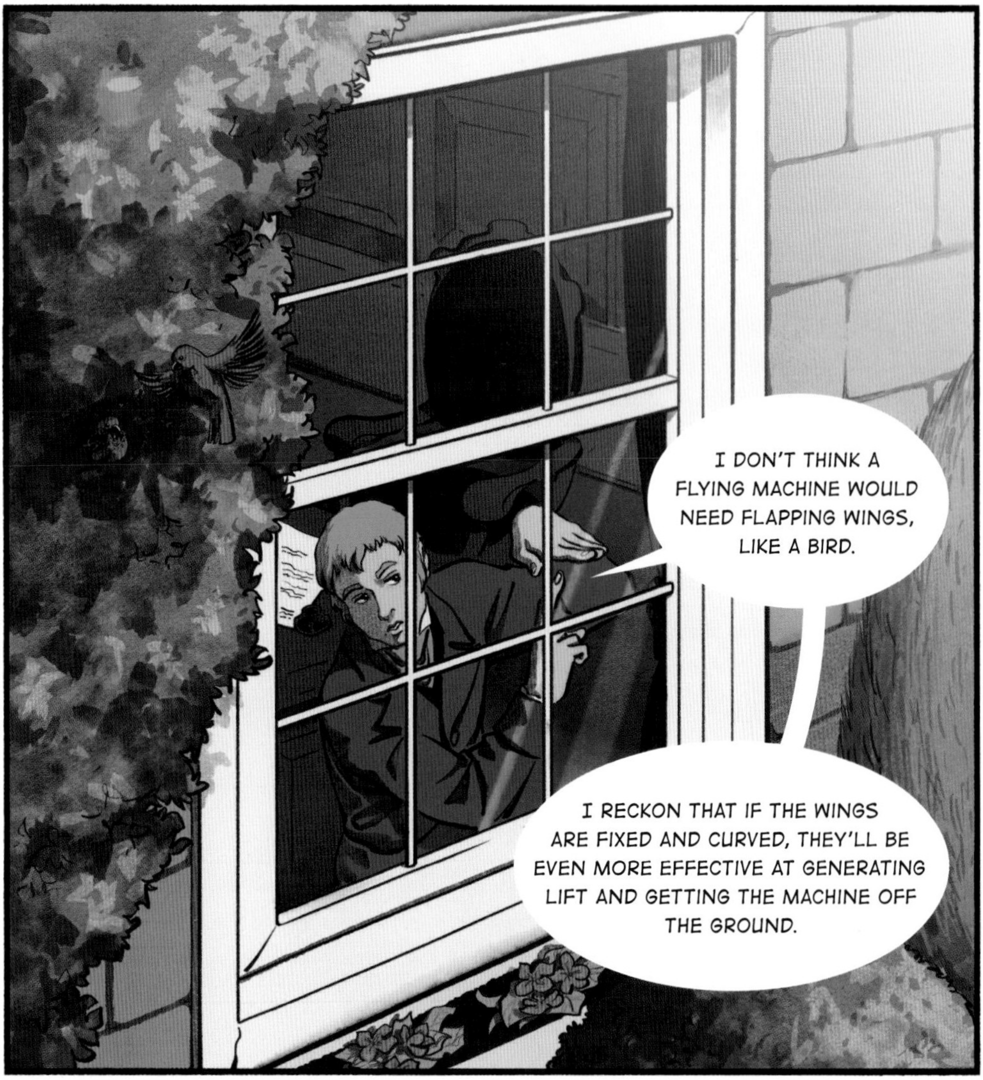
I DON'T THINK A FLYING MACHINE WOULD NEED FLAPPING WINGS, LIKE A BIRD.
I RECKON THAT IF THE WINGS ARE FIXED AND CURVED, THEY'LL BE EVEN MORE EFFECTIVE AT GENERATING LIFT AND GETTING THE MACHINE OFF THE GROUND.

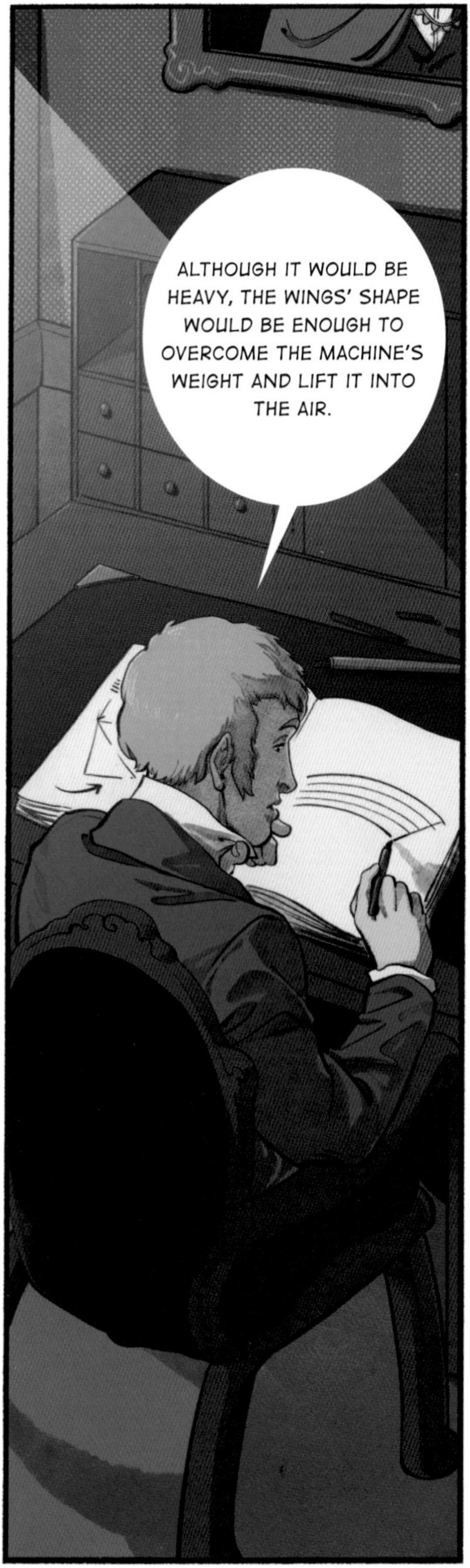
ALTHOUGH IT WOULD BE HEAVY, THE WINGS' SHAPE WOULD BE ENOUGH TO OVERCOME THE MACHINE'S WEIGHT AND LIFT IT INTO THE AIR.

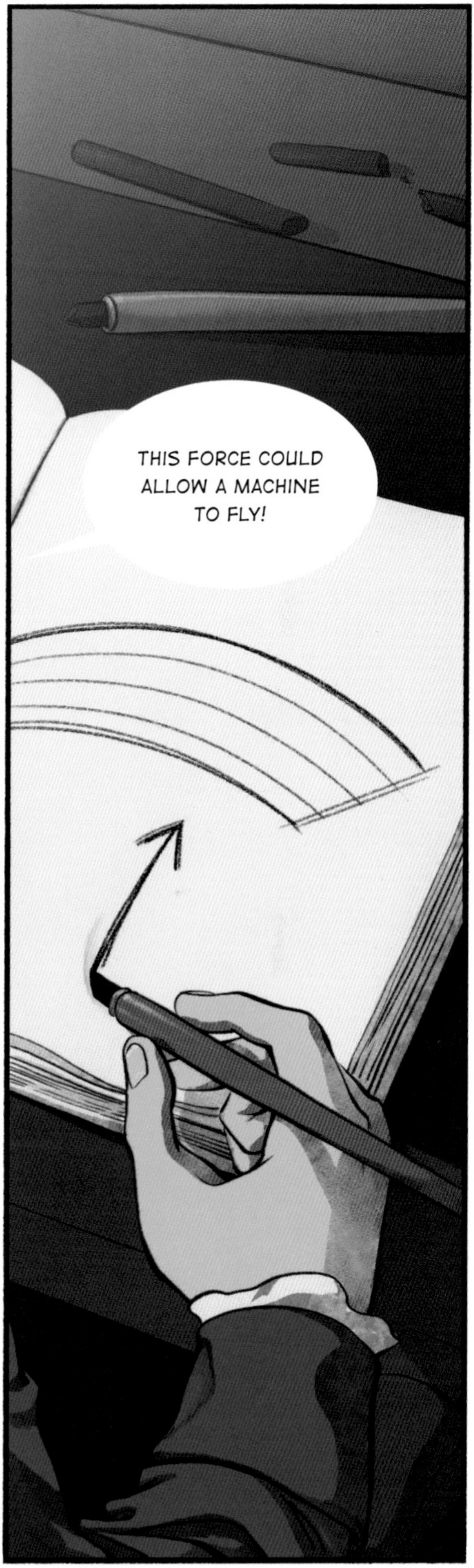
THIS FORCE COULD ALLOW A MACHINE TO FLY!

CONVINCED OF HIS IDEAS, GEORGE ENGRAVED THEM INTO A SILVER MEDALLION. HIS ETCHING IS NOW CONSIDERED THE FIRST RECORDED DRAWING OF A MODERN AIRPLANE.

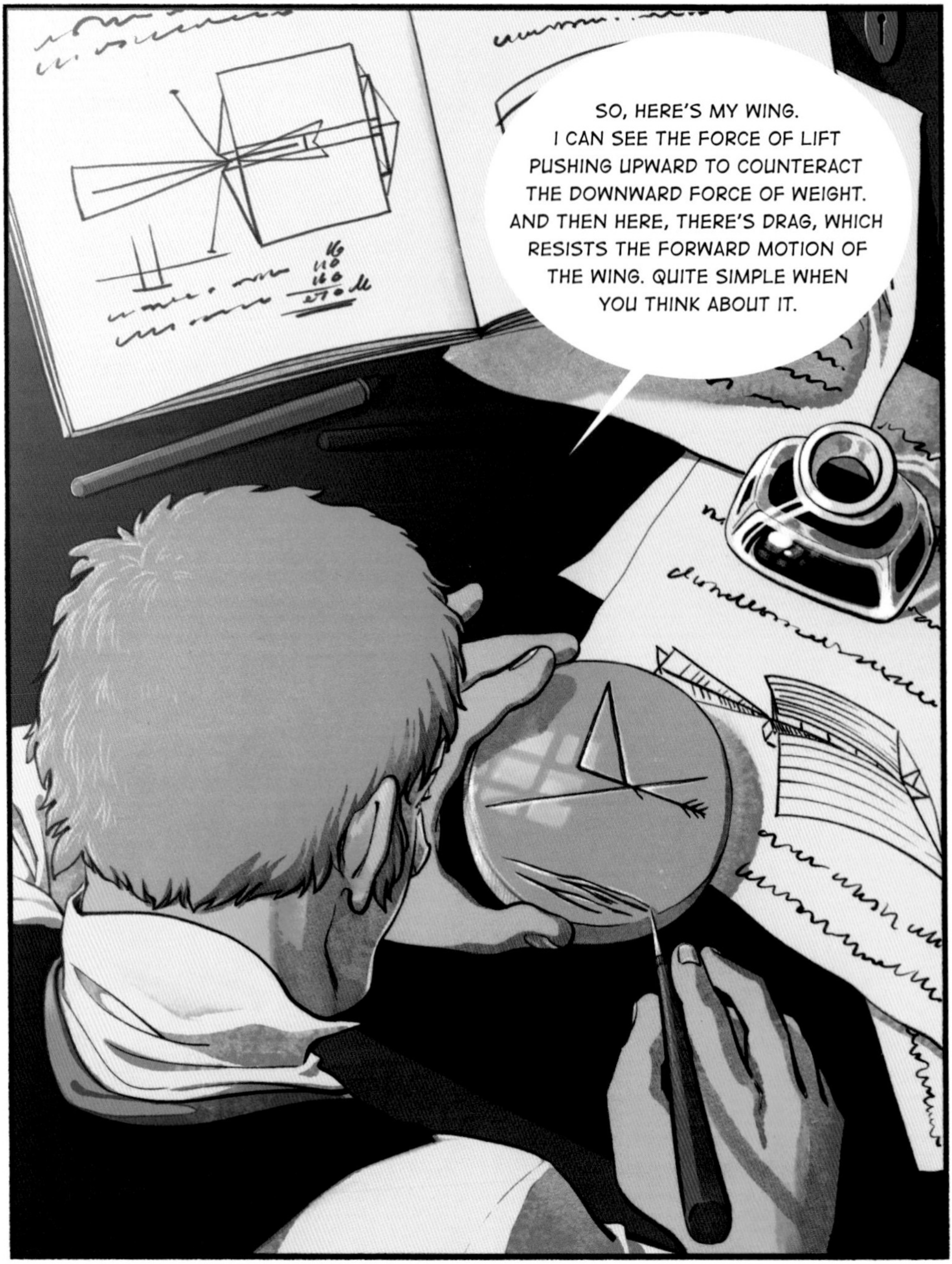
SO, HERE'S MY WING. I CAN SEE THE FORCE OF LIFT PUSHING UPWARD TO COUNTERACT THE DOWNWARD FORCE OF WEIGHT. AND THEN HERE, THERE'S DRAG, WHICH RESISTS THE FORWARD MOTION OF THE WING. QUITE SIMPLE WHEN YOU THINK ABOUT IT.

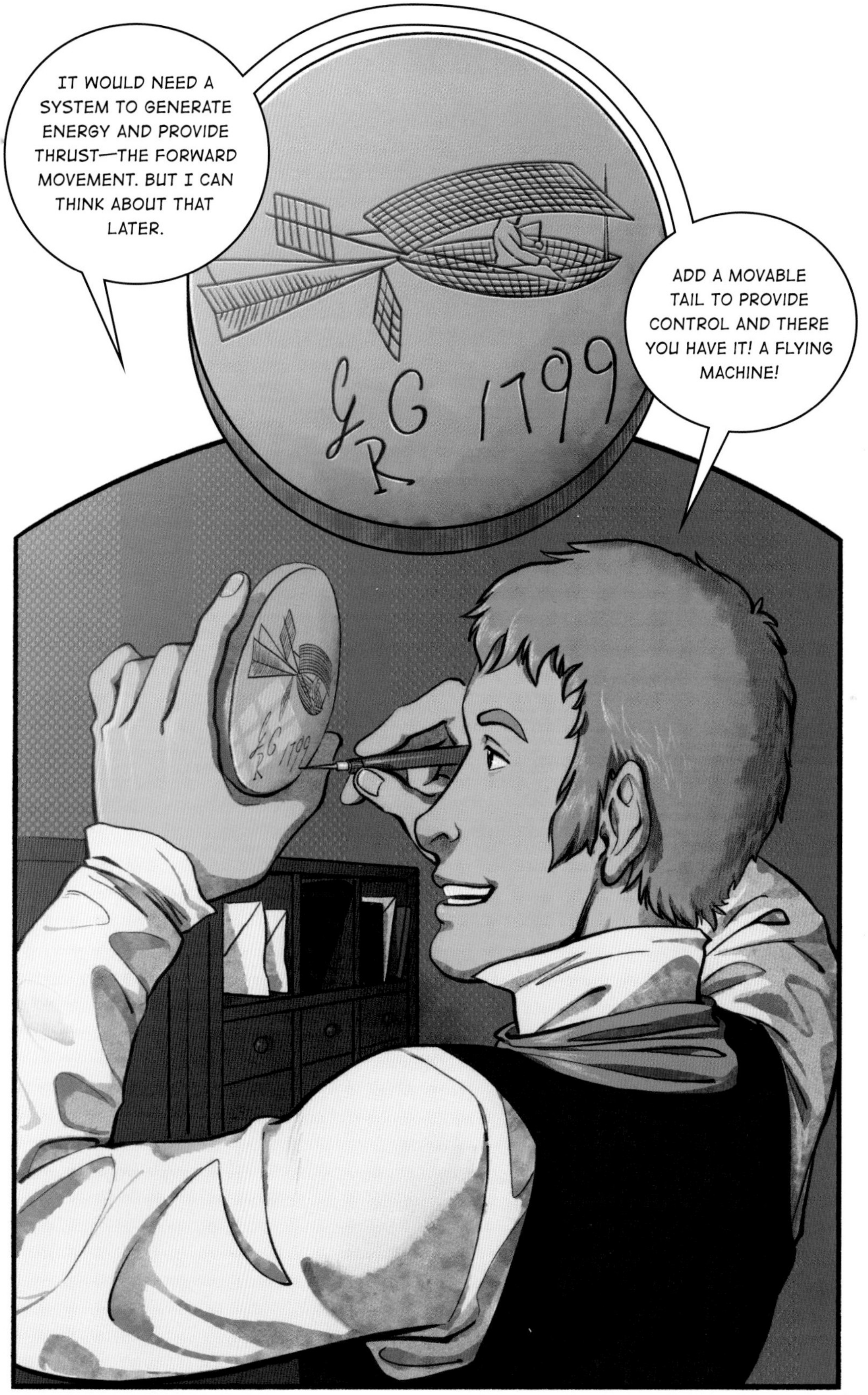
IT WOULD NEED A SYSTEM TO GENERATE ENERGY AND PROVIDE THRUST—THE FORWARD MOVEMENT. BUT I CAN THINK ABOUT THAT LATER.
ADD A MOVABLE TAIL TO PROVIDE CONTROL AND THERE YOU HAVE IT! A FLYING MACHINE!
GR G 1799

IN 1804, GEORGE BUILT A SUCCESSFUL MINIATURE GLIDING MACHINE LIKE THE ONE ENGRAVED ON HIS SILVER MEDALLION. IT HAD A SINGLE WING AND A MOVING TAIL. THOUGH SMALL, IT WAS THE FIRST RECORDED FIXED-WING AIRCRAFT CAPABLE OF FREE FLIGHT.

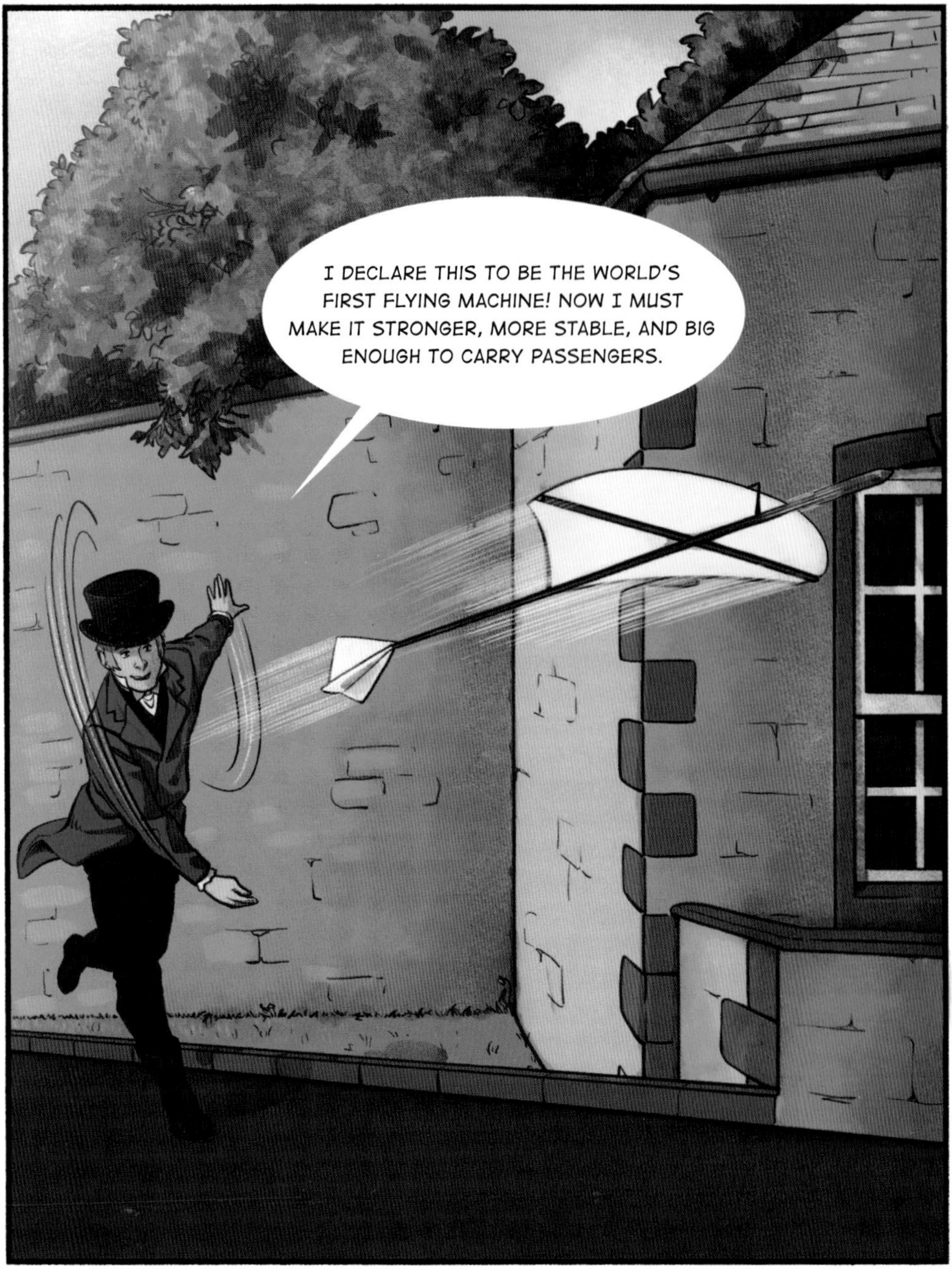
I DECLARE THIS TO BE THE WORLD'S FIRST FLYING MACHINE! NOW I MUST MAKE IT STRONGER, MORE STABLE, AND BIG ENOUGH TO CARRY PASSENGERS.

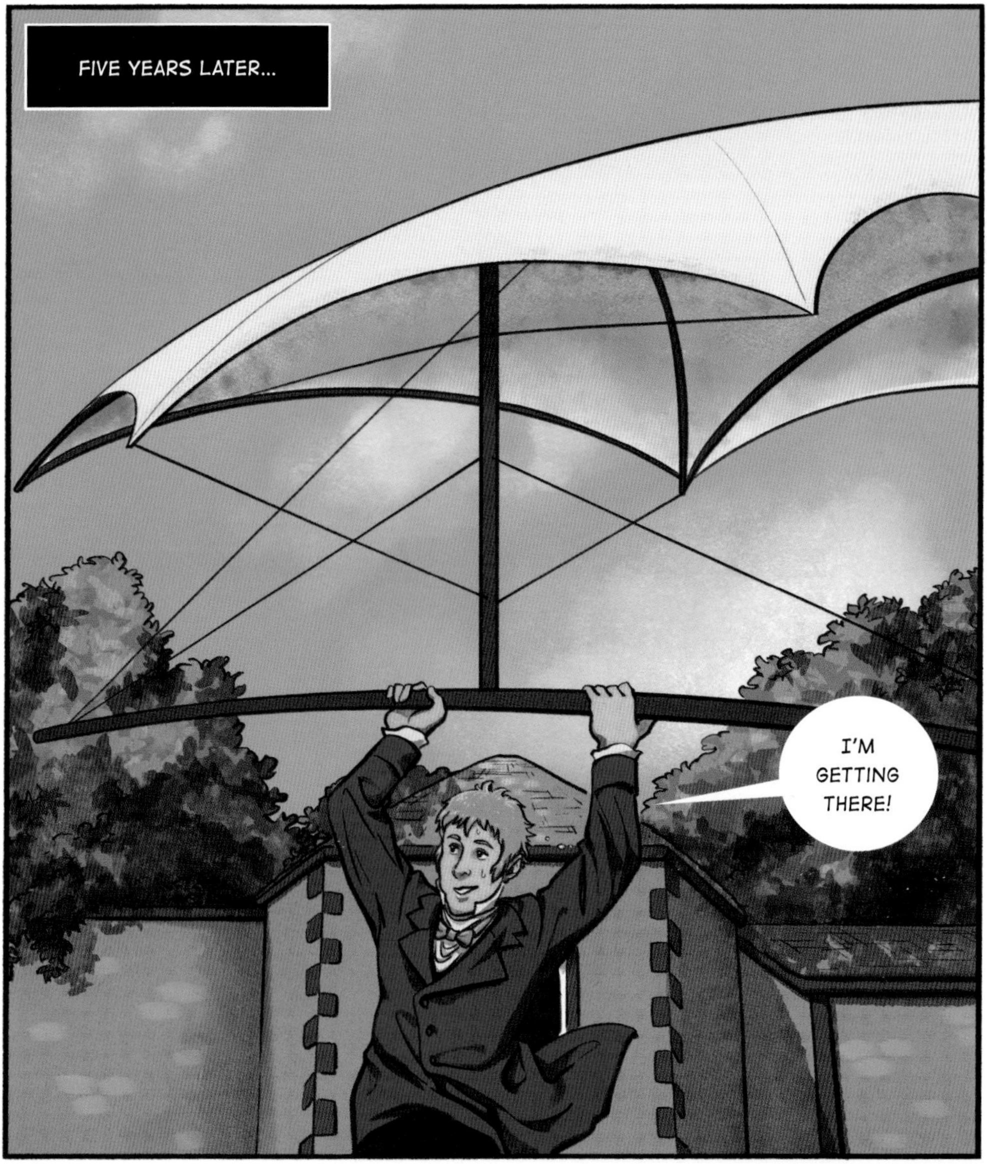
FIVE YEARS LATER...
I'M GETTING THERE!

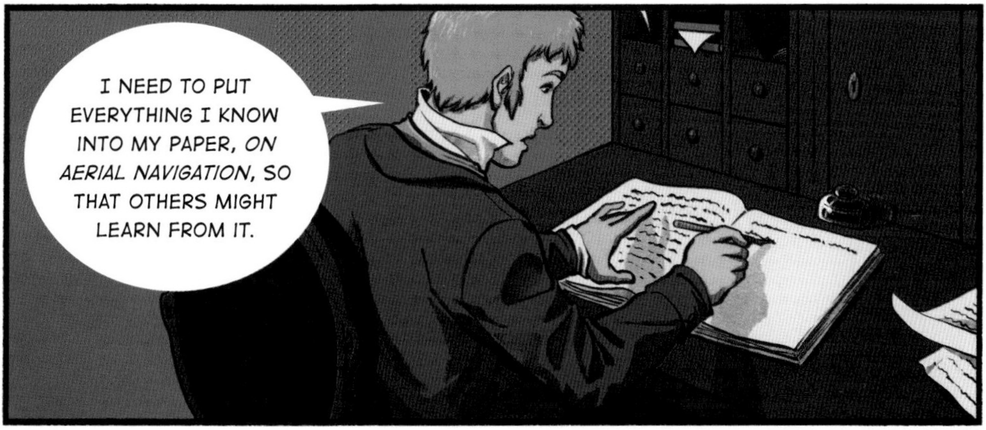
I NEED TO PUT EVERYTHING I KNOW INTO MY PAPER, *ON AERIAL NAVIGATION*, SO THAT OTHERS MIGHT LEARN FROM IT.

IN 1849, 45 YEARS AFTER BUILDING HIS FIRST MODEL GLIDER, GEORGE MADE A GLIDER ABLE TO CARRY THE 10-YEAR-OLD SON OF ONE OF HIS SERVANTS. TO EVERYONE'S SURPRISE, IT FLEW FOR SEVERAL FEET.

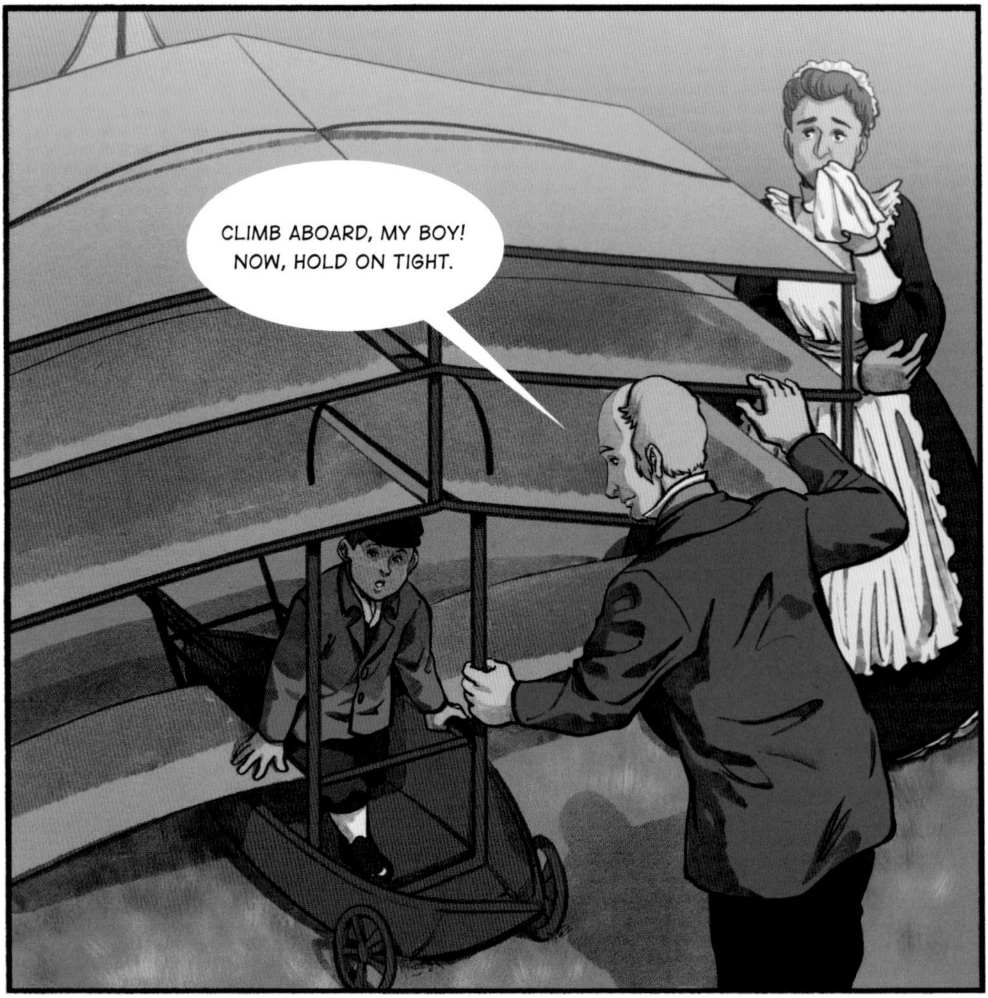
CLIMB ABOARD, MY BOY! NOW, HOLD ON TIGHT.

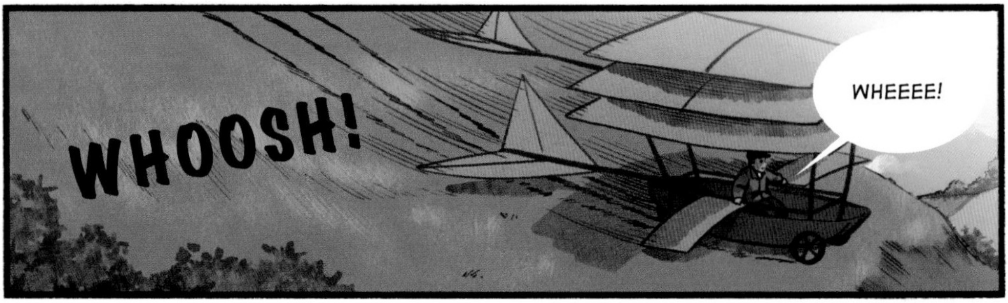
WHOOSH!
WHEEEE!

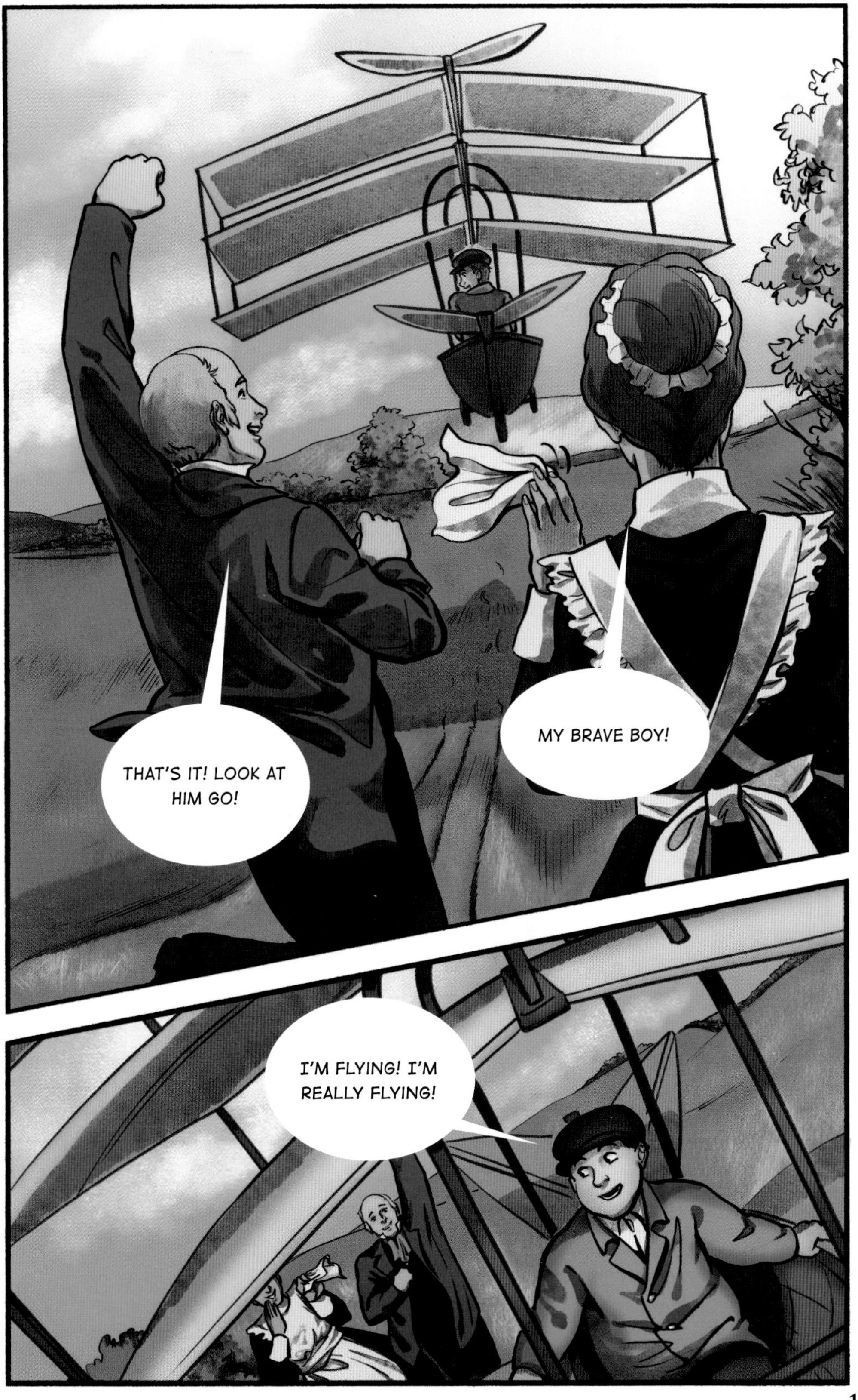
THAT'S IT! LOOK AT HIM GO!
MY BRAVE BOY!
I'M FLYING! I'M REALLY FLYING!

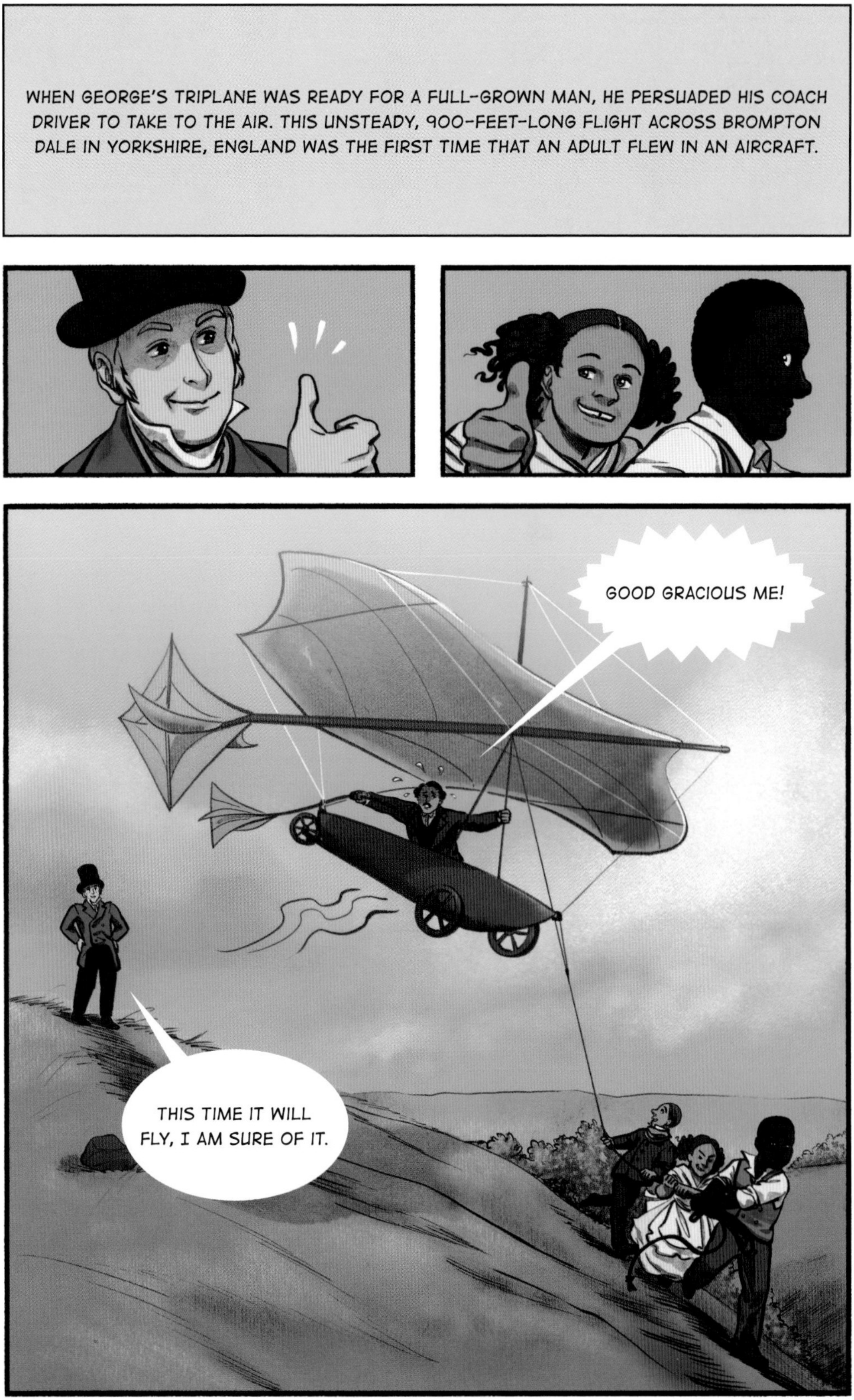
WHEN GEORGE'S TRIPLANE WAS READY FOR A FULL-GROWN MAN, HE PERSUADED HIS COACH DRIVER TO TAKE TO THE AIR. THIS UNSTEADY, 900-FEET-LONG FLIGHT ACROSS BROMPTON DALE IN YORKSHIRE, ENGLAND WAS THE FIRST TIME THAT AN ADULT FLEW IN AN AIRCRAFT.
GOOD GRACIOUS ME!
THIS TIME IT WILL FLY, I AM SURE OF IT.

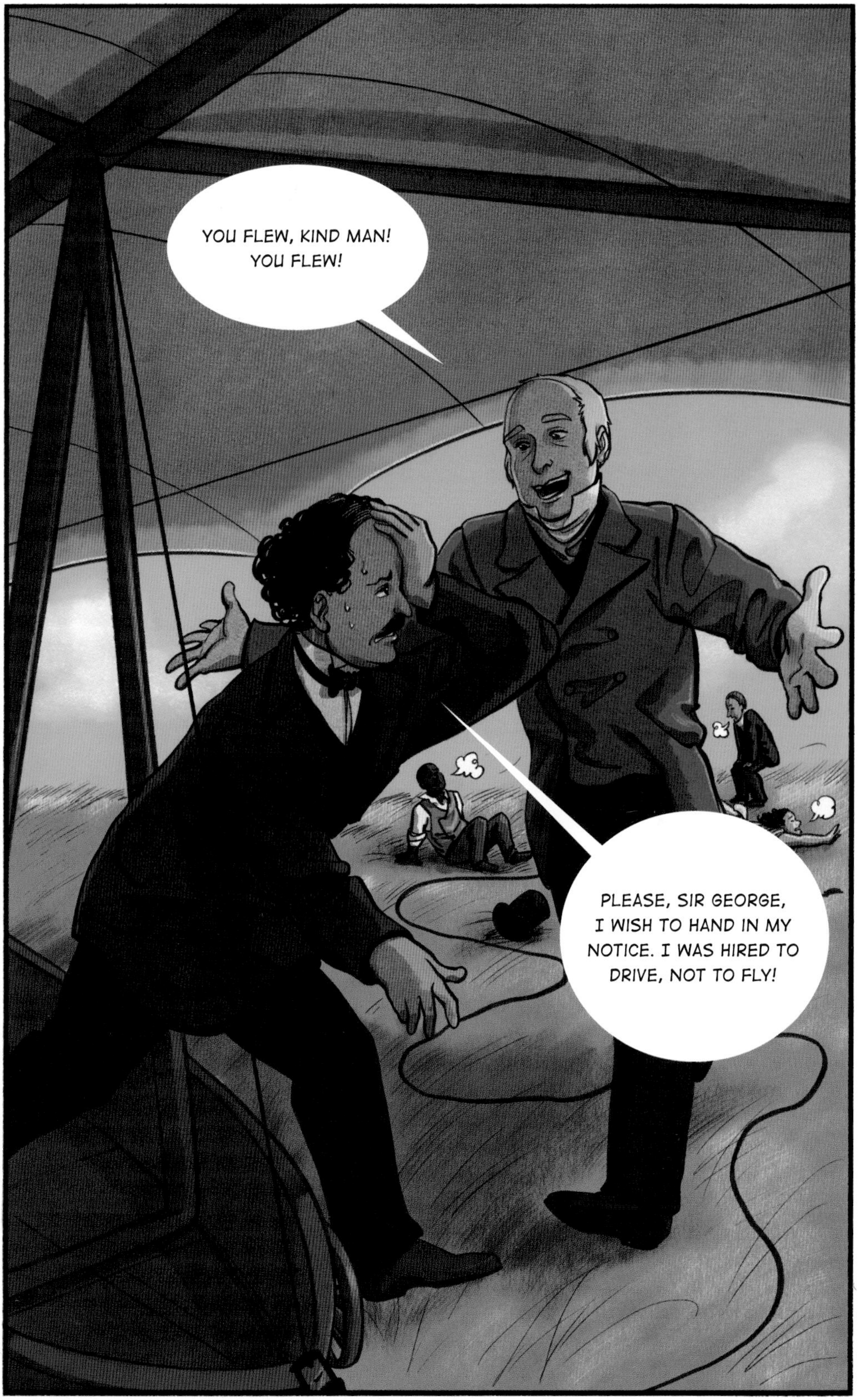
YOU FLEW, KIND MAN! YOU FLEW!
PLEASE, SIR GEORGE, I WISH TO HAND IN MY NOTICE. I WAS HIRED TO DRIVE, NOT TO FLY!

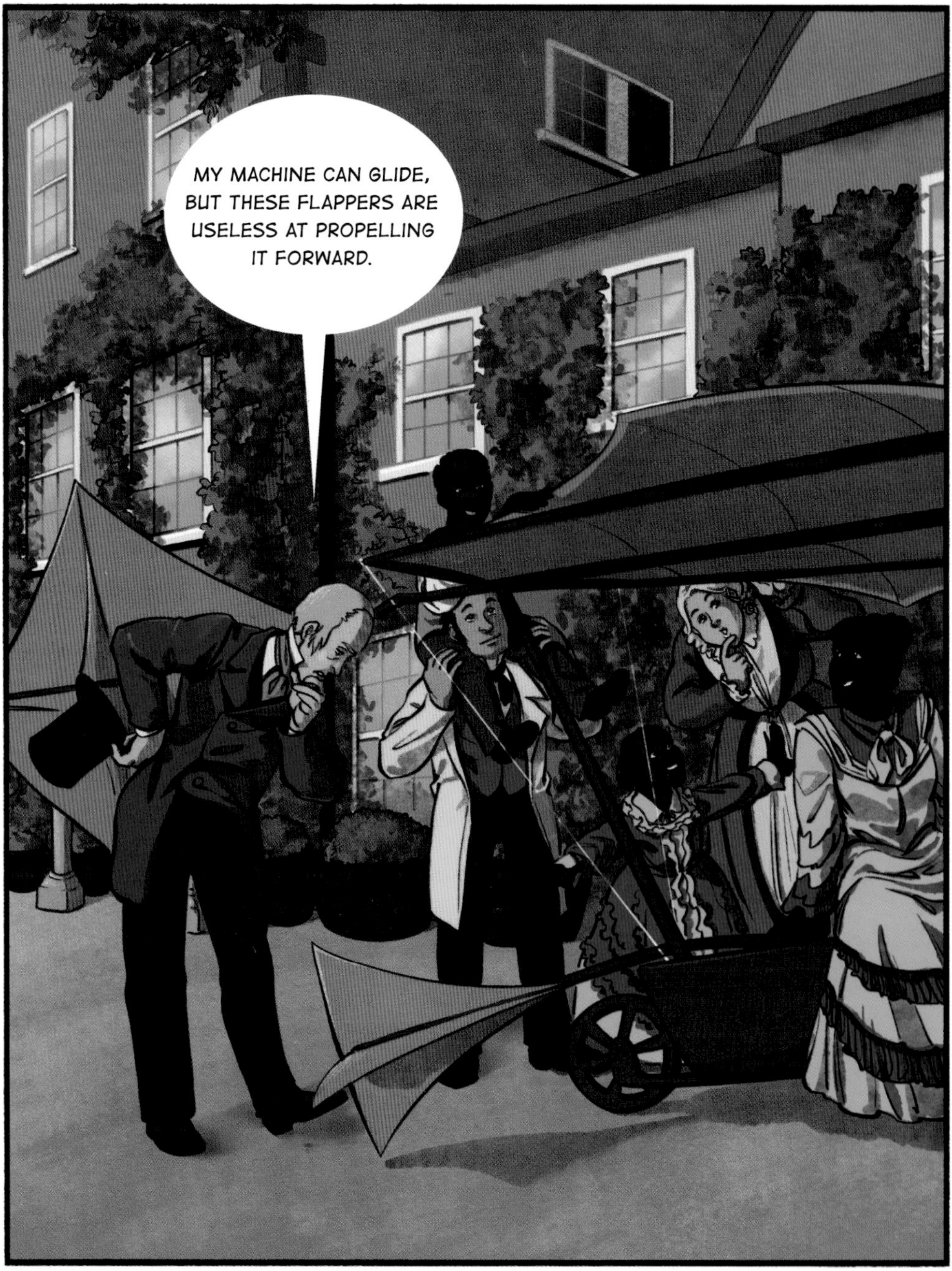
MY MACHINE CAN GLIDE, BUT THESE FLAPPERS ARE USELESS AT PROPELLING IT FORWARD.

GEORGE WAS AHEAD OF HIS TIME. IT WOULD BE QUITE A LONG WHILE BEFORE ANYONE WOULD INVENT AN ENGINE CAPABLE OF POWERING AN AIRCRAFT.

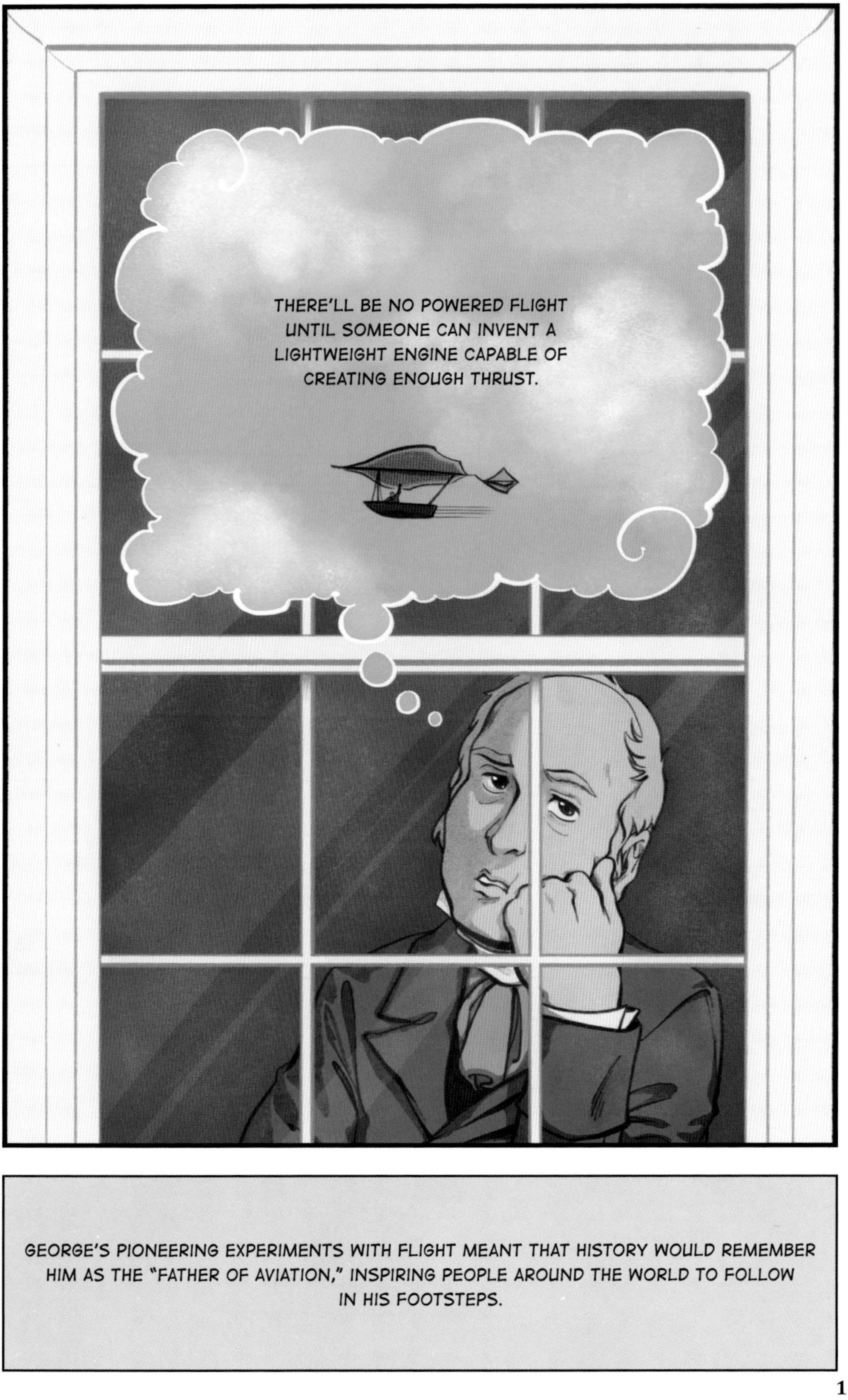
THERE'LL BE NO POWERED FLIGHT UNTIL SOMEONE CAN INVENT A LIGHTWEIGHT ENGINE CAPABLE OF CREATING ENOUGH THRUST.
GEORGE'S PIONEERING EXPERIMENTS WITH FLIGHT MEANT THAT HISTORY WOULD REMEMBER HIM AS THE "FATHER OF AVIATION," INSPIRING PEOPLE AROUND THE WORLD TO FOLLOW IN HIS FOOTSTEPS.

OTTO LILIENTHAL
(1848–1896)
THE FLYING MAN

AS CHILDREN, OTTO AND HIS YOUNGER BROTHER, GUSTAV, LOVED PLAYING OUTDOORS. THEY BECAME FASCINATED BY THE HUGE WHITE STORKS THAT LIVED IN THE MEADOWS NEAR THEIR HOUSE. IT WAS THEN THAT OTTO HAD HIS FIRST DREAMS OF FLYING.

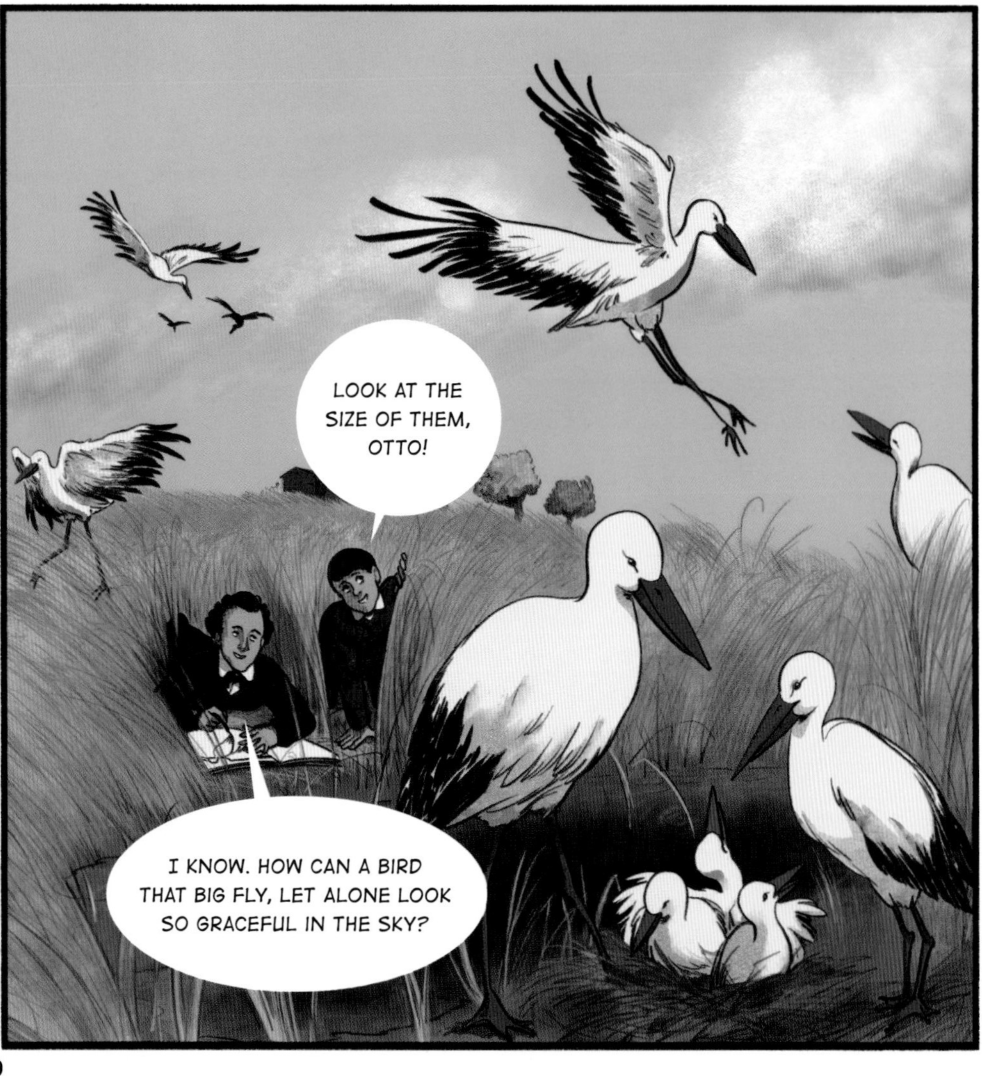
LOOK AT THE SIZE OF THEM, OTTO!
I KNOW. HOW CAN A BIRD THAT BIG FLY, LET ALONE LOOK SO GRACEFUL IN THE SKY?

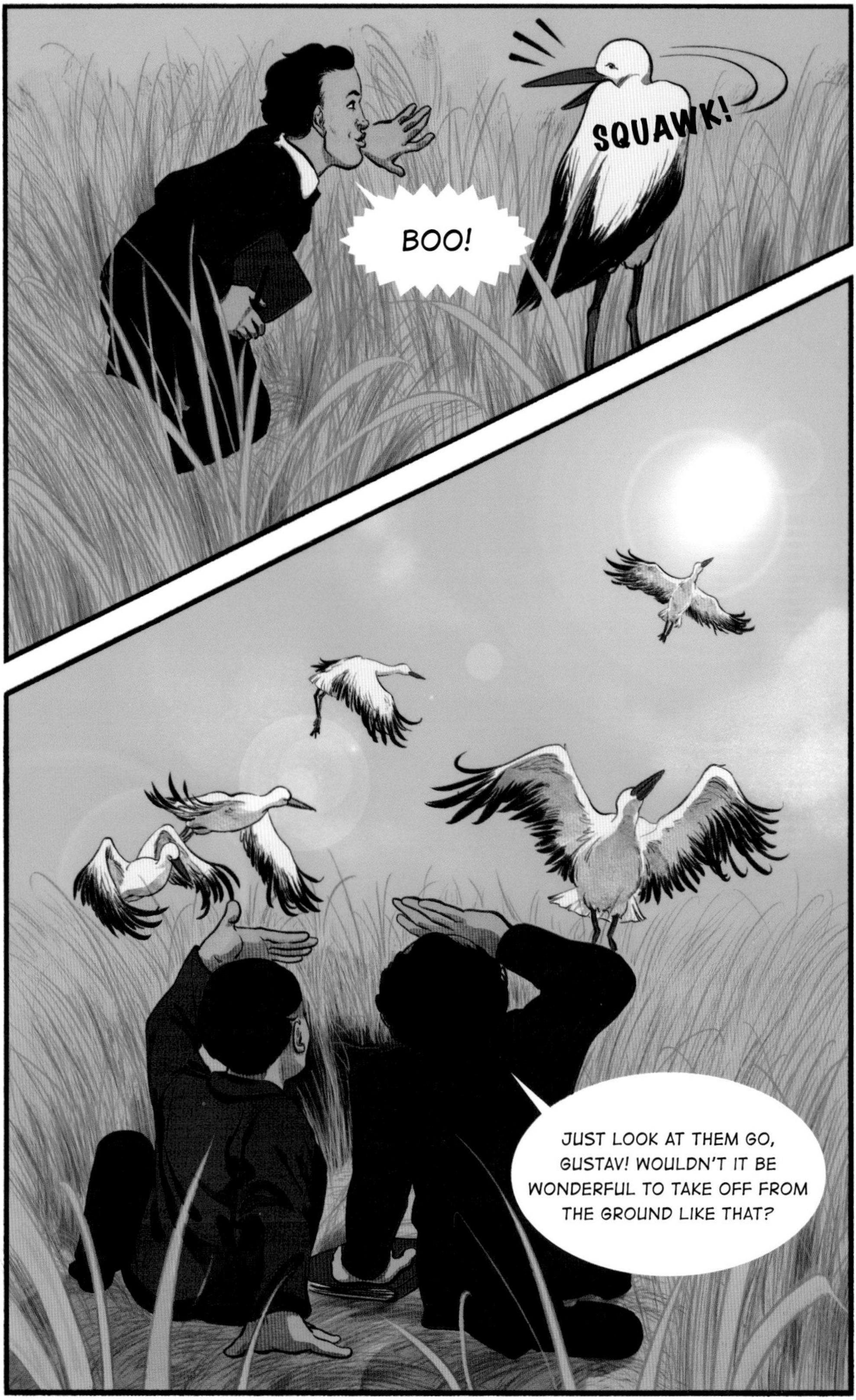
SQUAWK!
BOO!
JUST LOOK AT THEM GO, GUSTAV! WOULDN'T IT BE WONDERFUL TO TAKE OFF FROM THE GROUND LIKE THAT?

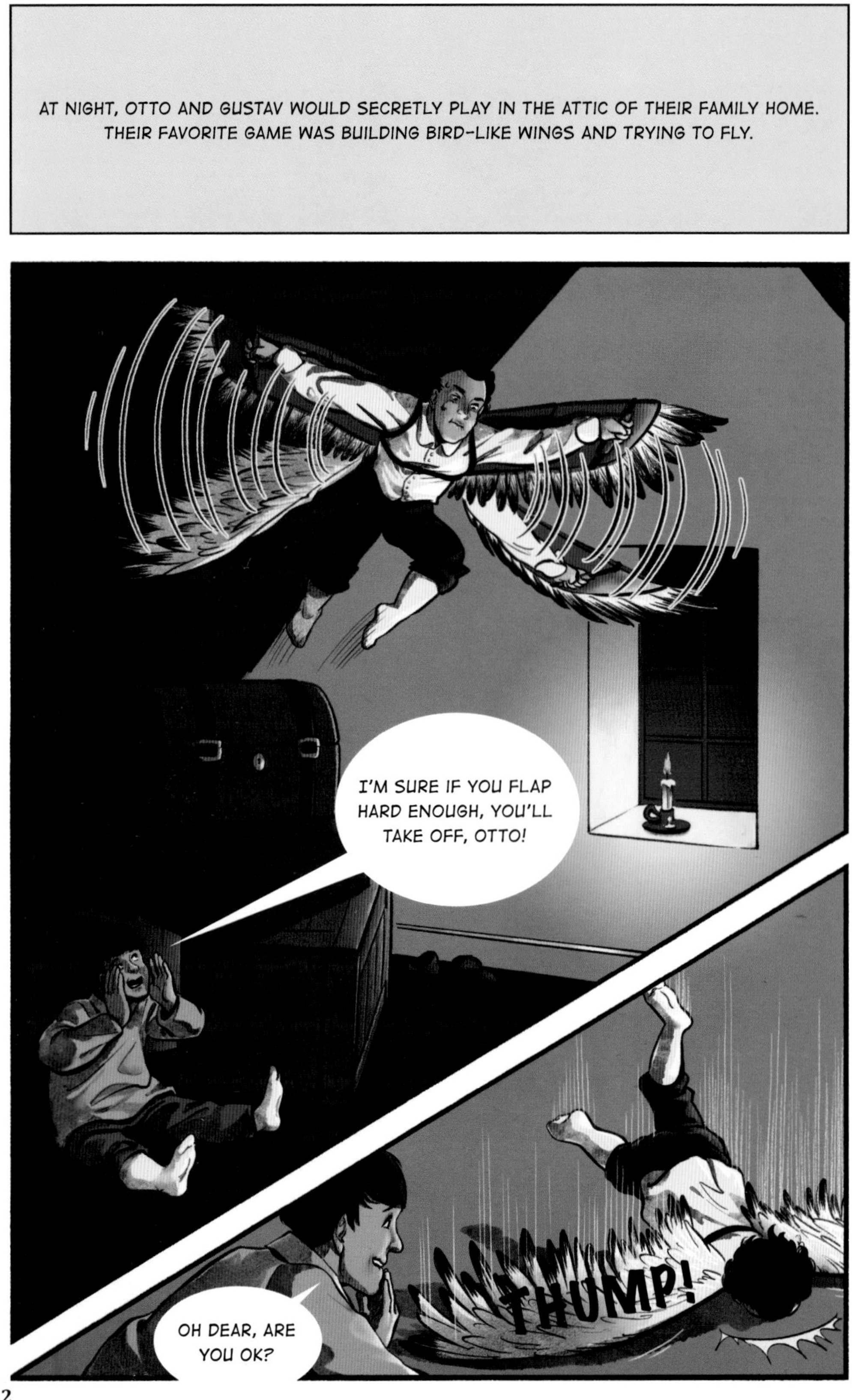
AT NIGHT, OTTO AND GUSTAV WOULD SECRETLY PLAY IN THE ATTIC OF THEIR FAMILY HOME. THEIR FAVORITE GAME WAS BUILDING BIRD-LIKE WINGS AND TRYING TO FLY.
I'M SURE IF YOU FLAP HARD ENOUGH, YOU'LL TAKE OFF, OTTO!
THUMP!
OH DEAR, ARE YOU OK?

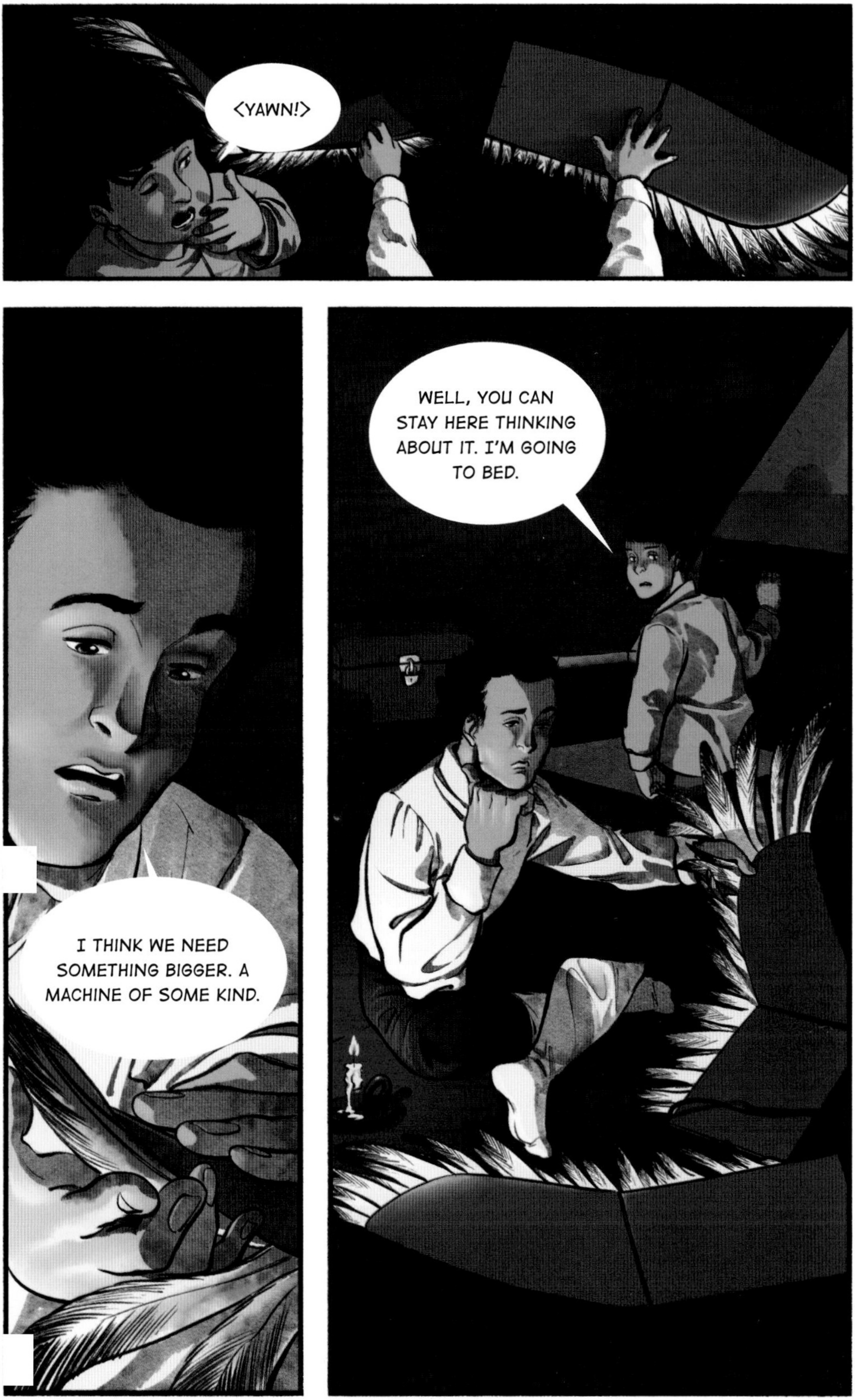
<YAWN!>
WELL, YOU CAN STAY HERE THINKING ABOUT IT. I'M GOING TO BED.
I THINK WE NEED SOMETHING BIGGER. A MACHINE OF SOME KIND.

OTTO TRAINED AS A MECHANICAL ENGINEER AT TECHNICAL SCHOOL AND THEN WORKED AT THE SCHWARTZKOPFF MACHINE TOOL FACTORY, BUT HIS THOUGHTS ALWAYS RETURNED TO FLYING. HIS PROGRESS WAS INTERRUPTED BY THE START OF THE FRANCO-PRUSSIAN WAR IN 1870.

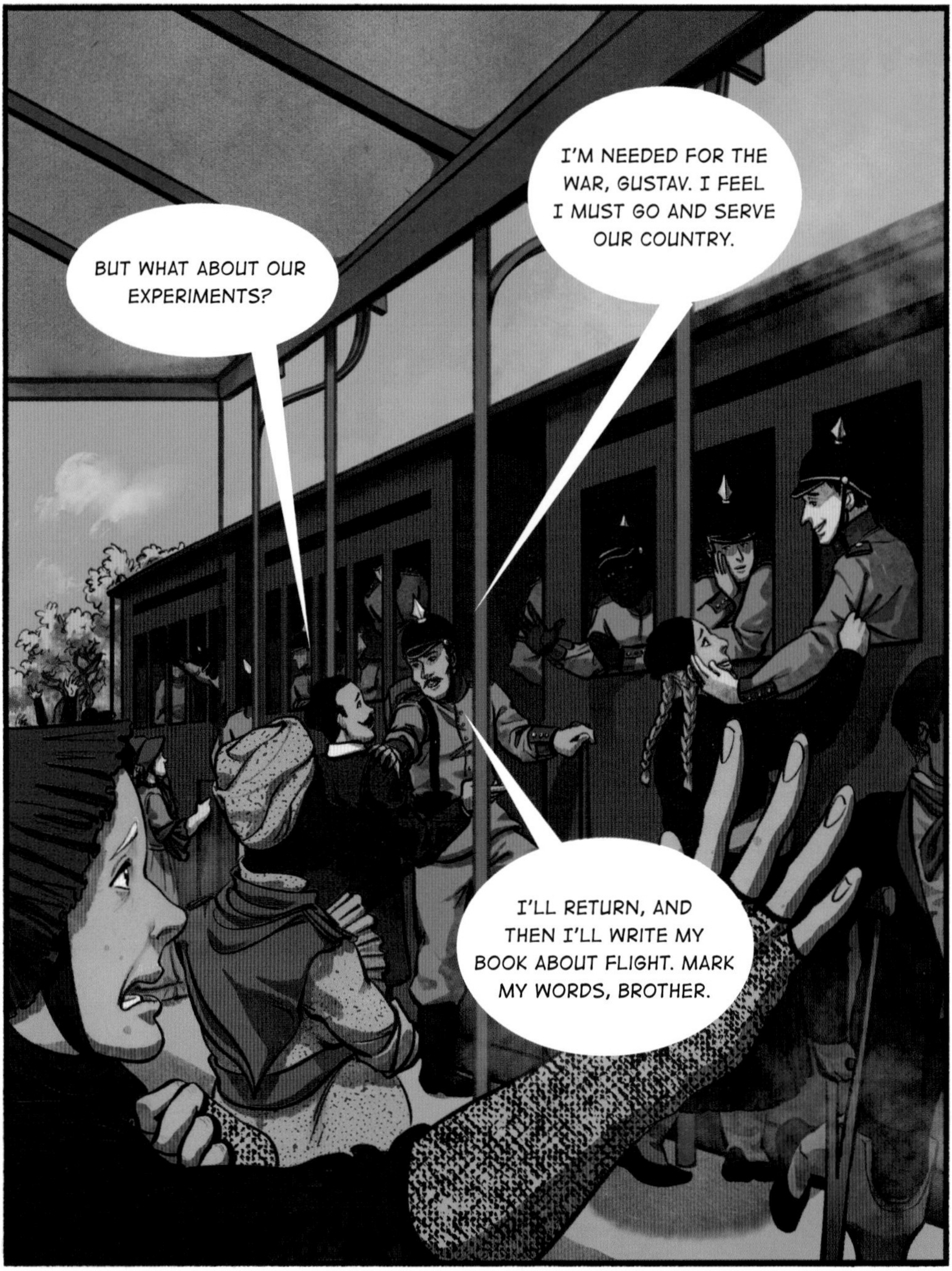
BUT WHAT ABOUT OUR EXPERIMENTS?
I'M NEEDED FOR THE WAR, GUSTAV. I FEEL I MUST GO AND SERVE OUR COUNTRY.
I'LL RETURN, AND THEN I'LL WRITE MY BOOK ABOUT FLIGHT. MARK MY WORDS, BROTHER.

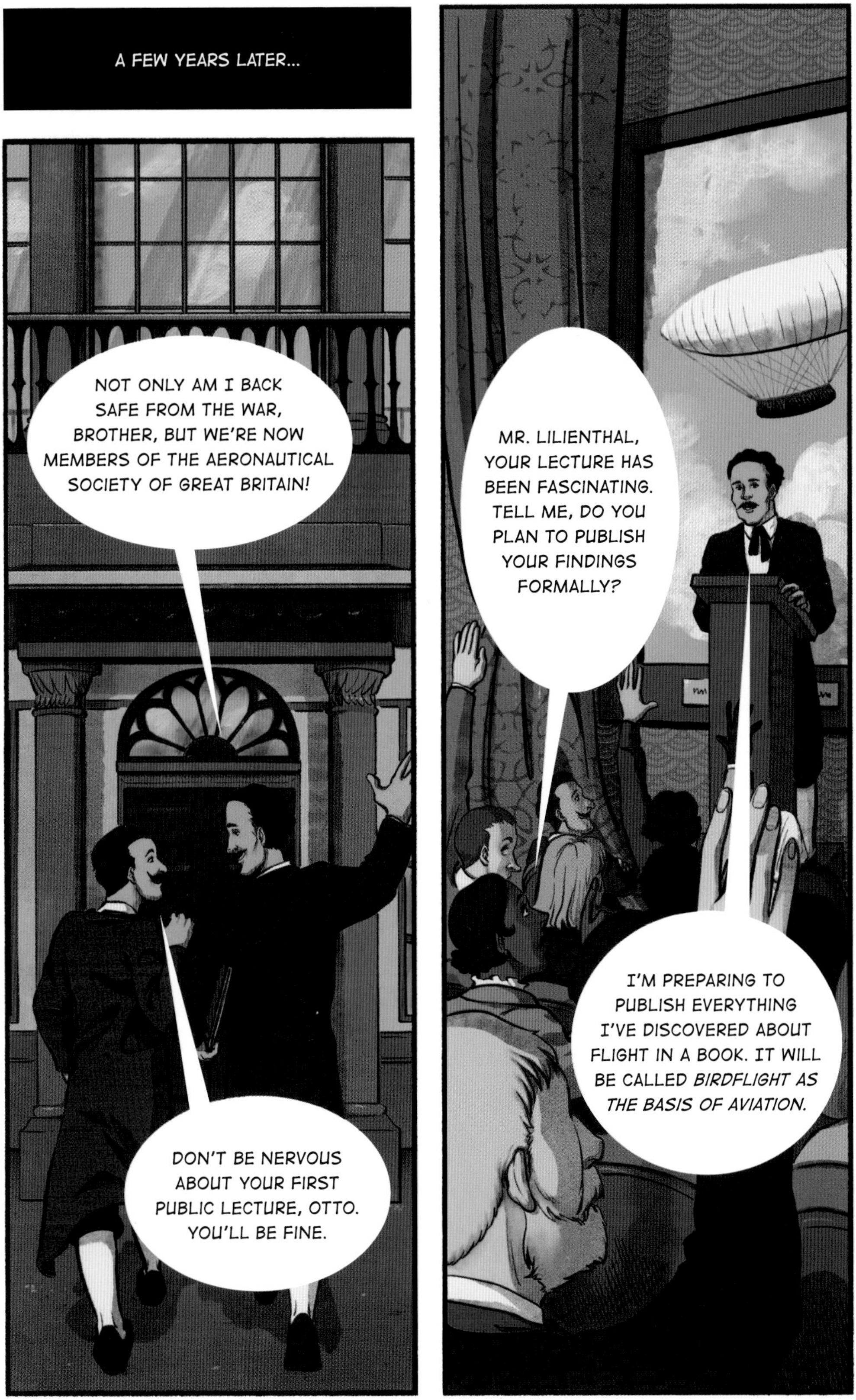
A FEW YEARS LATER...
NOT ONLY AM I BACK SAFE FROM THE WAR, BROTHER, BUT WE'RE NOW MEMBERS OF THE AERONAUTICAL SOCIETY OF GREAT BRITAIN!
DON'T BE NERVOUS ABOUT YOUR FIRST PUBLIC LECTURE, OTTO. YOU'LL BE FINE.
MR. LILIENTHAL, YOUR LECTURE HAS BEEN FASCINATING. TELL ME, DO YOU PLAN TO PUBLISH YOUR FINDINGS FORMALLY?
I'M PREPARING TO PUBLISH EVERYTHING I'VE DISCOVERED ABOUT FLIGHT IN A BOOK. IT WILL BE CALLED *BIRDFLIGHT AS THE BASIS OF AVIATION.*

BY HIS EARLY FORTIES, OTTO WAS FINALLY READY TO ACHIEVE HIS DREAM OF FLIGHT. IN 1891, HIS FIRST CONTRAPTION, THE DERWITZER GLIDER, CARRIED HIM FOR 79 FEET OVER THE GROUND.

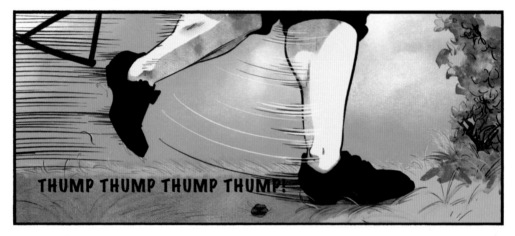

THUMP THUMP THUMP THUMP!

WHOOSH!

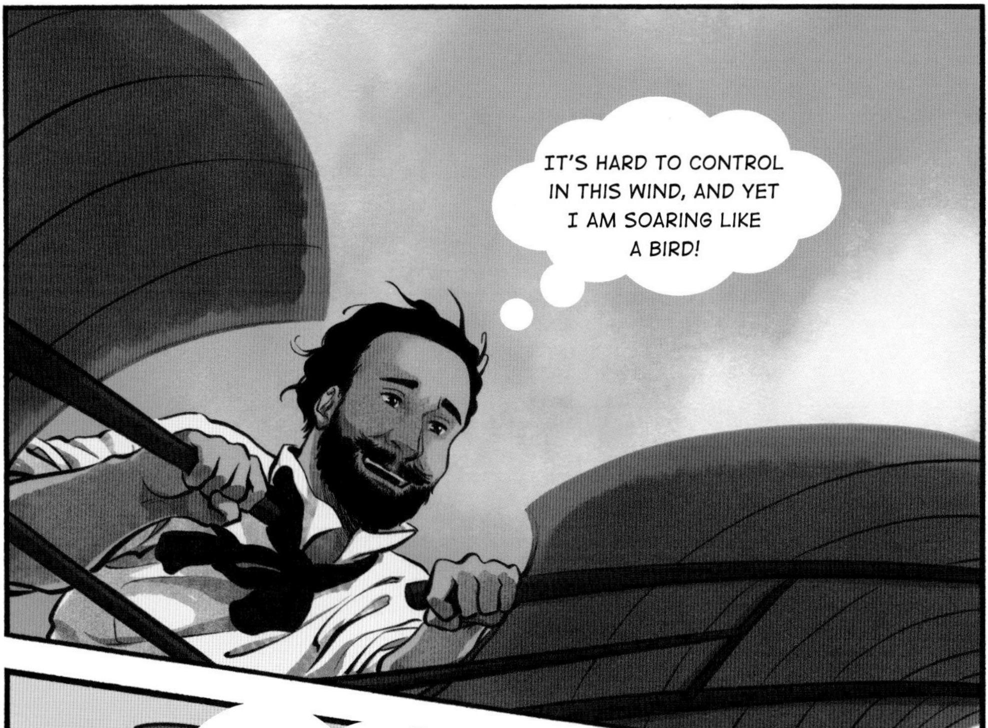
IT'S HARD TO CONTROL IN THIS WIND, AND YET I AM SOARING LIKE A BIRD!

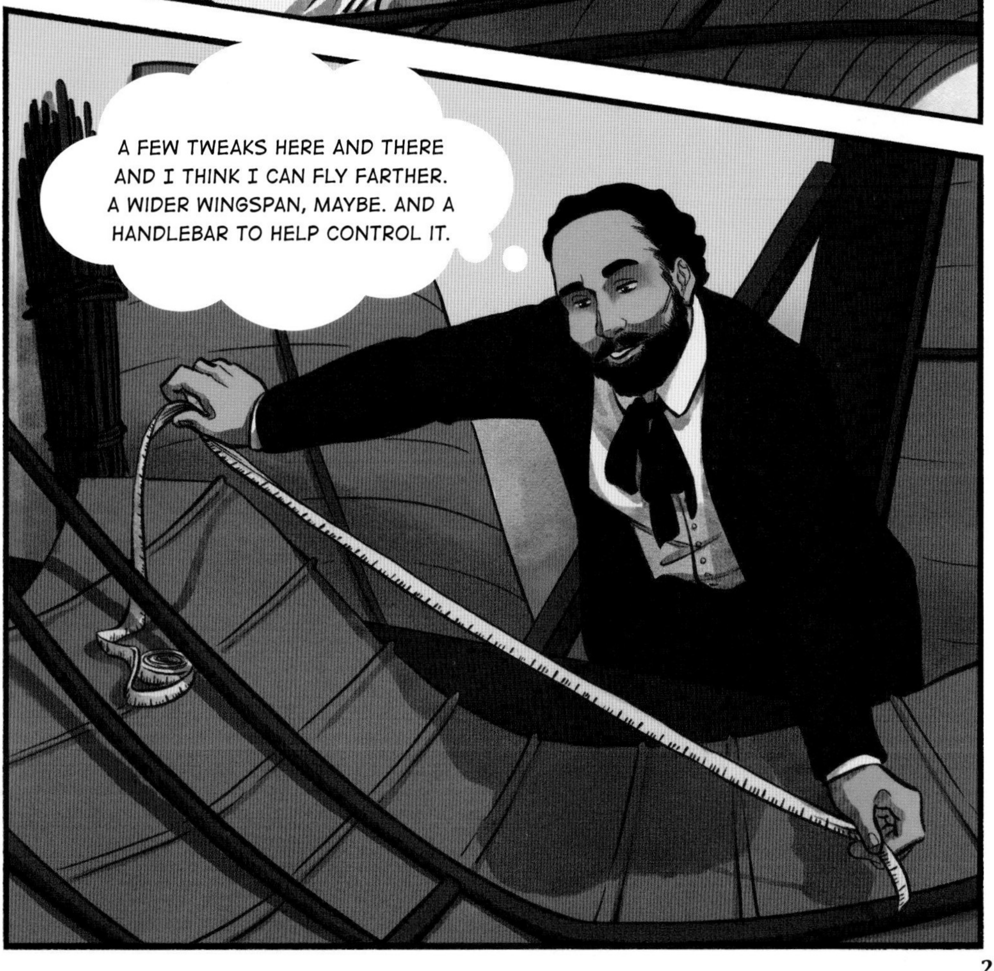
A FEW TWEAKS HERE AND THERE AND I THINK I CAN FLY FARTHER. A WIDER WINGSPAN, MAYBE. AND A HANDLEBAR TO HELP CONTROL IT.

OTTO CONTINUED TO IMPROVE UPON HIS DESIGNS AND BUILT A SPECIAL HILLTOP PLATFORM AS A LAUNCH SITE. HE RACKED UP OVER 2,000 FLIGHTS IN 16 DIFFERENT GLIDERS AND SOON BECAME FAMOUS.

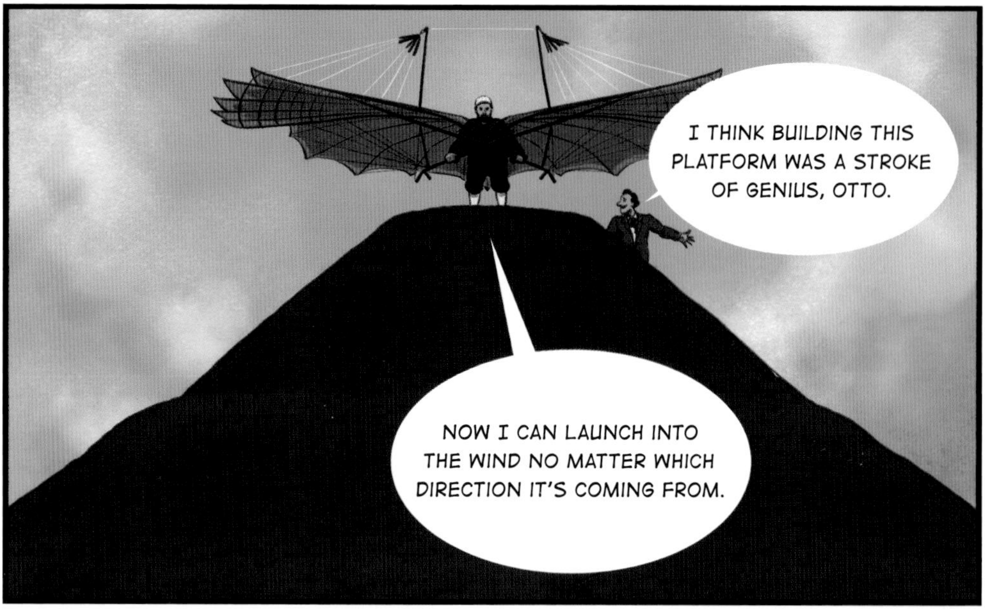
I THINK BUILDING THIS PLATFORM WAS A STROKE OF GENIUS, OTTO.
NOW I CAN LAUNCH INTO THE WIND NO MATTER WHICH DIRECTION IT'S COMING FROM.

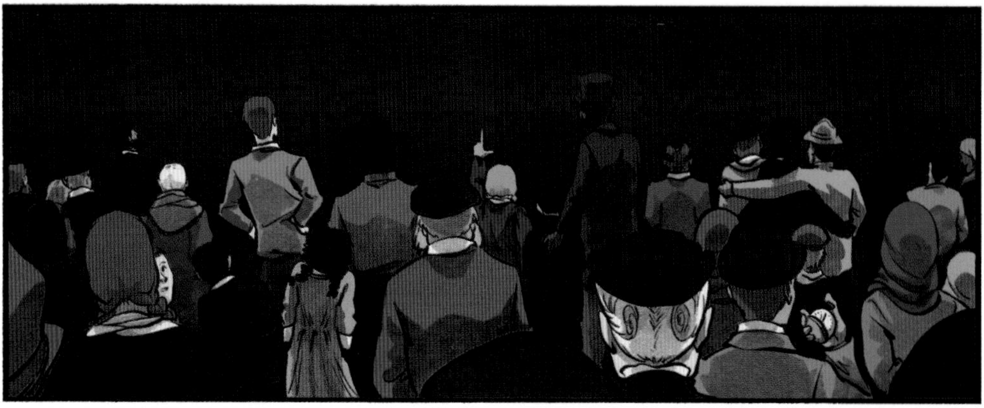

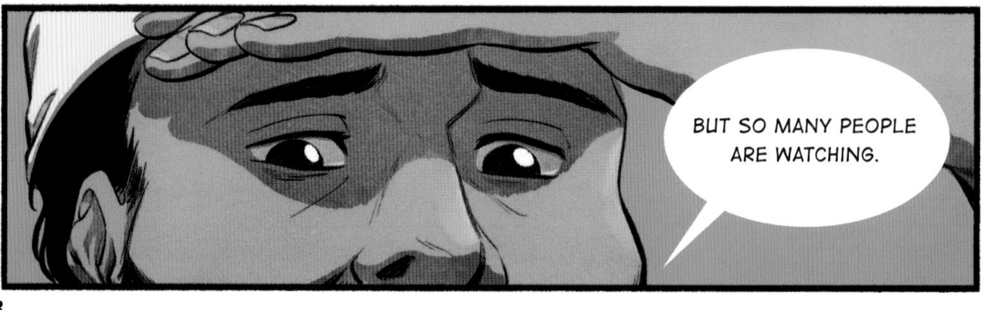
BUT SO MANY PEOPLE ARE WATCHING.

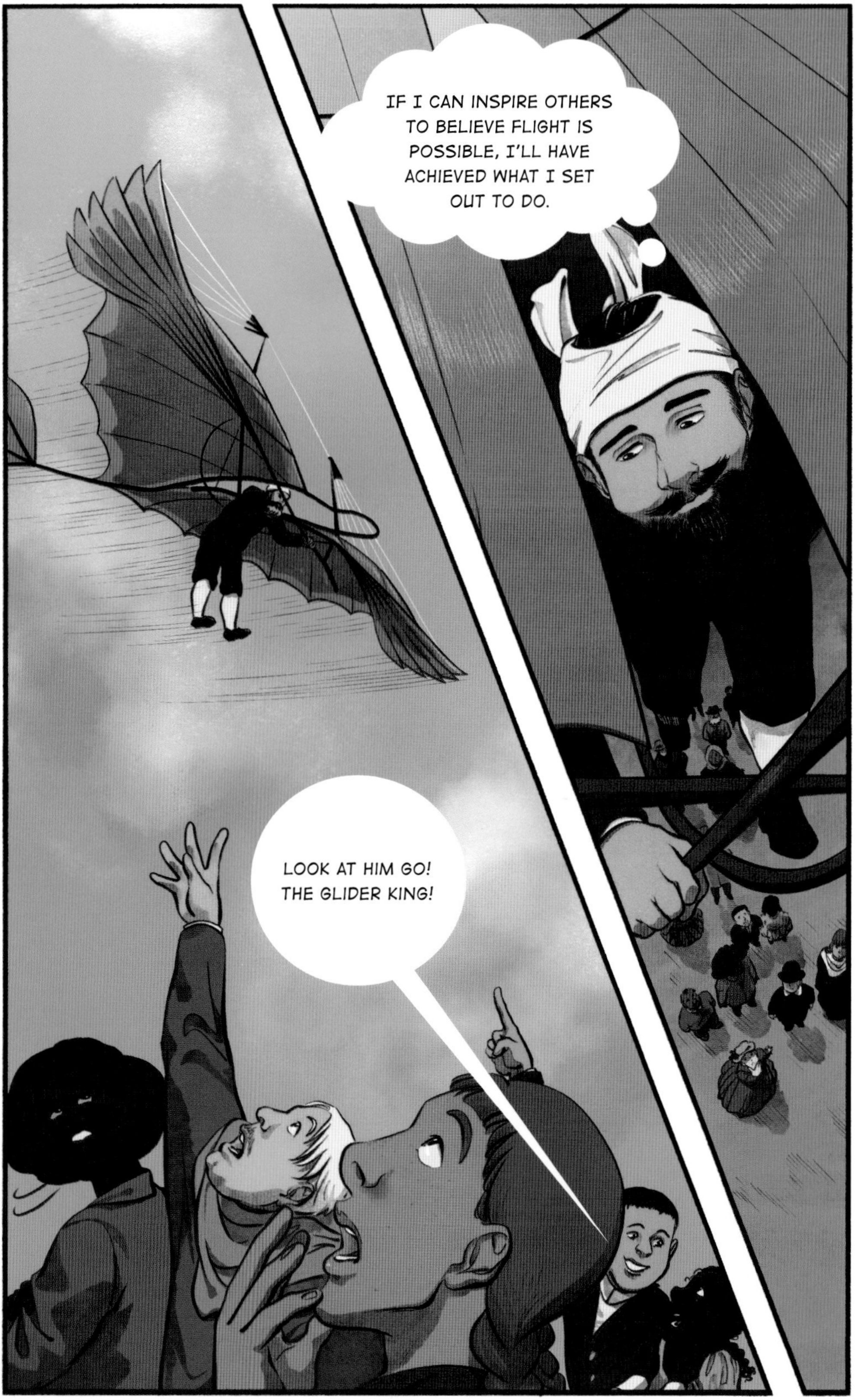
IF I CAN INSPIRE OTHERS TO BELIEVE FLIGHT IS POSSIBLE, I'LL HAVE ACHIEVED WHAT I SET OUT TO DO.
LOOK AT HIM GO! THE GLIDER KING!

IN THE LAST FEW YEARS OF HIS LIFE, MANY OF OTTO'S FLIGHTS WERE CAPTURED ON FILM BY EARLY PHOTOGRAPHERS. HE REALIZED THAT MANY OTHER PEOPLE MIGHT BE INSPIRED BY SEEING THESE IMAGES—PROOF THAT HUMANS COULD SOAR LIKE BIRDS.

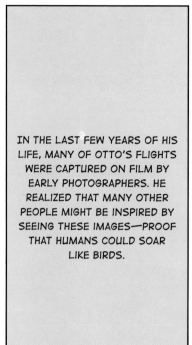

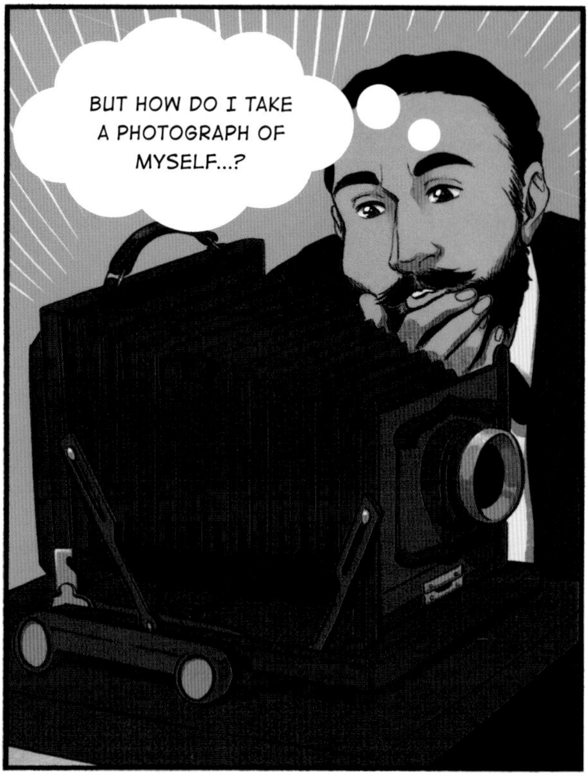
BUT HOW DO I TAKE A PHOTOGRAPH OF MYSELF...?

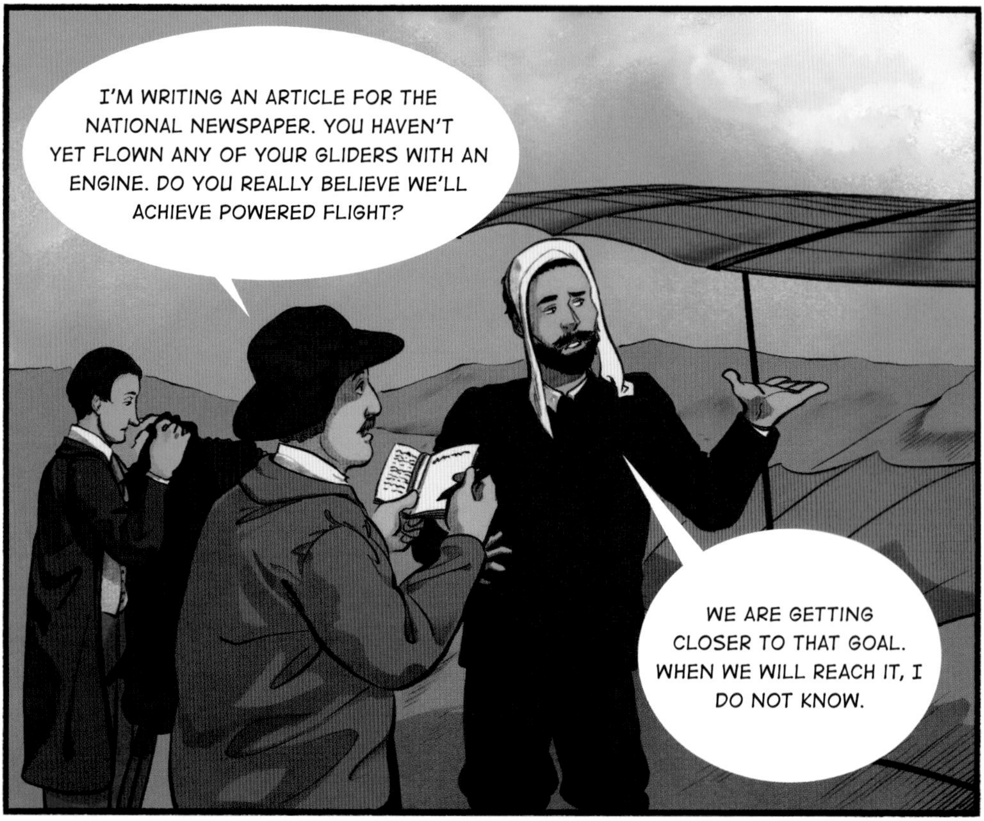
I'M WRITING AN ARTICLE FOR THE NATIONAL NEWSPAPER. YOU HAVEN'T YET FLOWN ANY OF YOUR GLIDERS WITH AN ENGINE. DO YOU REALLY BELIEVE WE'LL ACHIEVE POWERED FLIGHT?
WE ARE GETTING CLOSER TO THAT GOAL. WHEN WE WILL REACH IT, I DO NOT KNOW.

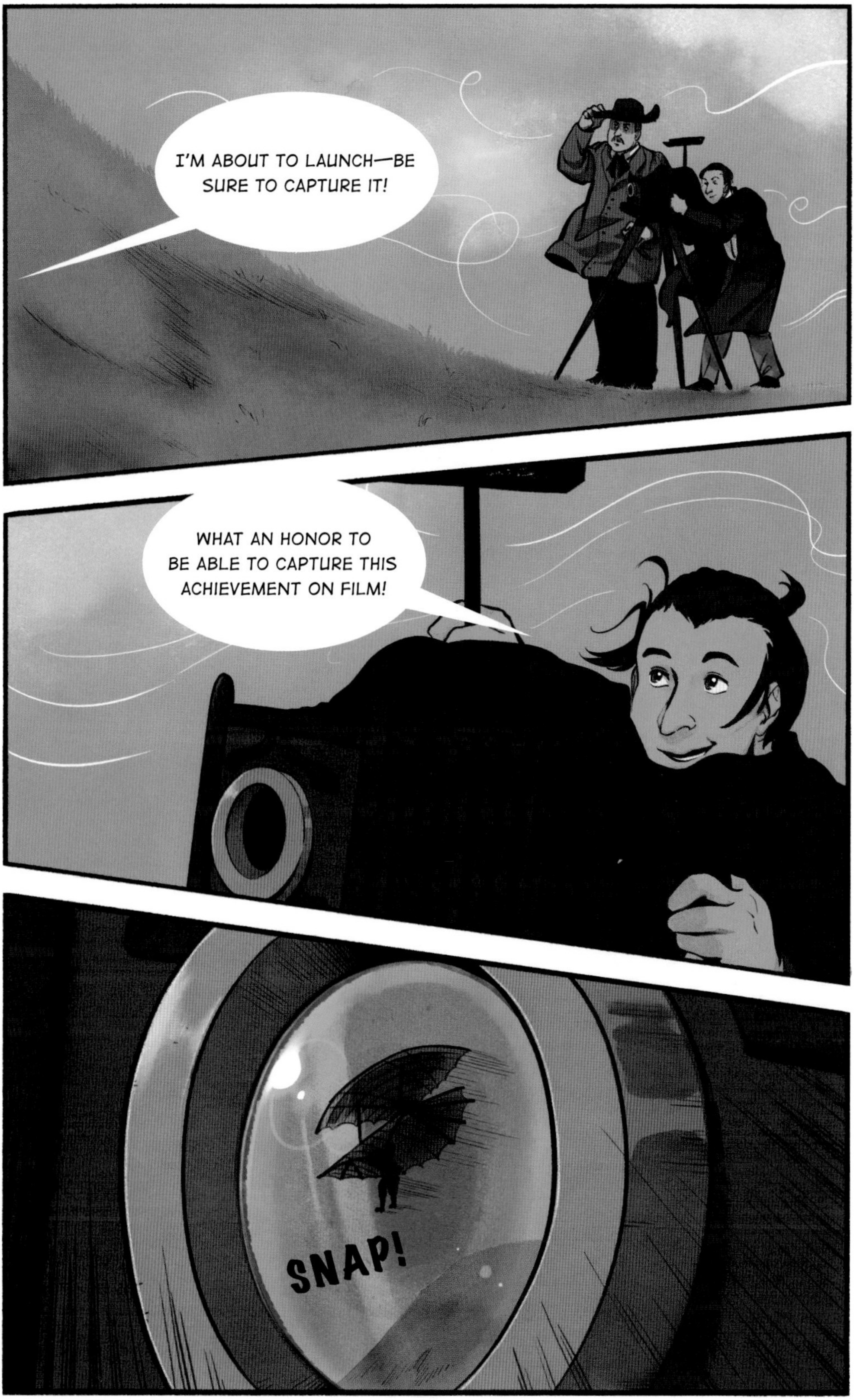
I'M ABOUT TO LAUNCH—BE SURE TO CAPTURE IT!
WHAT AN HONOR TO BE ABLE TO CAPTURE THIS ACHIEVEMENT ON FILM!
SNAP!

OTTO ENCOURAGED MANY OTHERS TO PURSUE THE PATH TO POWERED FLIGHT. UNFORTUNATELY, HE DIED IN A GLIDING ACCIDENT IN AUGUST 1896, AT THE AGE OF 48. A COUPLE OF MONTHS BEFORE HIS DEATH, OTTO GAVE A FINAL LECTURE AT THE TRADE EXHIBITION IN BERLIN, GERMANY.

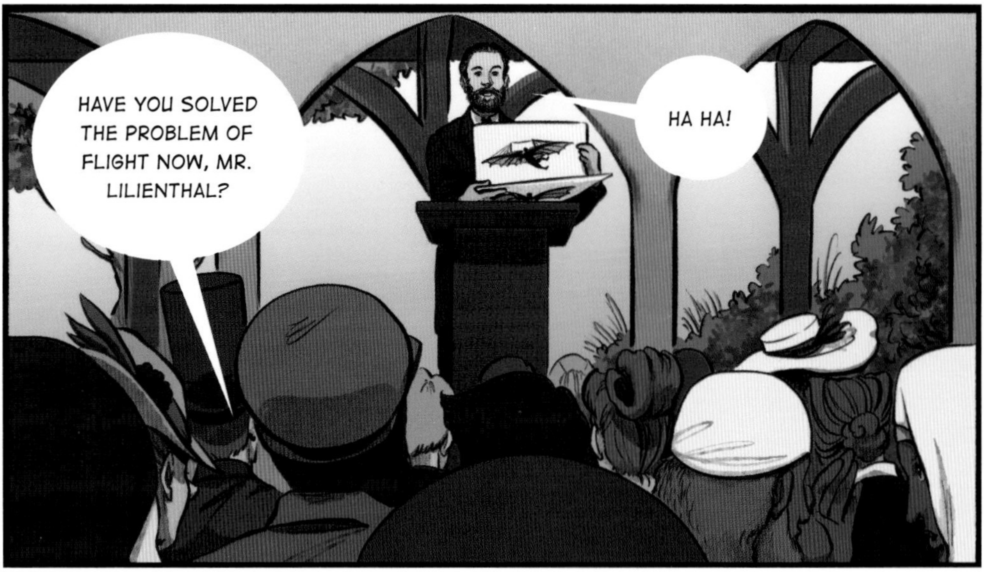
HAVE YOU SOLVED THE PROBLEM OF FLIGHT NOW, MR. LILIENTHAL?
HA HA!

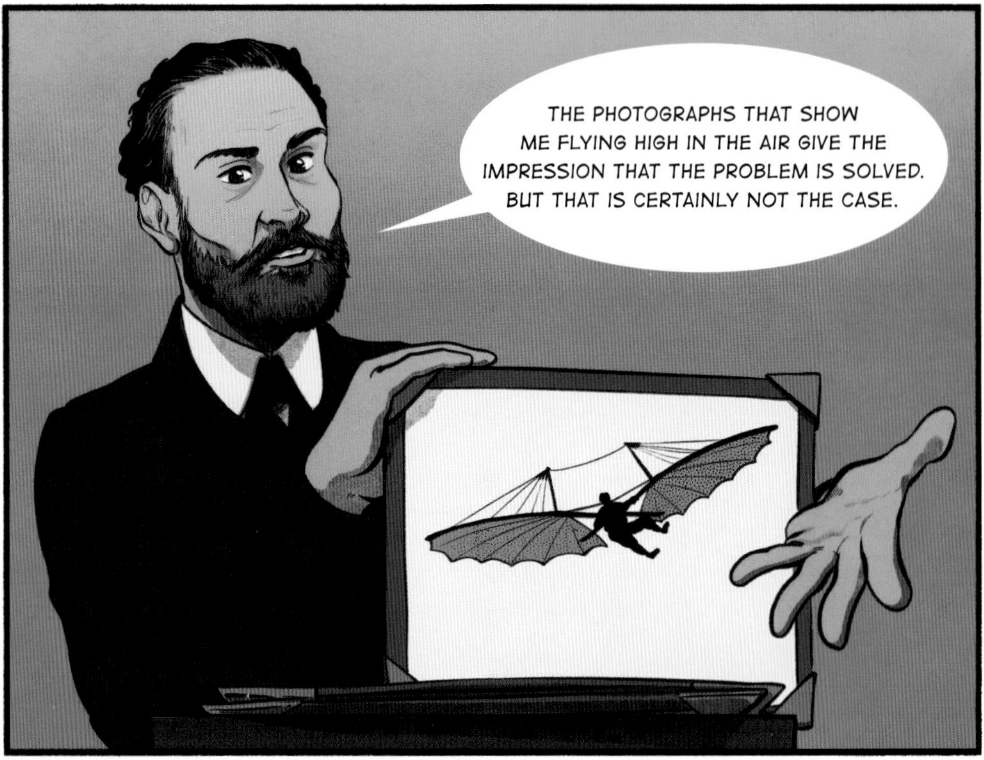
THE PHOTOGRAPHS THAT SHOW ME FLYING HIGH IN THE AIR GIVE THE IMPRESSION THAT THE PROBLEM IS SOLVED. BUT THAT IS CERTAINLY NOT THE CASE.

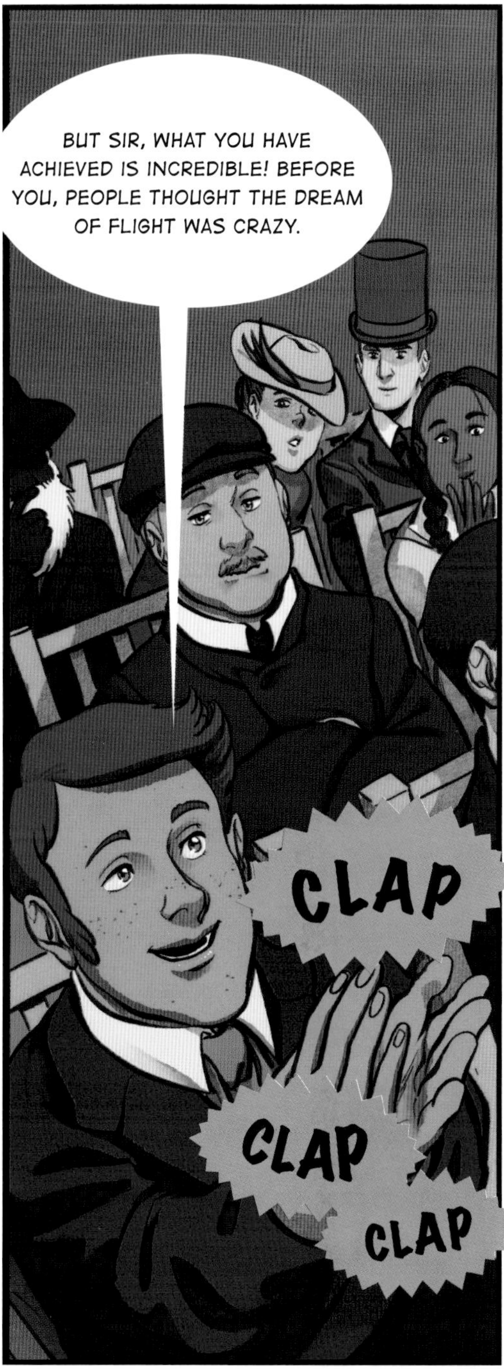
BUT SIR, WHAT YOU HAVE ACHIEVED IS INCREDIBLE! BEFORE YOU, PEOPLE THOUGHT THE DREAM OF FLIGHT WAS CRAZY.
CLAP
CLAP
CLAP

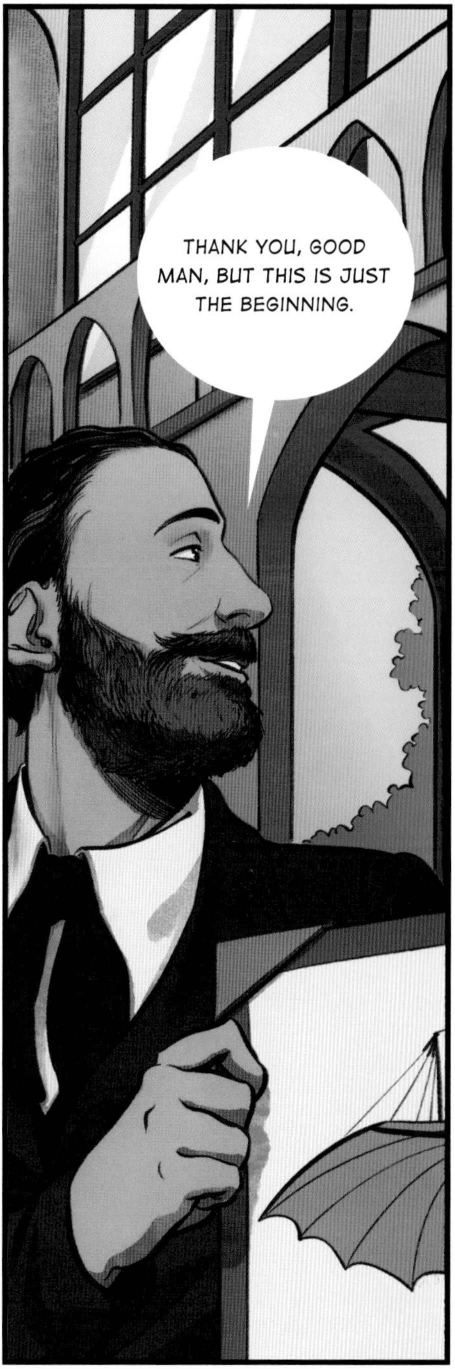
THANK YOU, GOOD MAN, BUT THIS IS JUST THE BEGINNING.

OTTO'S ACHIEVEMENTS WERE A DIRECT INSPIRATION FOR THE WRIGHT BROTHERS, WHO HEARD ABOUT HIS GLIDER FLIGHTS AS YOUNG MEN. HIS DEATH SPURRED THEM TO ACTION.

WILBUR & ORVILLE WRIGHT
(1867–1912; 1871–1948)
TAKE-OFF AT KITTY HAWK

JUST FOUR YEARS APART IN AGE, WILBUR AND ORVILLE SPENT THEIR CHILDHOOD PLAYING TOGETHER. ONE OF THEIR FAVORITE TOYS WAS A FLYING MACHINE THEIR FATHER BROUGHT BACK FROM HIS TRAVELS. THIS SEEMINGLY MAGICAL DEVICE INSPIRED AN EARLY LOVE OF AVIATION IN THE TWO BROTHERS.

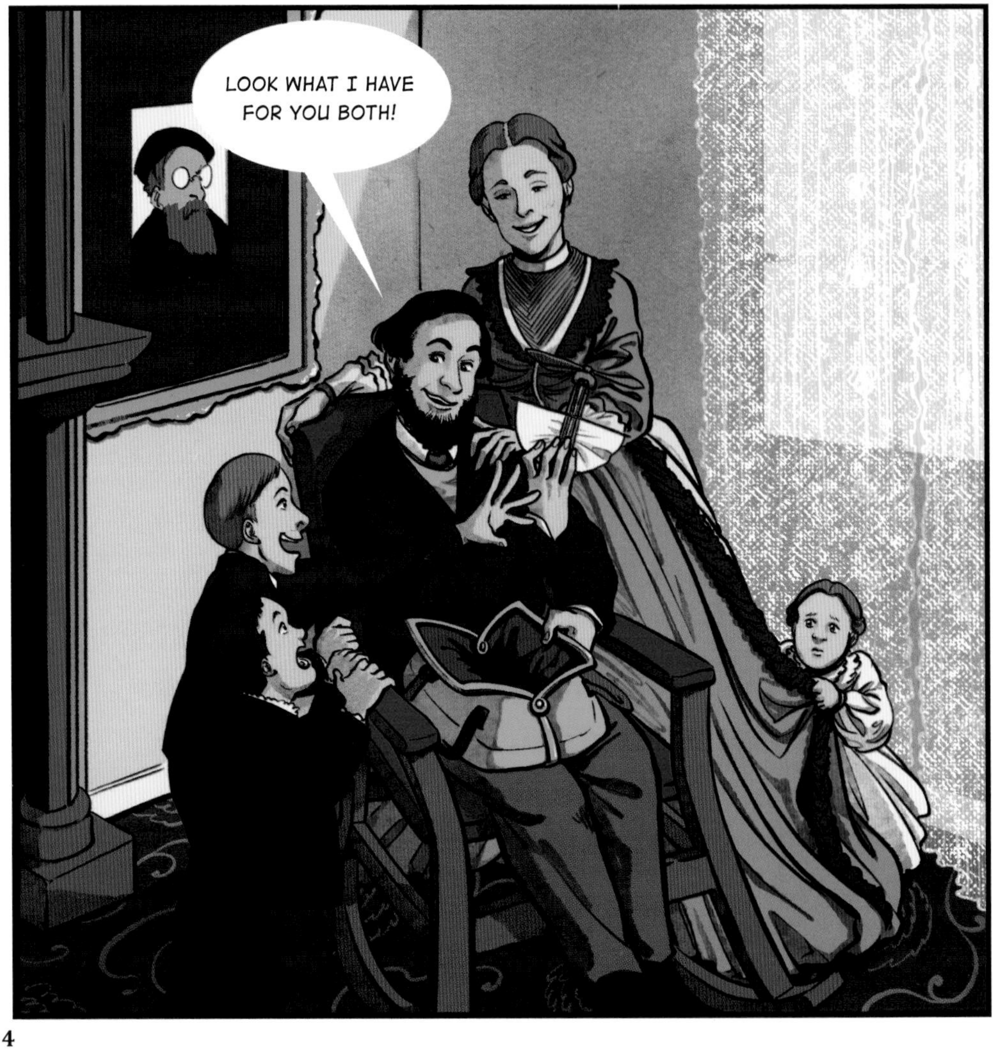
LOOK WHAT I HAVE FOR YOU BOTH!

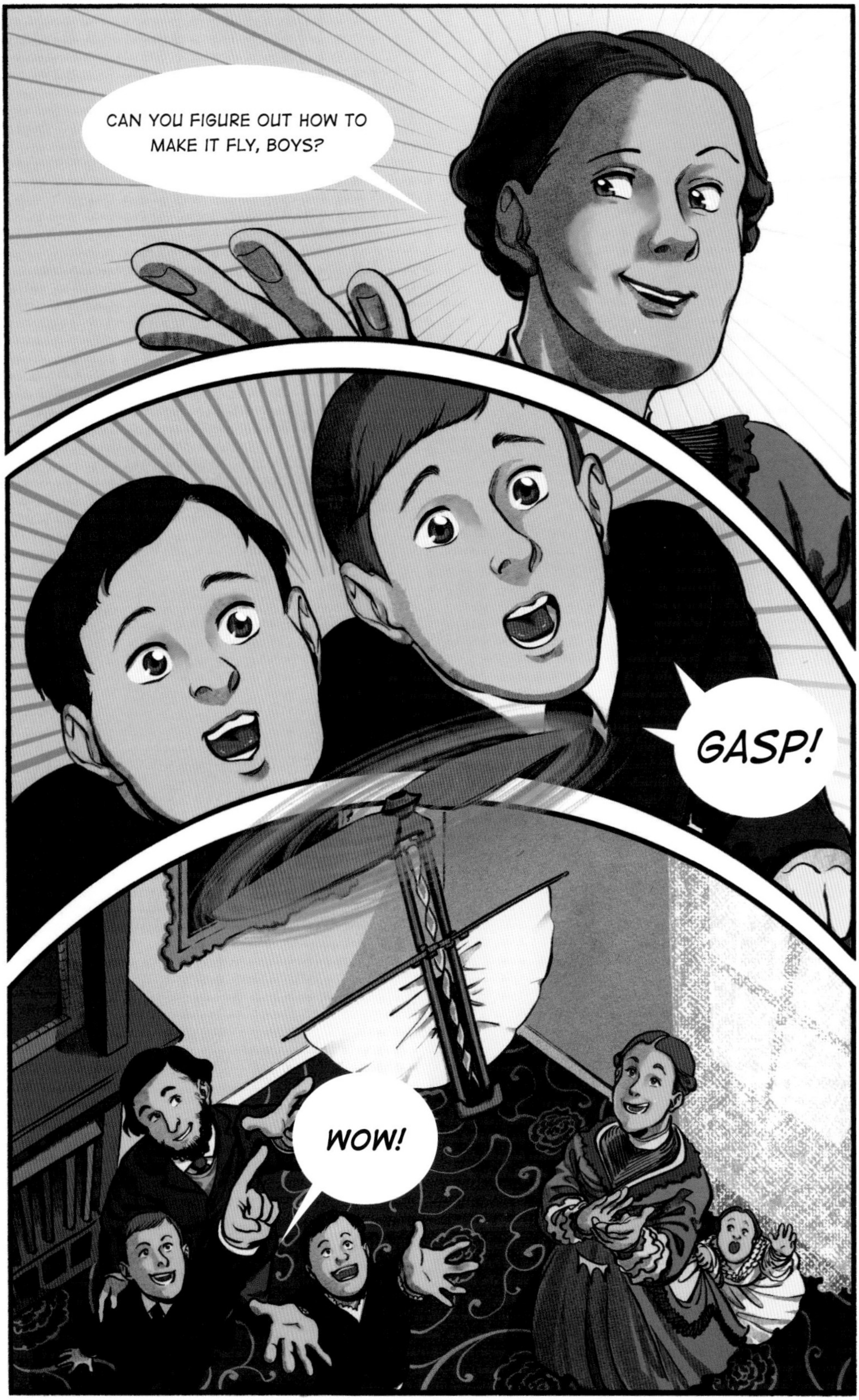
CAN YOU FIGURE OUT HOW TO MAKE IT FLY, BOYS?
GASP!
WOW!

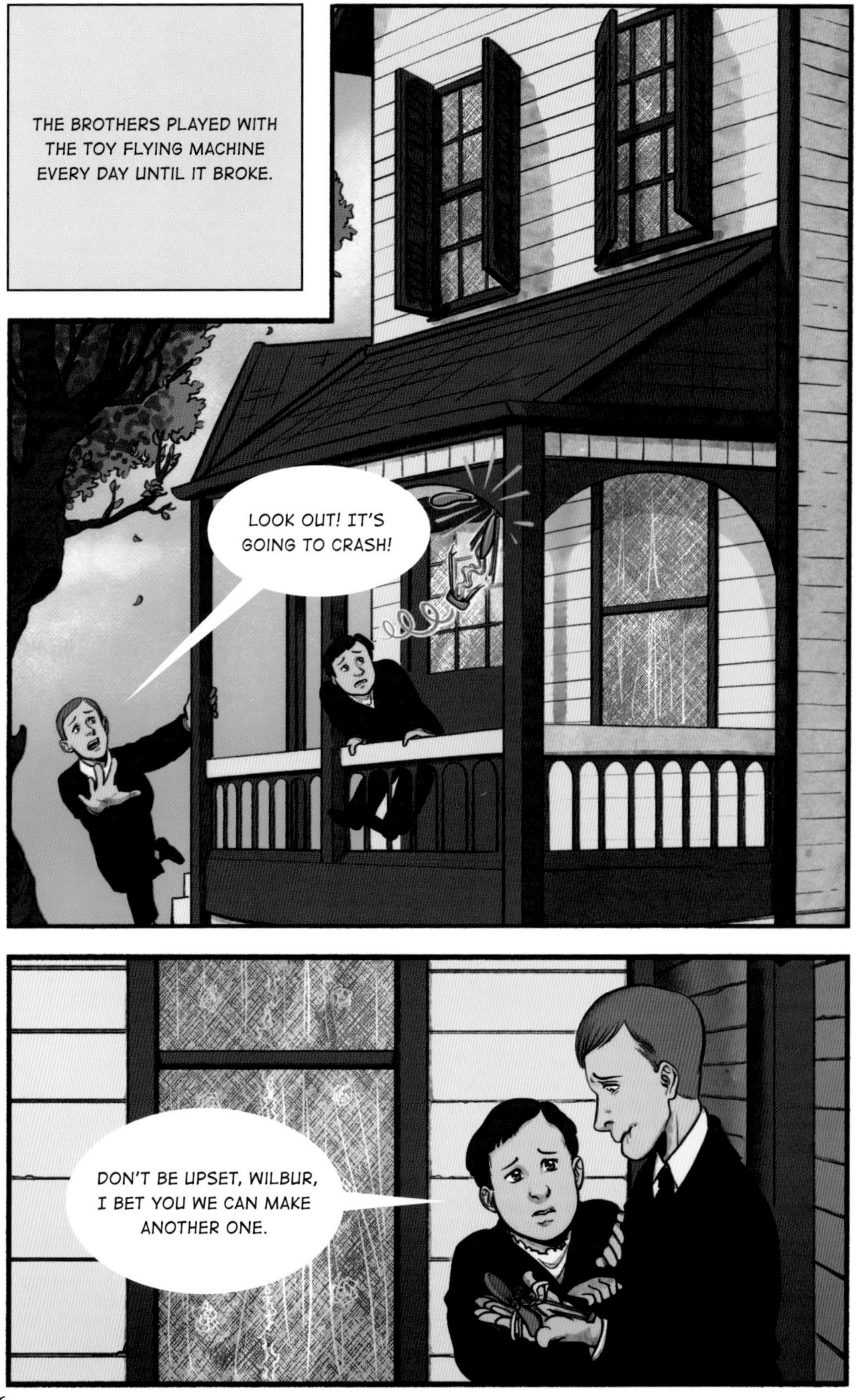
THE BROTHERS PLAYED WITH THE TOY FLYING MACHINE EVERY DAY UNTIL IT BROKE.
LOOK OUT! IT'S GOING TO CRASH!
DON'T BE UPSET, WILBUR, I BET YOU WE CAN MAKE ANOTHER ONE.

SO THEY COPIED IT AND BUILT THEIR OWN VERSIONS, TRYING TO MAKE THEM BIGGER AND BETTER THAN THE ORIGINAL.

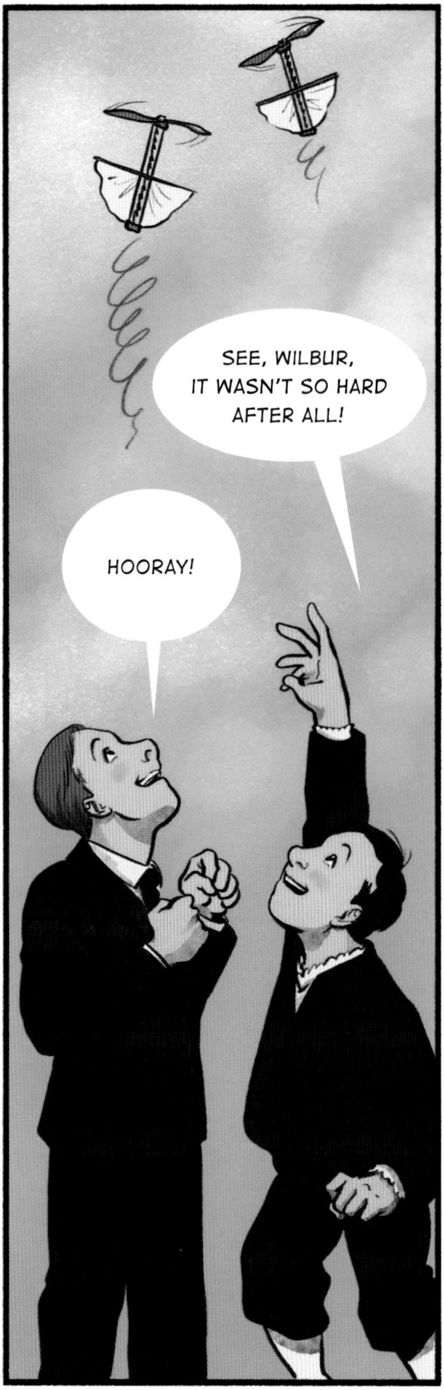
SEE, WILBUR, IT WASN'T SO HARD AFTER ALL!
HOORAY!

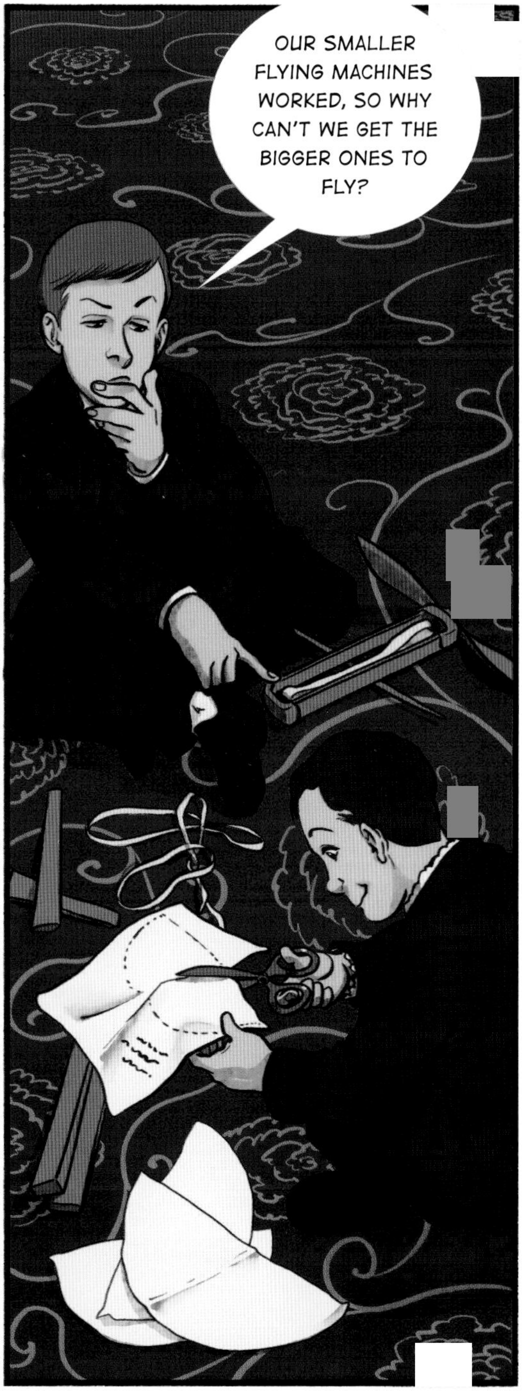
OUR SMALLER FLYING MACHINES WORKED, SO WHY CAN'T WE GET THE BIGGER ONES TO FLY?

AS TEENAGERS, WILBUR AND ORVILLE PURCHASED THEIR FIRST BICYCLES AND FELL IN LOVE WITH CROSS-COUNTRY CYCLING. IN THEIR TWENTIES, THEY DECIDED TO OPEN A STORE—WRIGHT CYCLE CO.—TO SELL AND BUILD BICYCLES OF THEIR OWN DESIGNS.

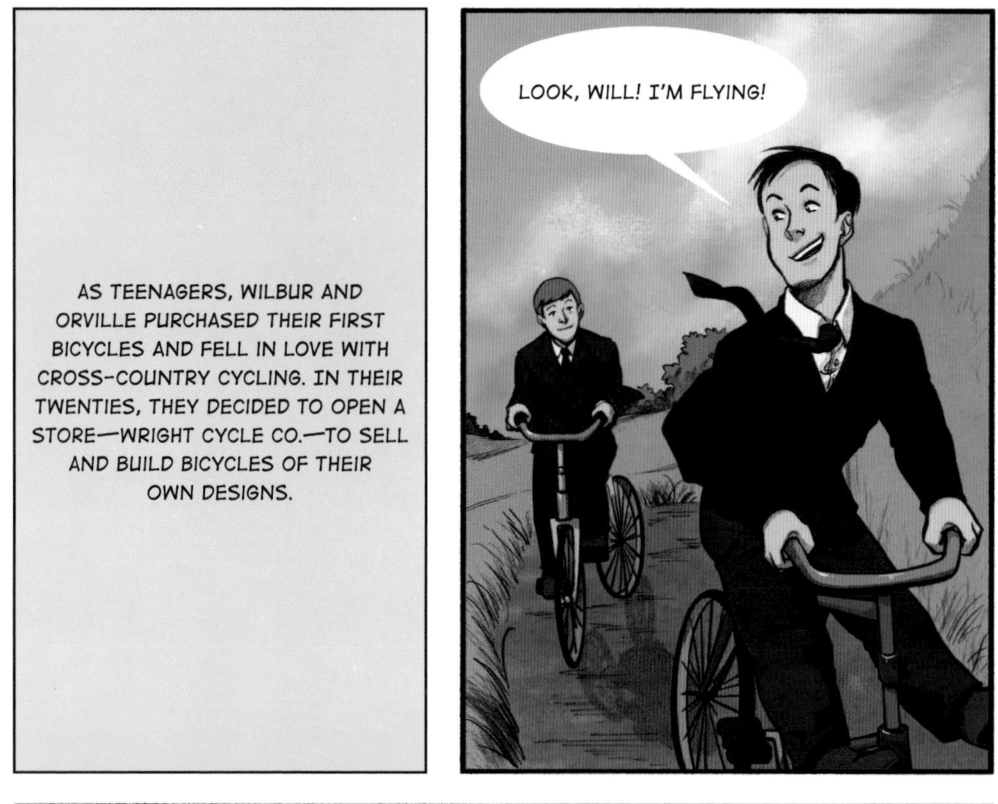
LOOK, WILL! I'M FLYING!

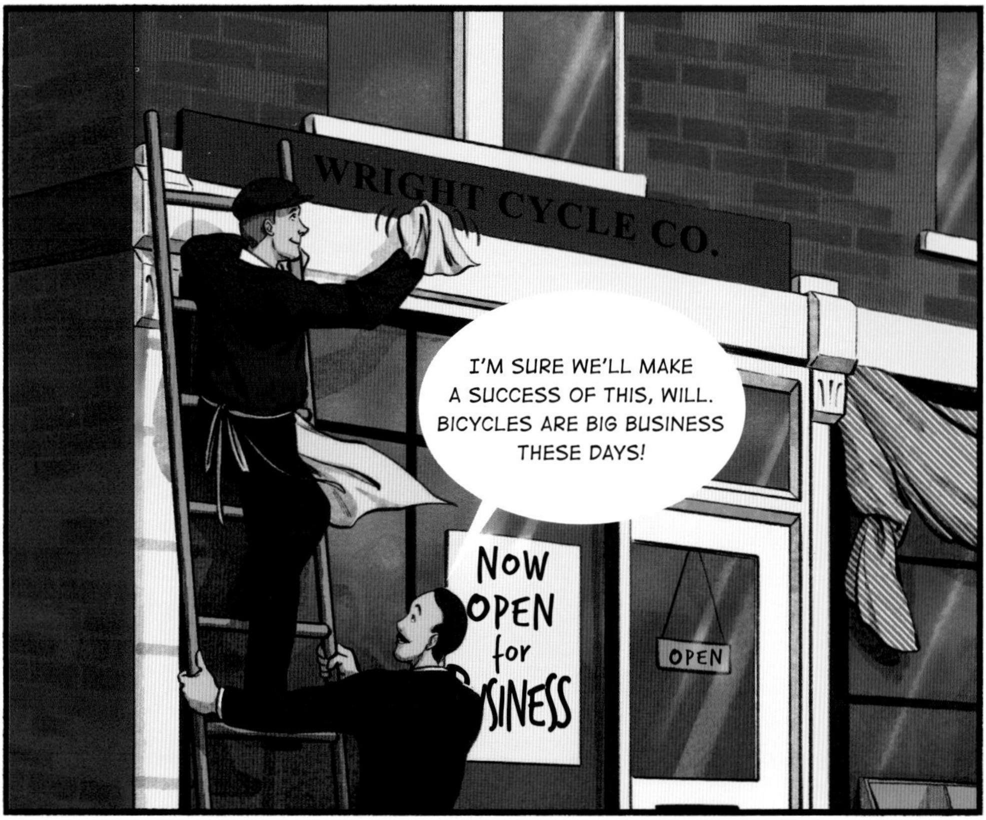
WRIGHT CYCLE CO.
I'M SURE WE'LL MAKE A SUCCESS OF THIS, WILL. BICYCLES ARE BIG BUSINESS THESE DAYS!
NOW OPEN for
OPEN

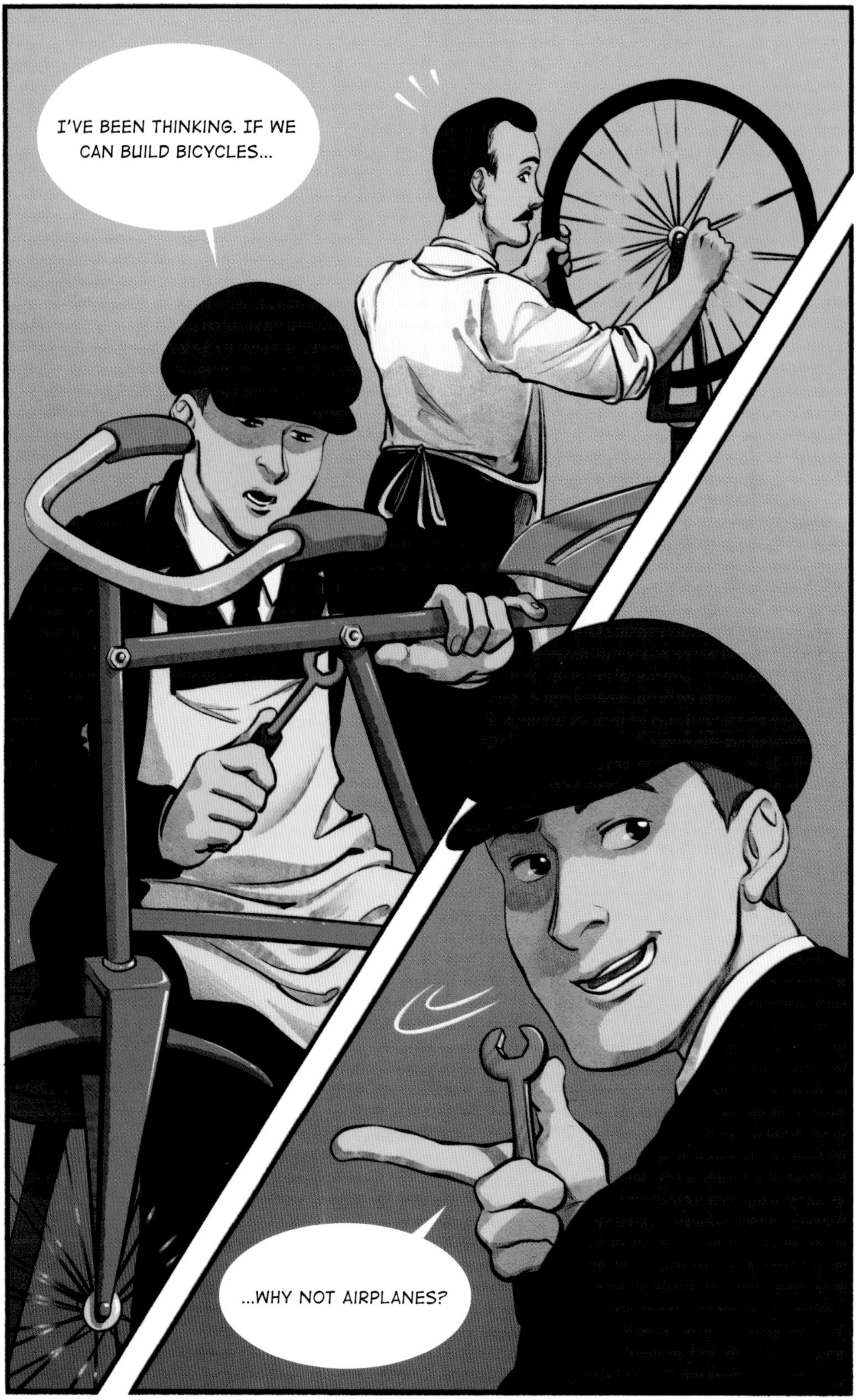
I'VE BEEN THINKING. IF WE CAN BUILD BICYCLES...
...WHY NOT AIRPLANES?

THE BROTHERS IMPROVED THEIR MECHANICAL SKILLS BY DESIGNING AND BUILDING BICYCLES. SOON, BUSINESS WAS BOOMING, WHICH GAVE THEM THE MONEY TO SPEND ON DESIGNING PLANES.

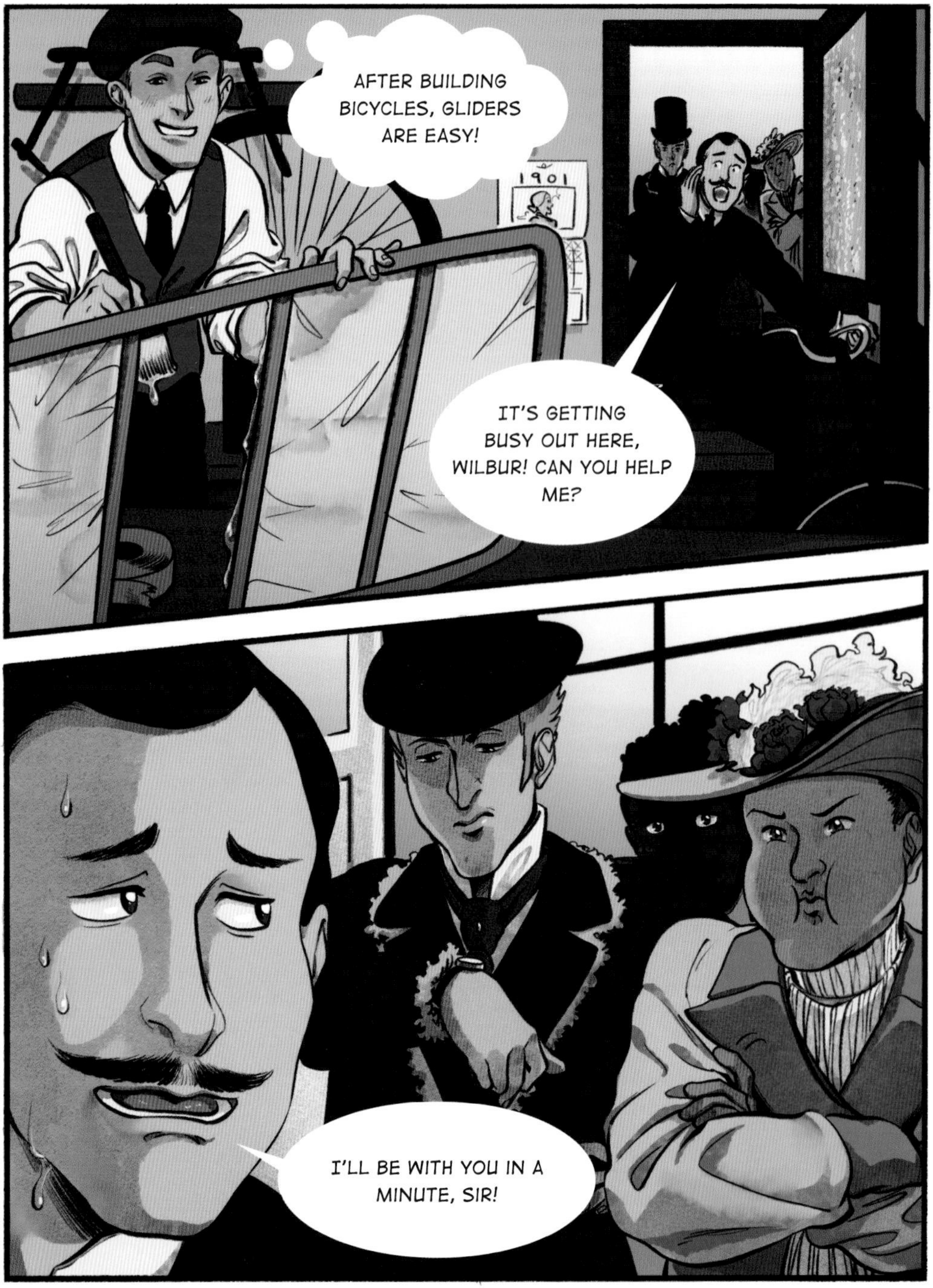
AFTER BUILDING BICYCLES, GLIDERS ARE EASY!
1901
IT'S GETTING BUSY OUT HERE, WILBUR! CAN YOU HELP ME?
I'LL BE WITH YOU IN A MINUTE, SIR!

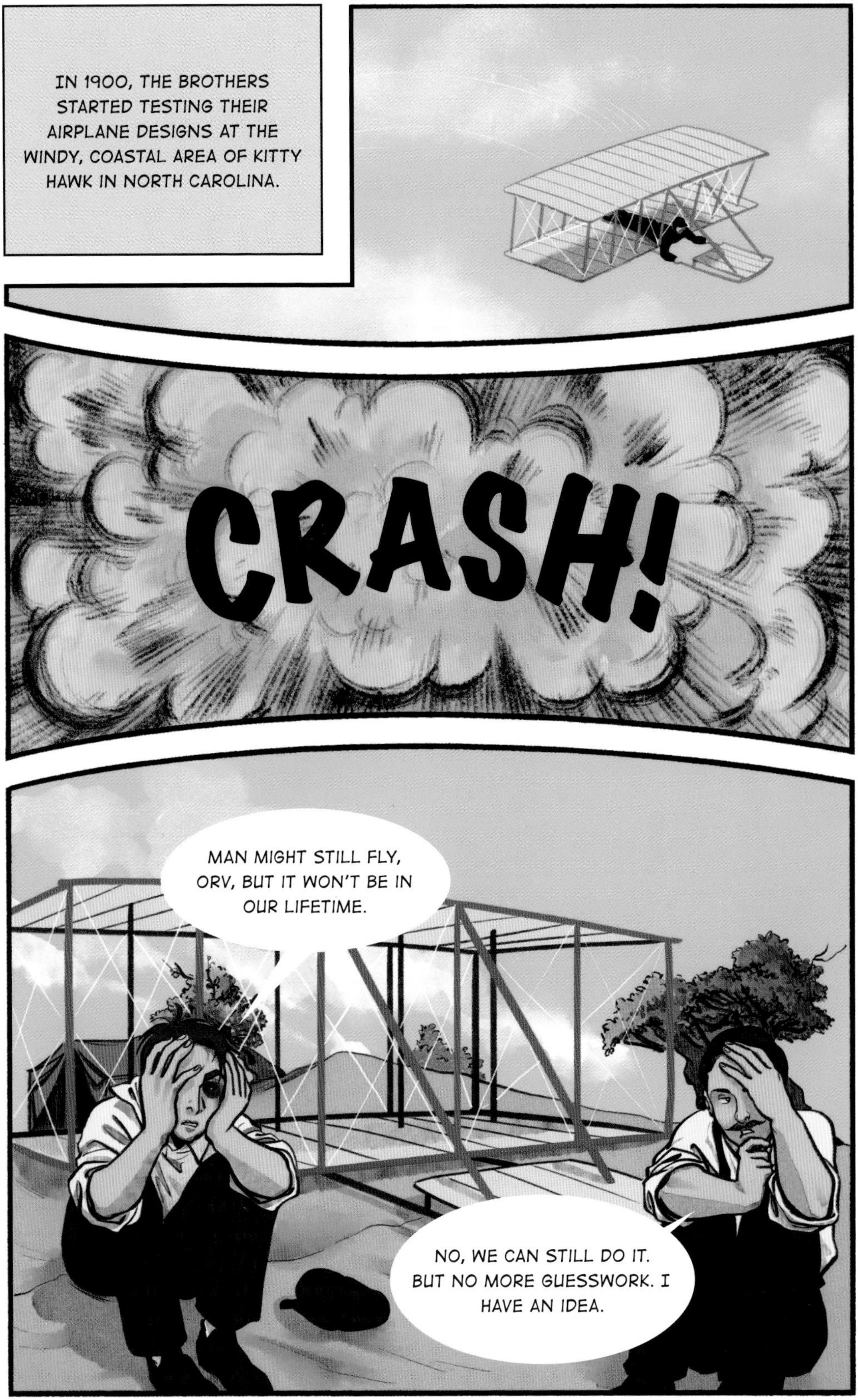
IN 1900, THE BROTHERS STARTED TESTING THEIR AIRPLANE DESIGNS AT THE WINDY, COASTAL AREA OF KITTY HAWK IN NORTH CAROLINA.
CRASH!
MAN MIGHT STILL FLY, ORV, BUT IT WON'T BE IN OUR LIFETIME.
NO, WE CAN STILL DO IT. BUT NO MORE GUESSWORK. I HAVE AN IDEA.

IN 1901, THE BROTHERS BUILT A WIND TUNNEL—THE SECOND IN THE WORLD—AT THE BACK OF THEIR BICYCLE STORE. THEY WANTED TO MEASURE THE EFFECT OF THE IMPORTANT AERODYNAMIC FORCES OF LIFT AND DRAG ON HUNDREDS OF MODEL WINGS. THEIR LABORIOUS TESTING GAVE THEM THE MOST DETAILED DATA IN THE WORLD FOR DESIGNING AIRCRAFT.

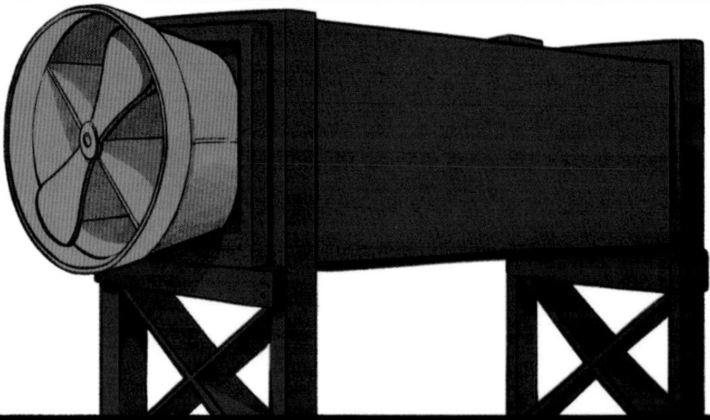

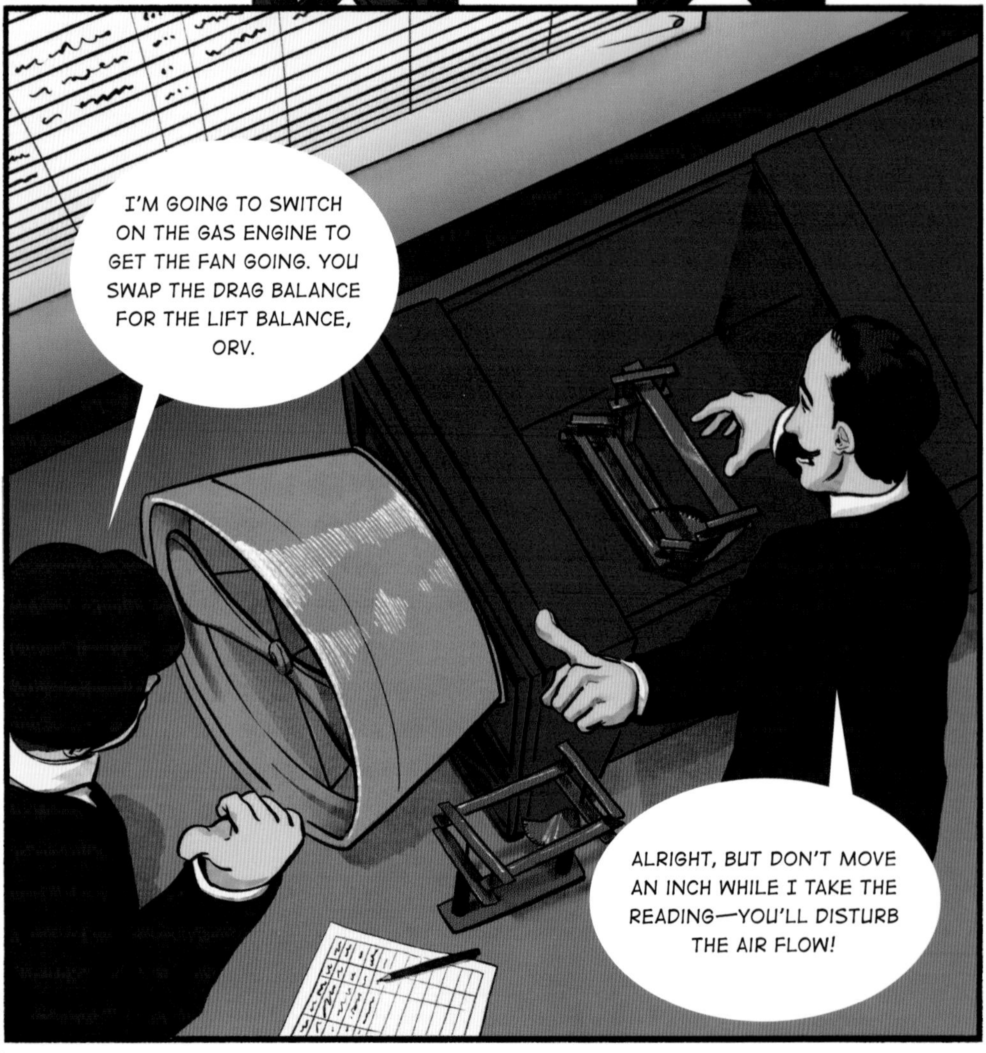

I'M GOING TO SWITCH ON THE GAS ENGINE TO GET THE FAN GOING. YOU SWAP THE DRAG BALANCE FOR THE LIFT BALANCE, ORV.
ALRIGHT, BUT DON'T MOVE AN INCH WHILE I TAKE THE READING—YOU'LL DISTURB THE AIR FLOW!

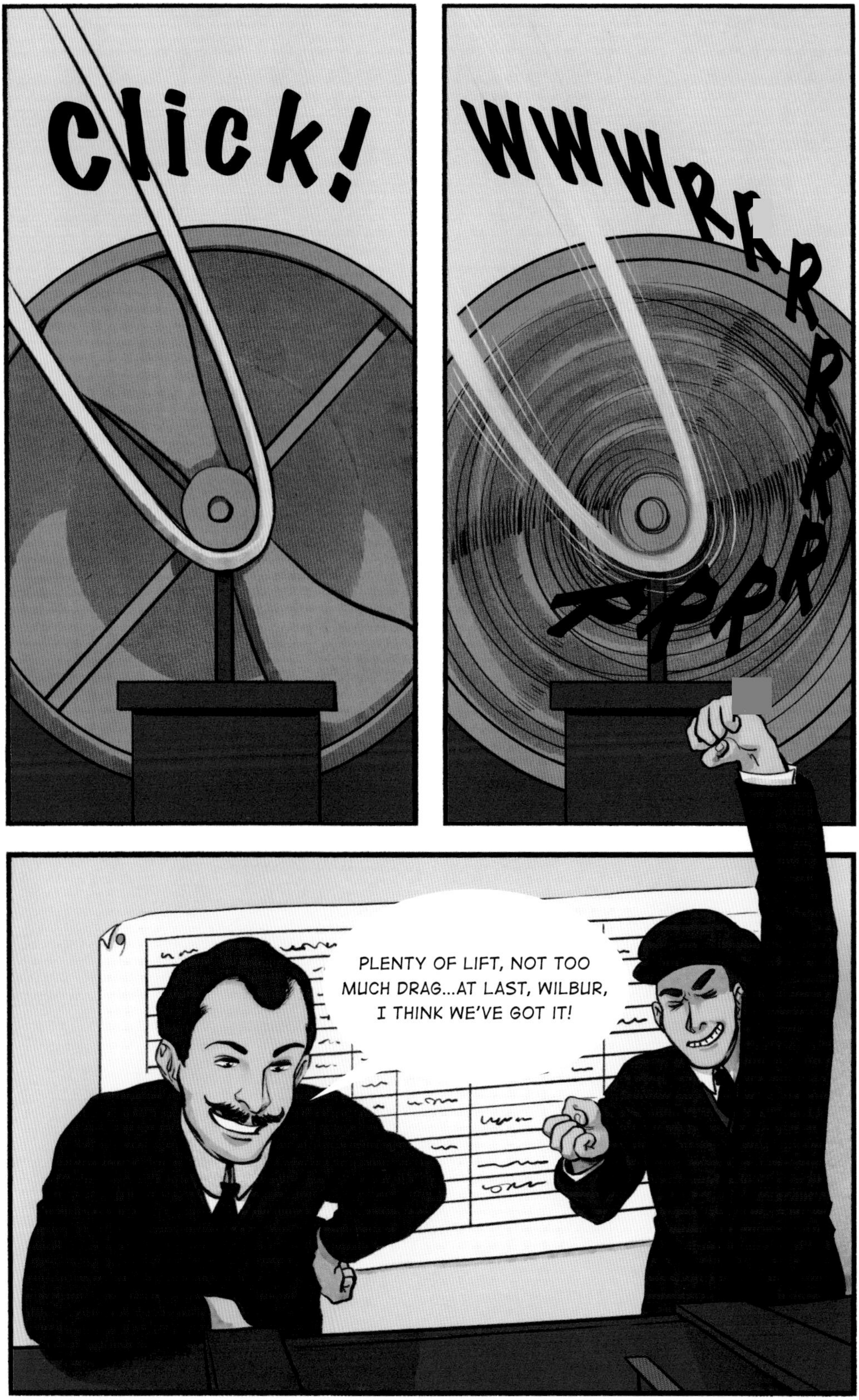
Click!
WWWRRRRRRRRRR
PLENTY OF LIFT, NOT TOO MUCH DRAG...AT LAST, WILBUR, I THINK WE'VE GOT IT!

AFTER THREE YEARS OF TESTING GLIDERS AT KITTY HAWK, NORTH CAROLINA, THE BROTHERS HAD PERFECTED THEIR STEERING SYSTEM AND HAD BUILT THEIR OWN ENGINE AND PROPELLERS. ON DECEMBER 17, 1903, THEY BELIEVED THEY WERE READY TO MAKE HISTORY.

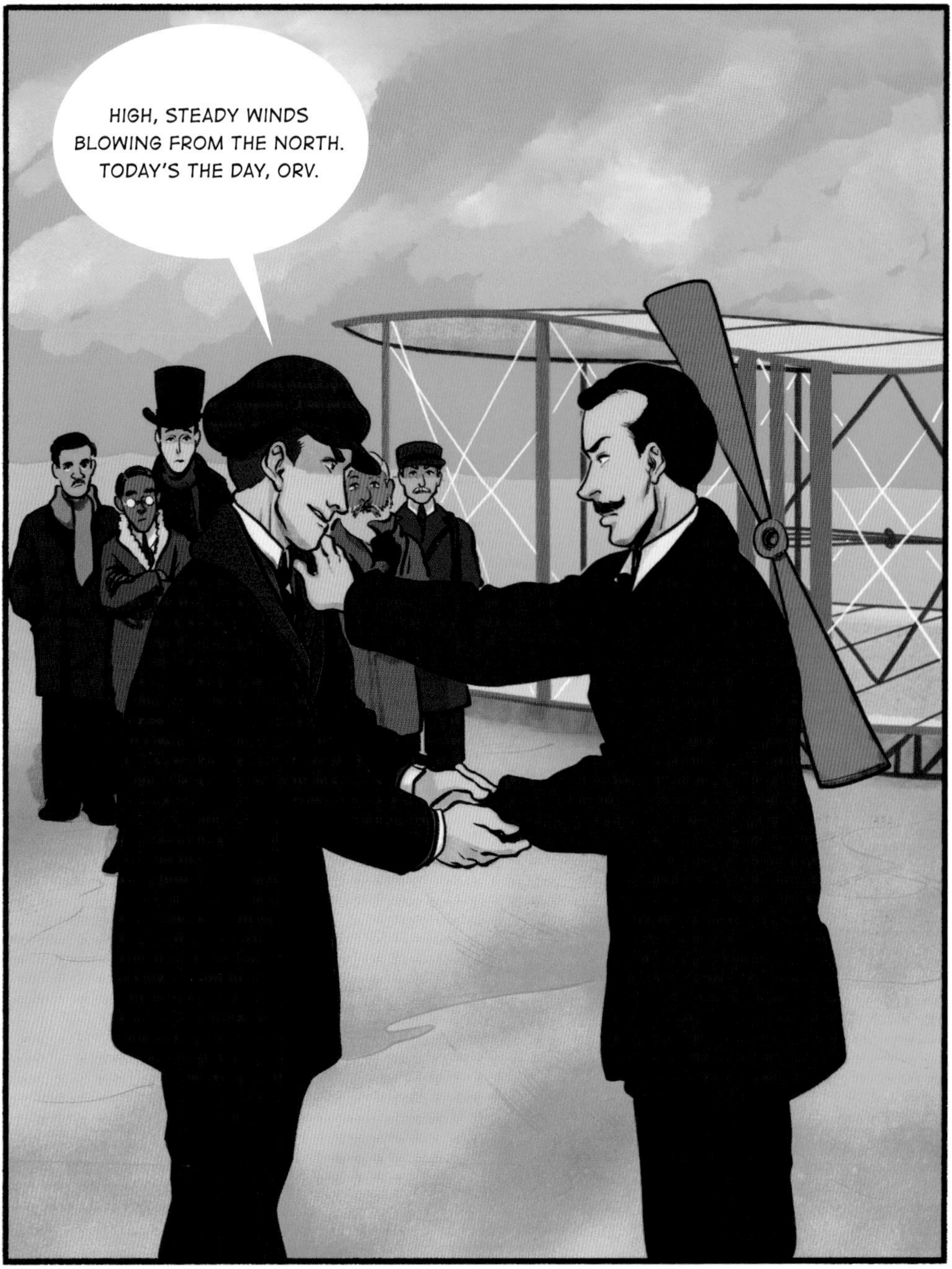
HIGH, STEADY WINDS BLOWING FROM THE NORTH. TODAY'S THE DAY, ORV.

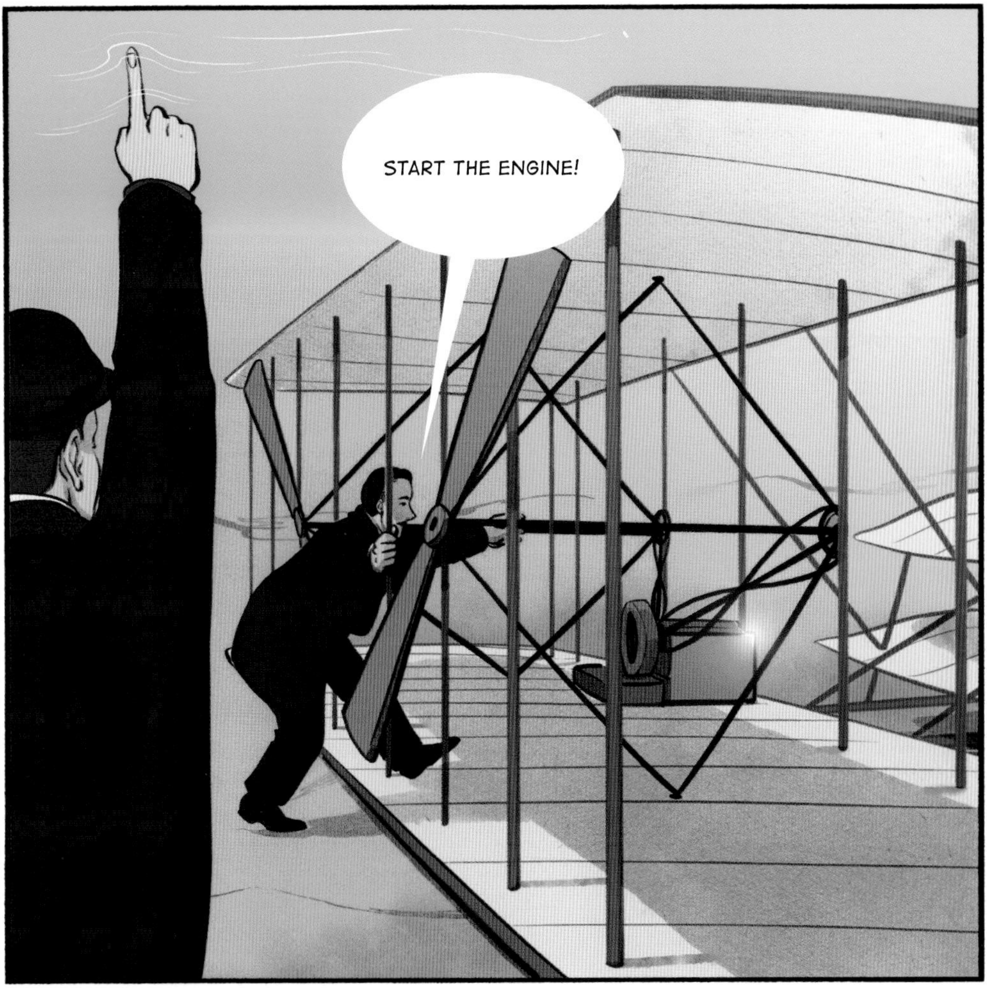
START THE ENGINE!

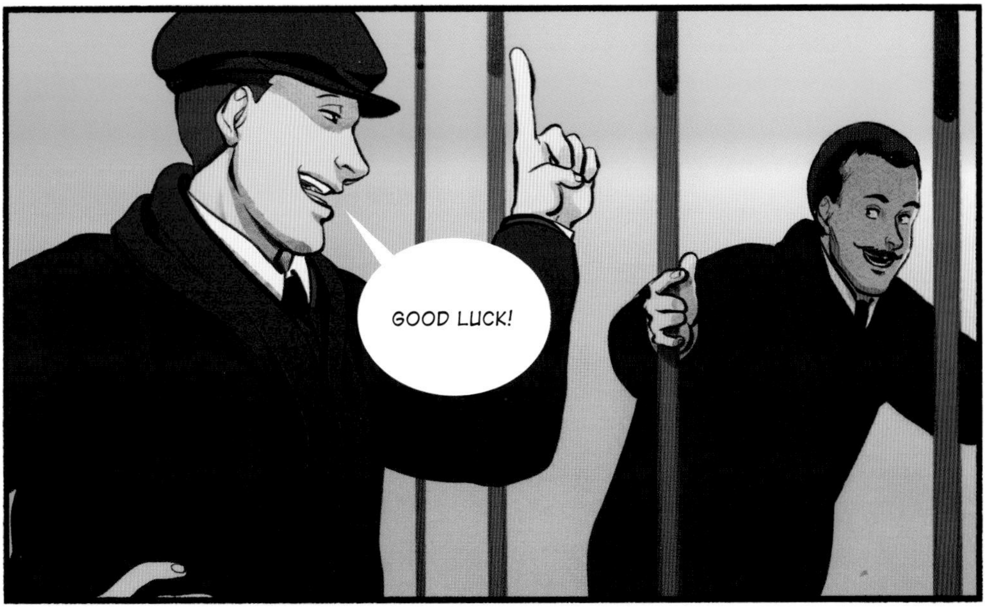
GOOD LUCK!

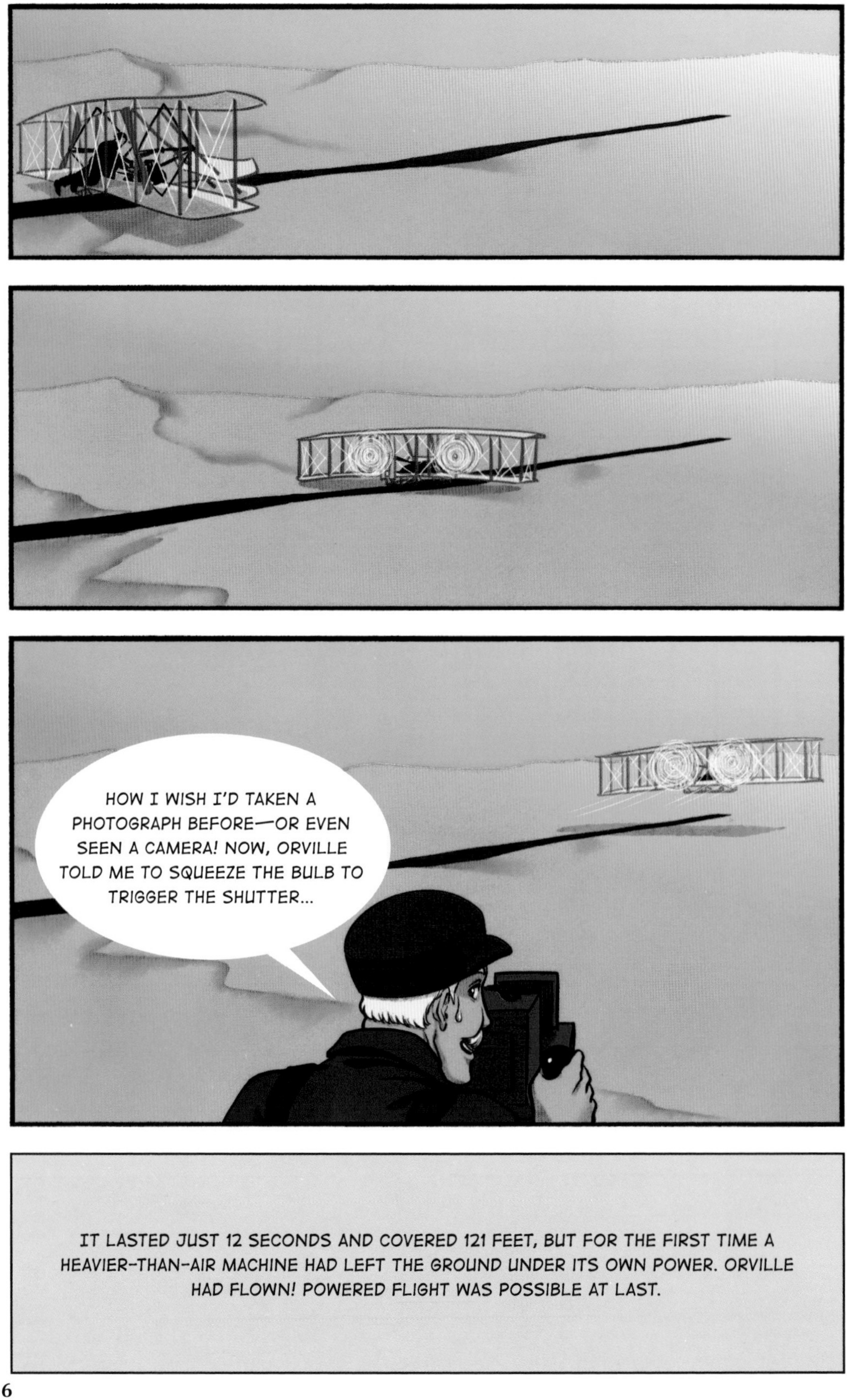
HOW I WISH I'D TAKEN A PHOTOGRAPH BEFORE—OR EVEN SEEN A CAMERA! NOW, ORVILLE TOLD ME TO SQUEEZE THE BULB TO TRIGGER THE SHUTTER...
IT LASTED JUST 12 SECONDS AND COVERED 121 FEET, BUT FOR THE FIRST TIME A HEAVIER-THAN-AIR MACHINE HAD LEFT THE GROUND UNDER ITS OWN POWER. ORVILLE HAD FLOWN! POWERED FLIGHT WAS POSSIBLE AT LAST.

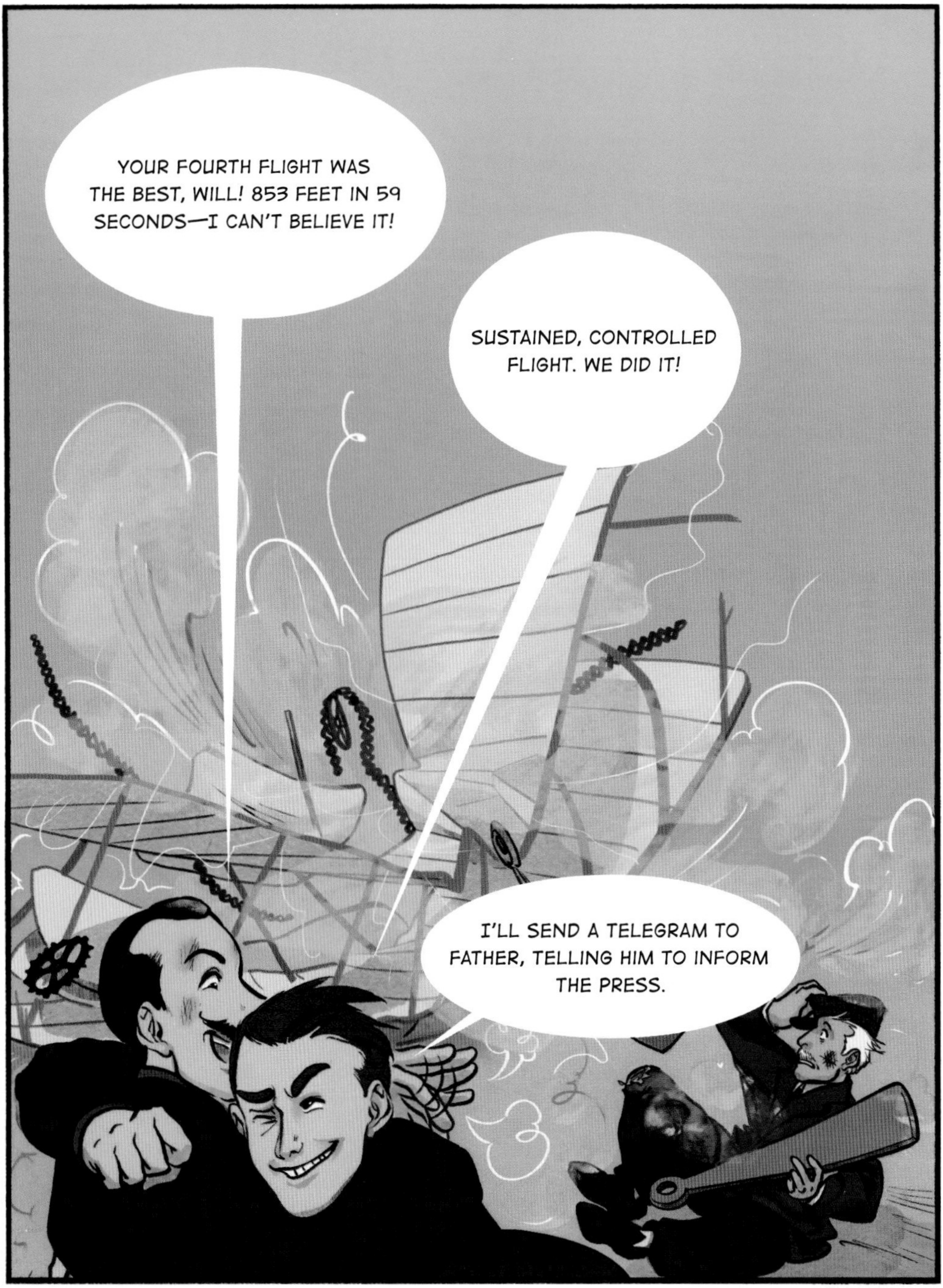
YOUR FOURTH FLIGHT WAS THE BEST, WILL! 853 FEET IN 59 SECONDS—I CAN'T BELIEVE IT!
SUSTAINED, CONTROLLED FLIGHT. WE DID IT!
I'LL SEND A TELEGRAM TO FATHER, TELLING HIM TO INFORM THE PRESS.

WILBUR AND ORVILLE'S ACHIEVEMENT AT THE START OF THE TWENTIETH CENTURY CHANGED THE WORLD FOREVER. FROM THIS POINT ON, AIRPLANES AND AVIATION TECHNOLOGIES DEVELOPED VERY QUICKLY.

ALBERTO SANTOS-DUMONT (1873–1932) THE KING OF CONTROVERSY

ALBERTO GREW UP WITH HIS SIX BROTHERS AND SISTERS ON HIS FAMILY'S COFFEE PLANTATION. HIS FATHER WAS A SKILLED ENGINEER AND INVESTED IN THE LATEST TECHNOLOGIES TO RUN THE BUSINESS. ALBERTO LOVED THE MACHINERY AND LIVING BENEATH THE BLUE, OPEN SKIES OF BRAZIL.

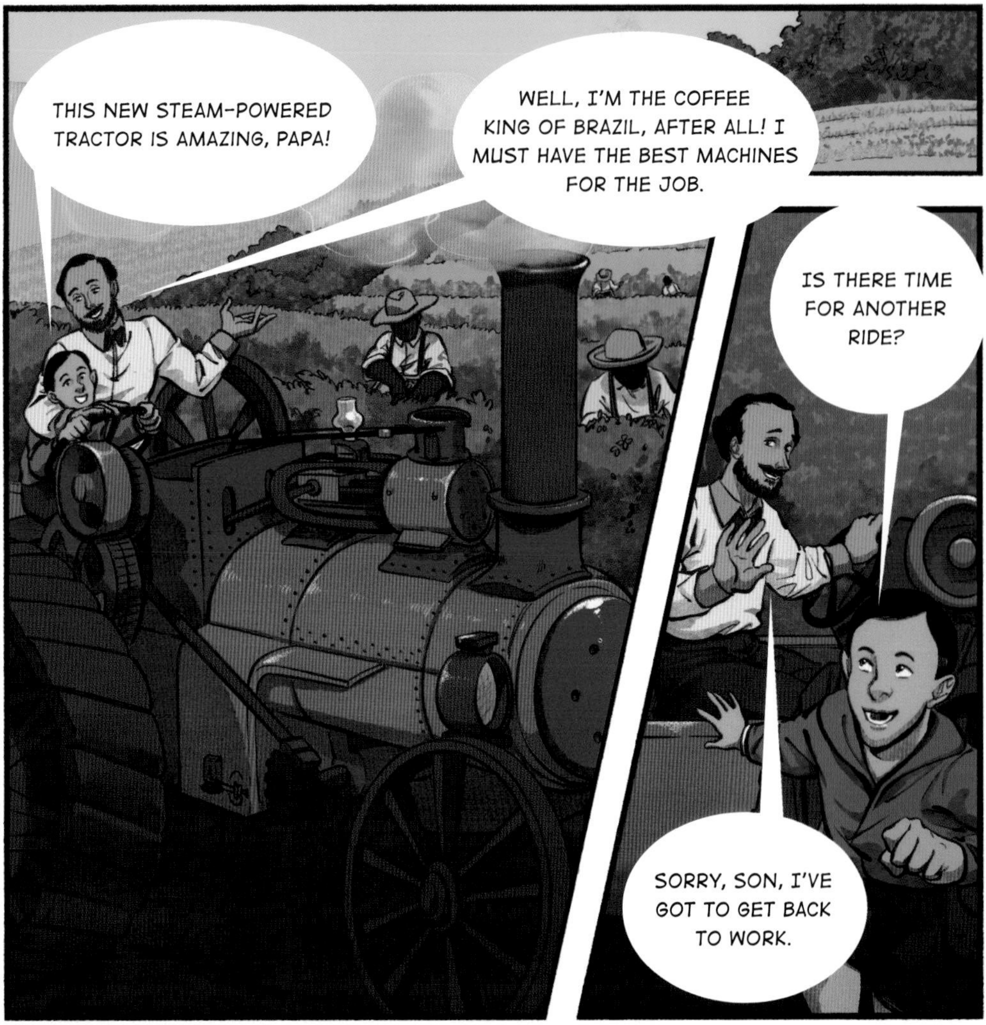
THIS NEW STEAM-POWERED TRACTOR IS AMAZING, PAPA!
WELL, I'M THE COFFEE KING OF BRAZIL, AFTER ALL! I MUST HAVE THE BEST MACHINES FOR THE JOB.
IS THERE TIME FOR ANOTHER RIDE?
SORRY, SON, I'VE GOT TO GET BACK TO WORK.

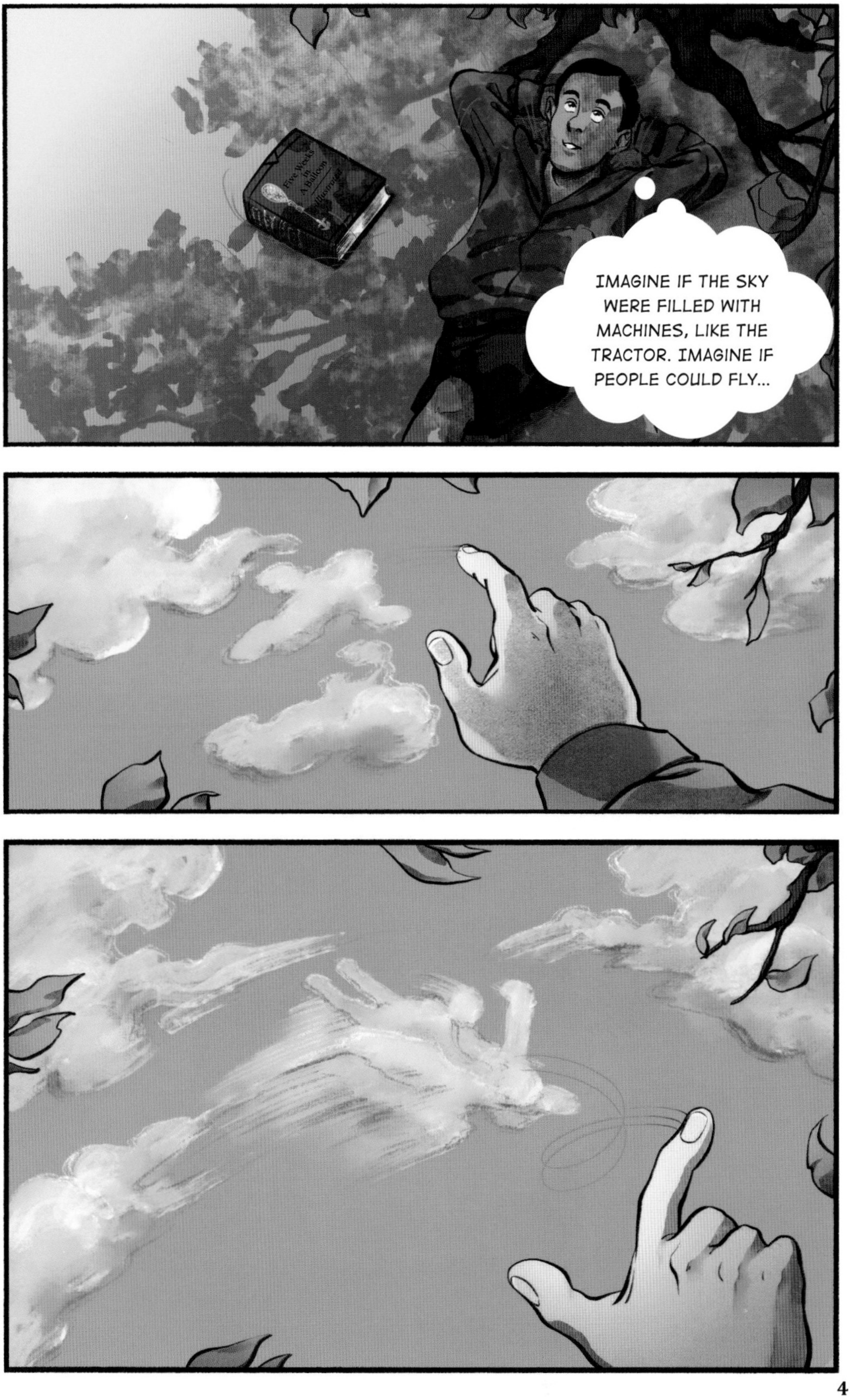
Five Weeks in A Balloon
IMAGINE IF THE SKY WERE FILLED WITH MACHINES, LIKE THE TRACTOR. IMAGINE IF PEOPLE COULD FLY...

AFTER A HORSE RIDING ACCIDENT LEFT ALBERTO'S FATHER UNABLE TO WORK, HE SOLD THE COFFEE PLANTATION. AT AGE 18, ALBERTO WAS SENT TO LIVE WITH RELATIVES IN PARIS, FRANCE. THOUGH HE WAS SAD TO BE AWAY FROM EVERYTHING HE KNEW AND LOVED, HE WAS STILL INTRIGUED WITH THE IDEA OF FLOATING IN THE CLOUDS.

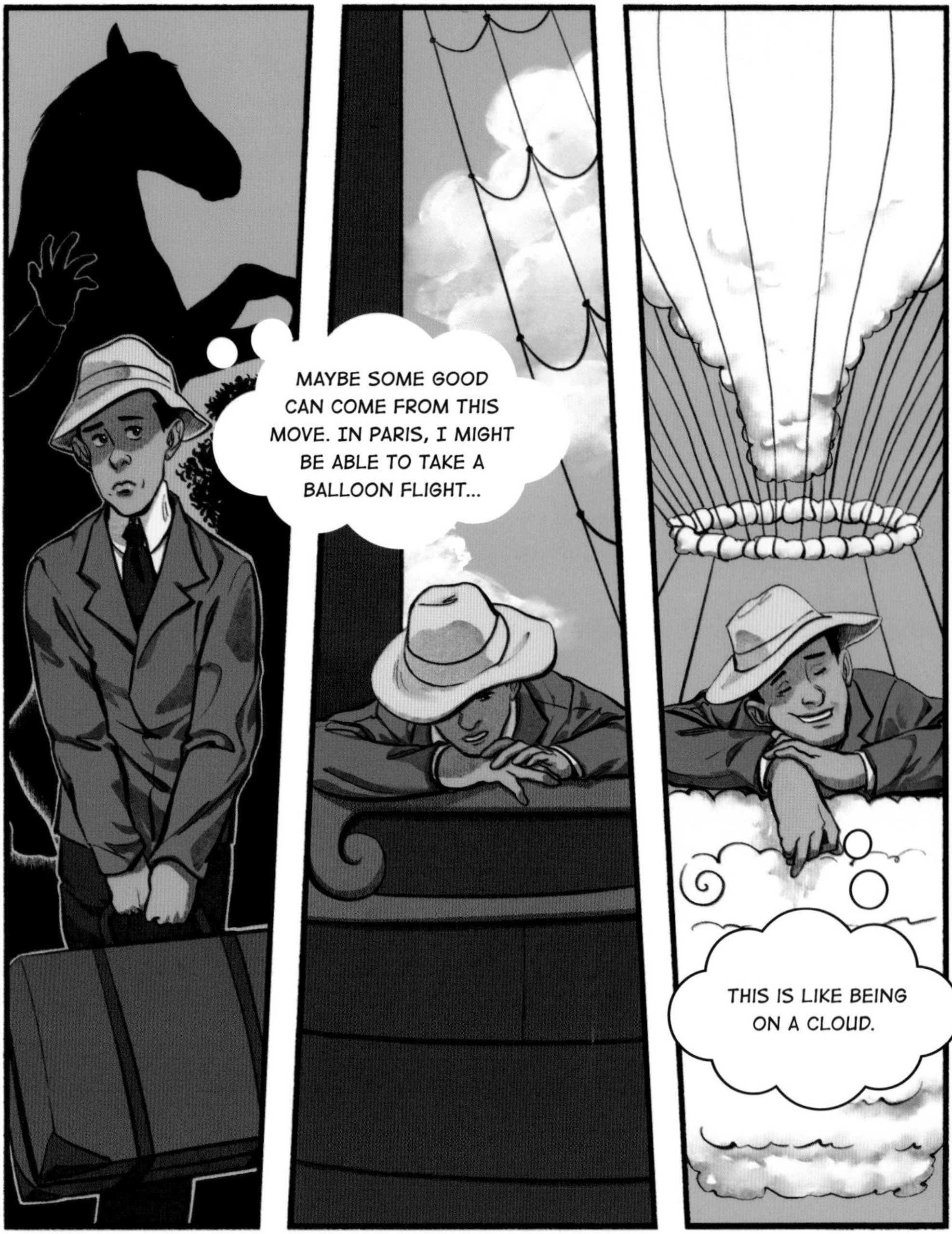
MAYBE SOME GOOD CAN COME FROM THIS MOVE. IN PARIS, I MIGHT BE ABLE TO TAKE A BALLOON FLIGHT...
THIS IS LIKE BEING ON A CLOUD.

HOT AIR BALLOONS HAD BEEN AROUND FOR OVER 100 YEARS WHEN ALBERTO TOOK HIS FIRST FLIGHT, BUT IT WAS AN EXCITING NEW EXPERIENCE FOR HIM.

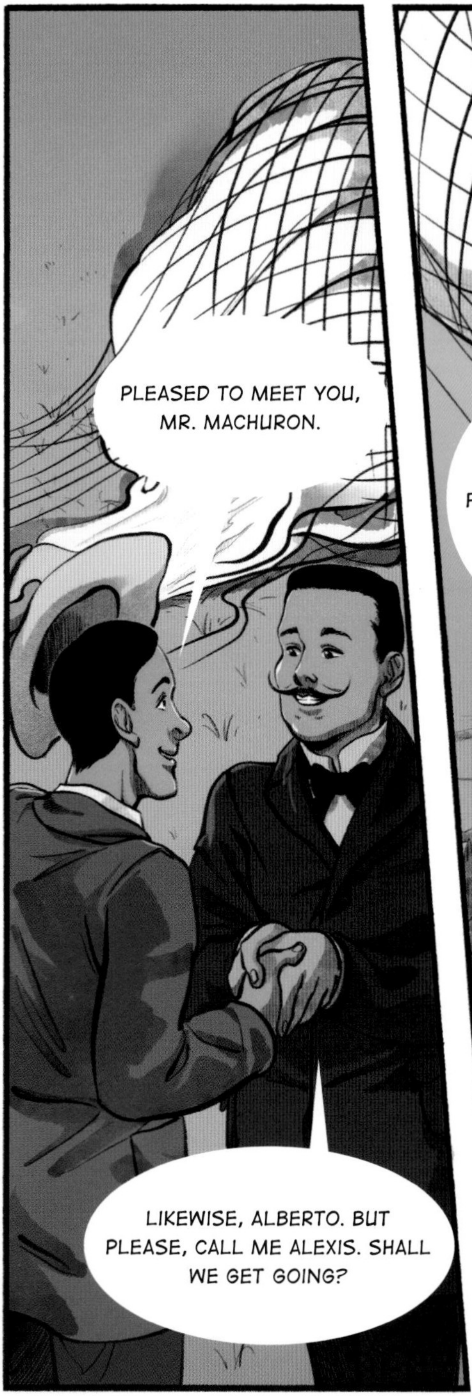
PLEASED TO MEET YOU, MR. MACHURON.
LIKEWISE, ALBERTO. BUT PLEASE, CALL ME ALEXIS. SHALL WE GET GOING?

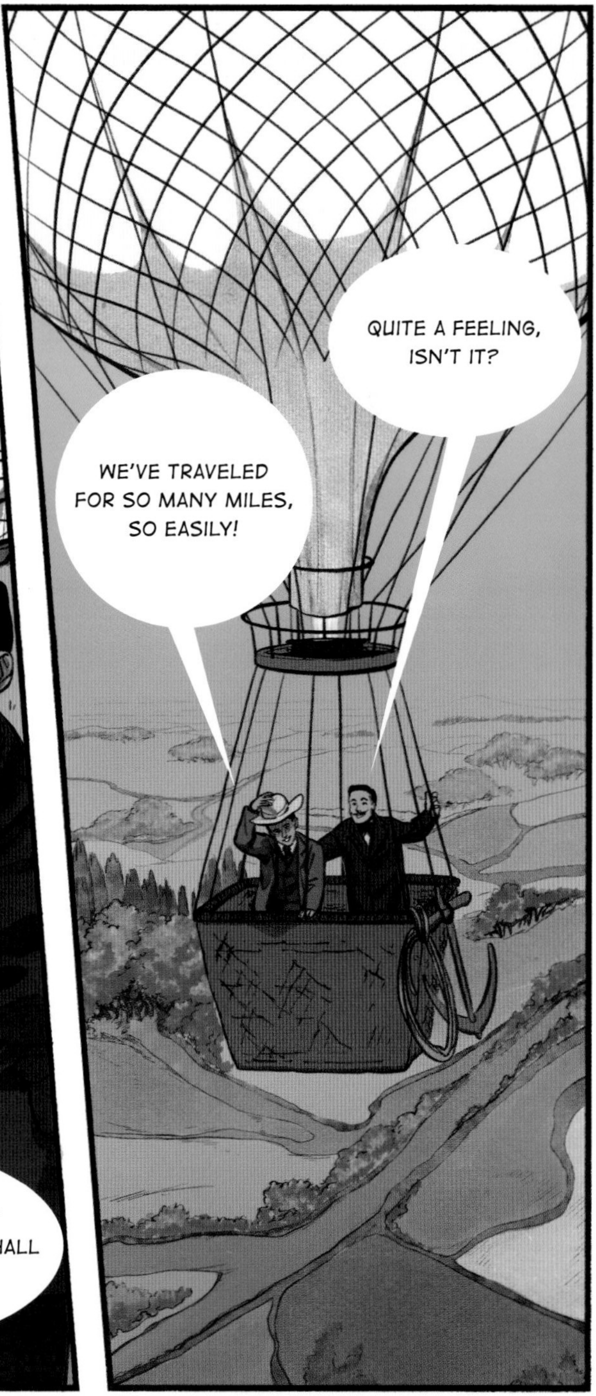
QUITE A FEELING, ISN'T IT?
WE'VE TRAVELED FOR SO MANY MILES, SO EASILY!

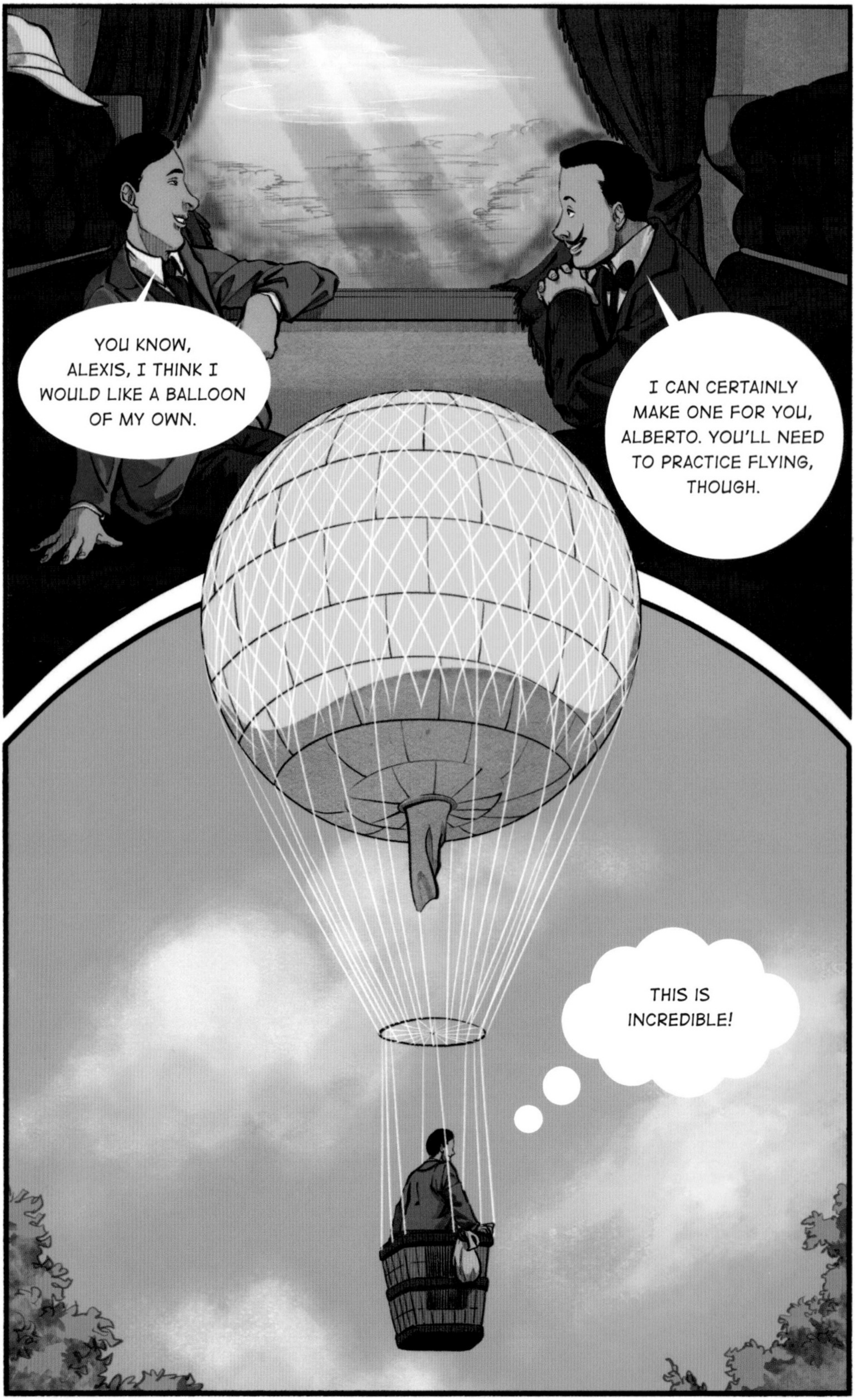
YOU KNOW, ALEXIS, I THINK I WOULD LIKE A BALLOON OF MY OWN.
I CAN CERTAINLY MAKE ONE FOR YOU, ALBERTO. YOU'LL NEED TO PRACTICE FLYING, THOUGH.
THIS IS INCREDIBLE!

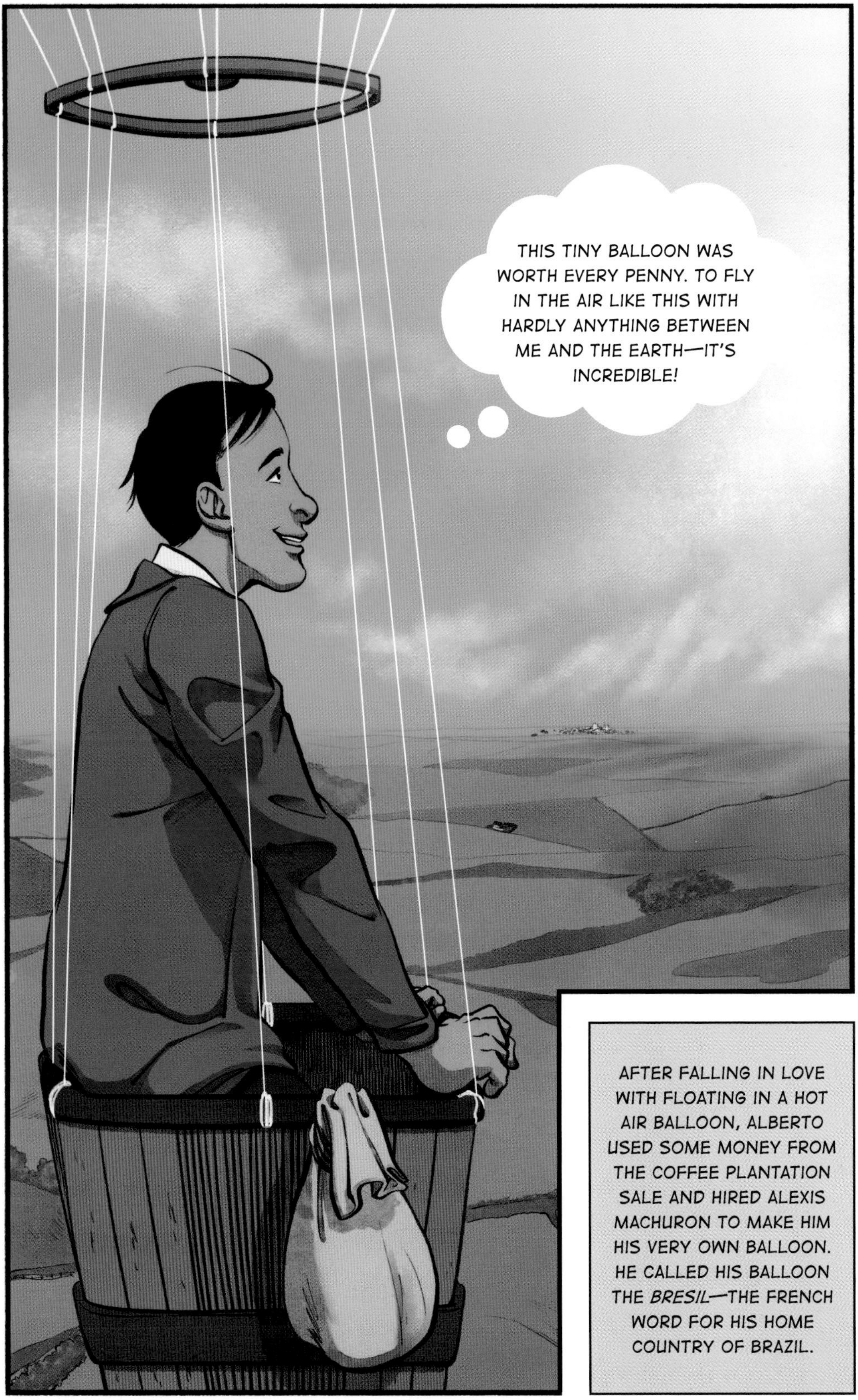
THIS TINY BALLOON WAS WORTH EVERY PENNY. TO FLY IN THE AIR LIKE THIS WITH HARDLY ANYTHING BETWEEN ME AND THE EARTH—IT'S INCREDIBLE!
AFTER FALLING IN LOVE WITH FLOATING IN A HOT AIR BALLOON, ALBERTO USED SOME MONEY FROM THE COFFEE PLANTATION SALE AND HIRED ALEXIS MACHURON TO MAKE HIM HIS VERY OWN BALLOON. HE CALLED HIS BALLOON THE *BRESIL*—THE FRENCH WORD FOR HIS HOME COUNTRY OF BRAZIL.

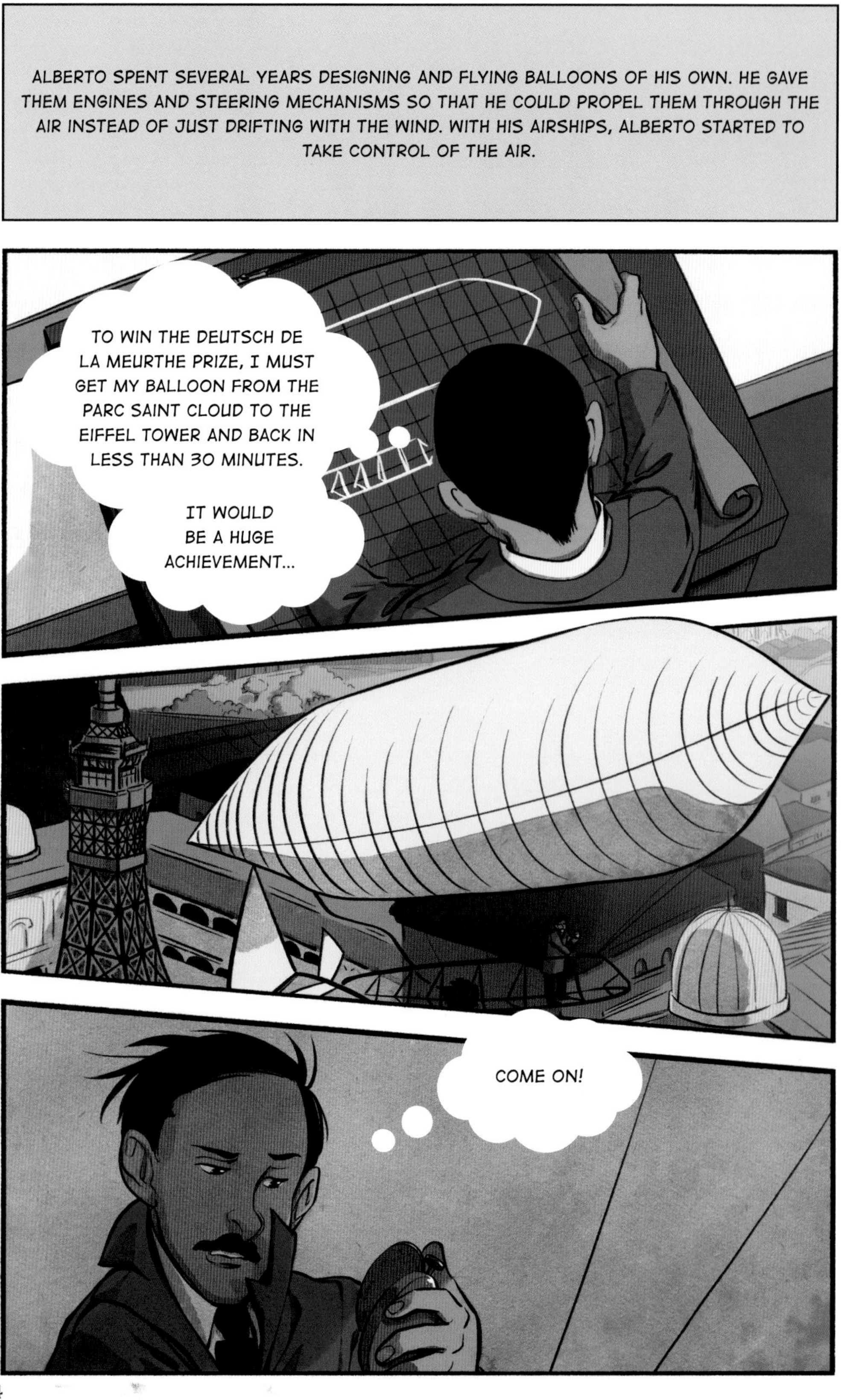
ALBERTO SPENT SEVERAL YEARS DESIGNING AND FLYING BALLOONS OF HIS OWN. HE GAVE THEM ENGINES AND STEERING MECHANISMS SO THAT HE COULD PROPEL THEM THROUGH THE AIR INSTEAD OF JUST DRIFTING WITH THE WIND. WITH HIS AIRSHIPS, ALBERTO STARTED TO TAKE CONTROL OF THE AIR.
TO WIN THE DEUTSCH DE LA MEURTHE PRIZE, I MUST GET MY BALLOON FROM THE PARC SAINT CLOUD TO THE EIFFEL TOWER AND BACK IN LESS THAN 30 MINUTES.
IT WOULD BE A HUGE ACHIEVEMENT...
COME ON!

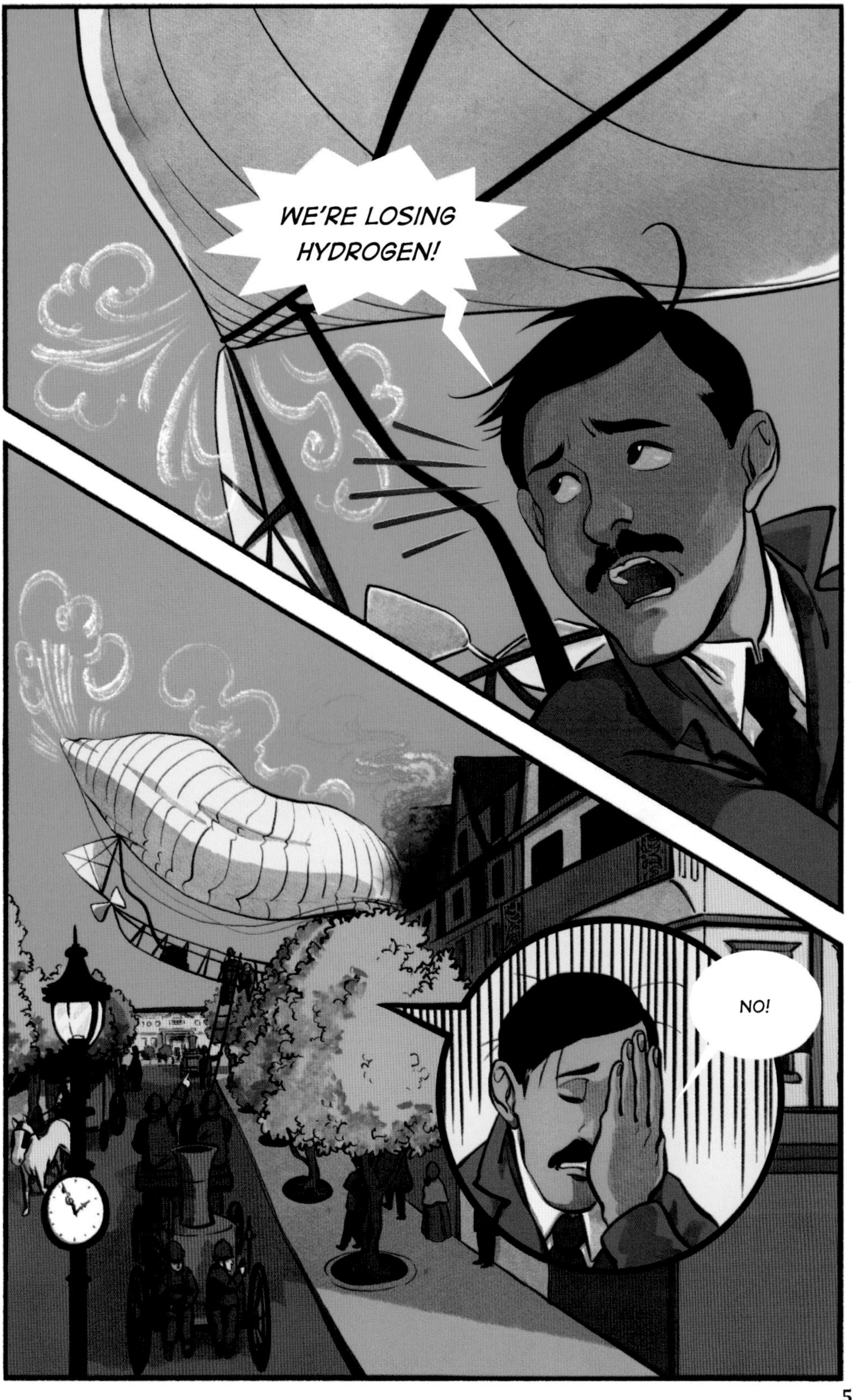
WE'RE LOSING HYDROGEN!
NO!

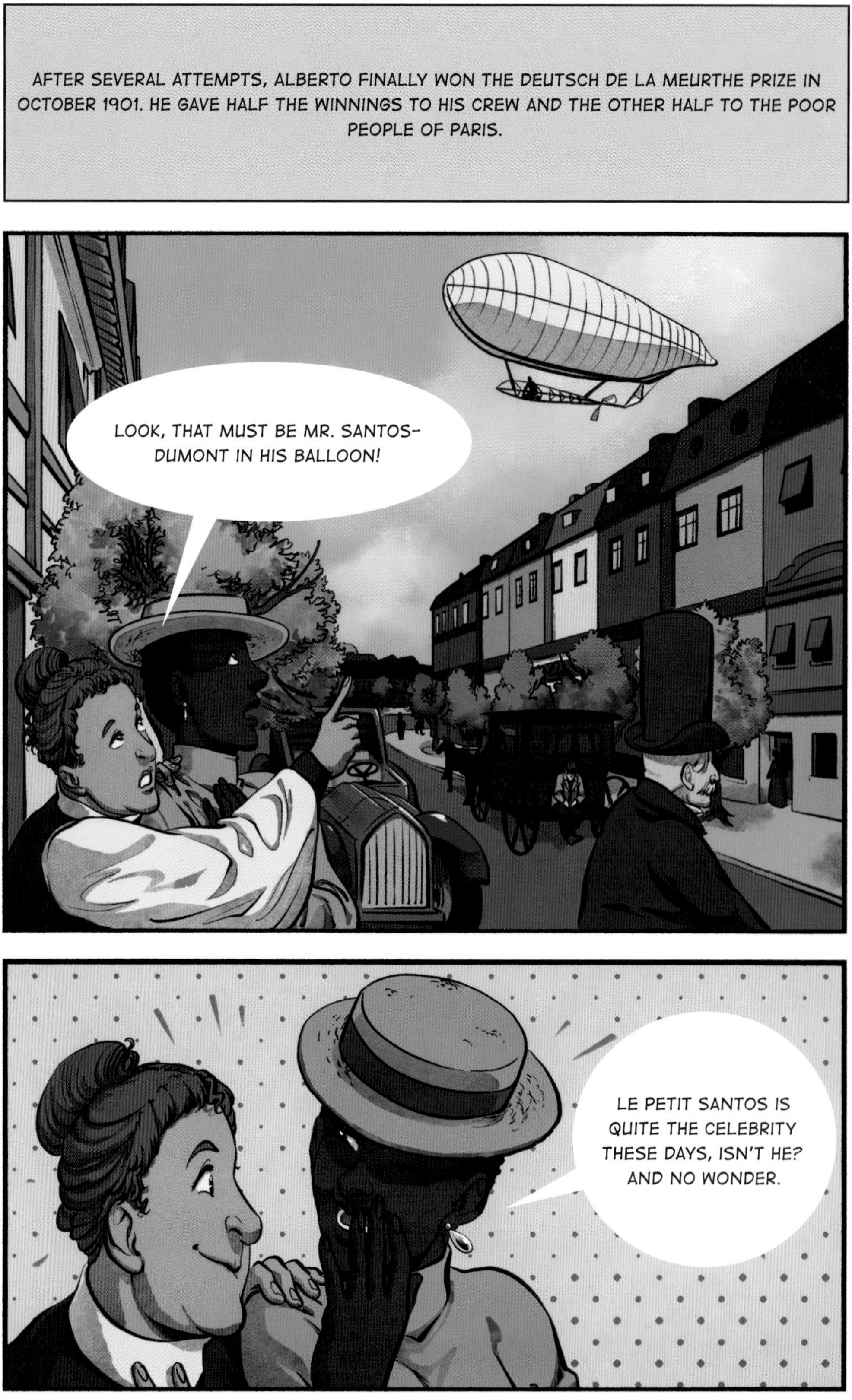
AFTER SEVERAL ATTEMPTS, ALBERTO FINALLY WON THE DEUTSCH DE LA MEURTHE PRIZE IN OCTOBER 1901. HE GAVE HALF THE WINNINGS TO HIS CREW AND THE OTHER HALF TO THE POOR PEOPLE OF PARIS.
LOOK, THAT MUST BE MR. SANTOS-DUMONT IN HIS BALLOON!
LE PETIT SANTOS IS QUITE THE CELEBRITY THESE DAYS, ISN'T HE? AND NO WONDER.

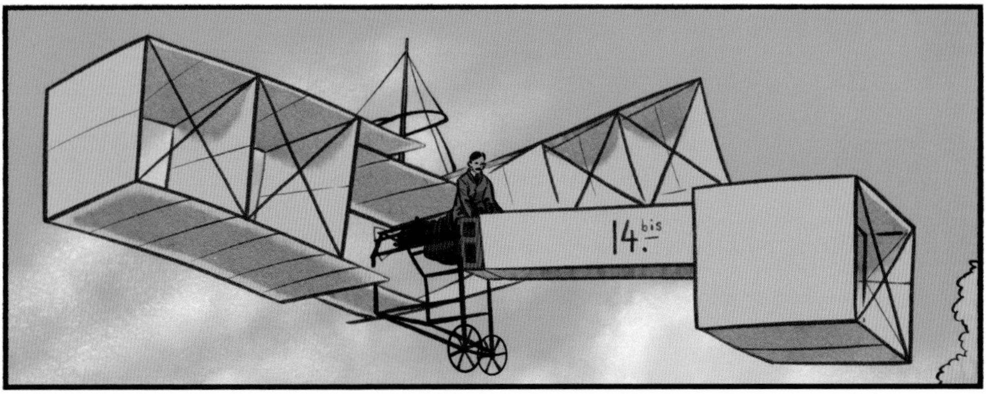
14.bis

AFTER SEVERAL YEARS OF BREAKING RECORDS WITH HIS BALLOONS AND AIRSHIPS, ALBERTO STARTED WORKING ON AIRPLANES.

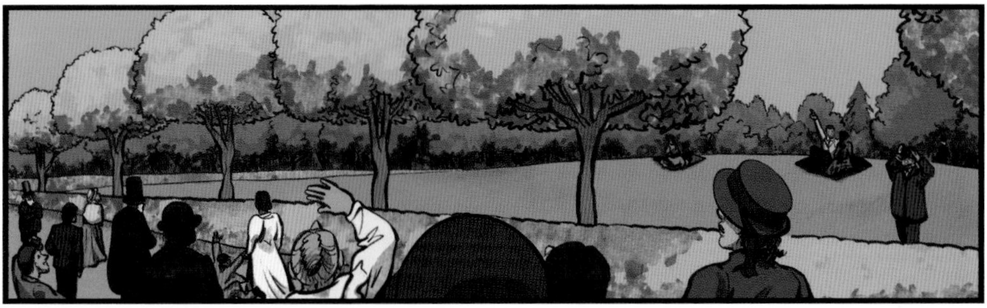

WHEN HIS *NO. 14-BIS* PLANE LIFTED OFF IN 1906, MANY BELIEVED HE WAS THE FIRST PERSON TO ACHIEVE MANNED, POWERED, HEAVIER-THAN-AIR FLIGHT. TODAY, THAT HONOR IS USUALLY AWARDED TO THE WRIGHT BROTHERS.

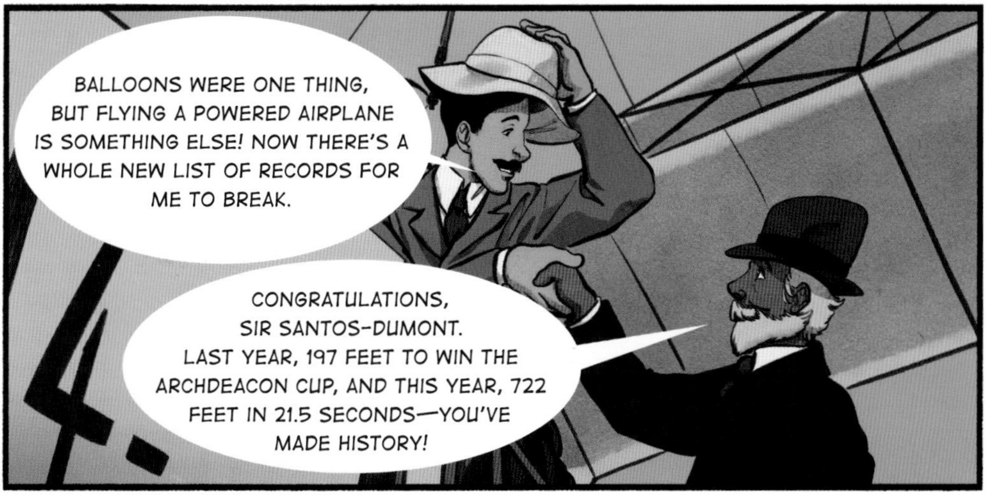
BALLOONS WERE ONE THING, BUT FLYING A POWERED AIRPLANE IS SOMETHING ELSE! NOW THERE'S A WHOLE NEW LIST OF RECORDS FOR ME TO BREAK.
CONGRATULATIONS, SIR SANTOS-DUMONT. LAST YEAR, 197 FEET TO WIN THE ARCHDEACON CUP, AND THIS YEAR, 722 FEET IN 21.5 SECONDS—YOU'VE MADE HISTORY!

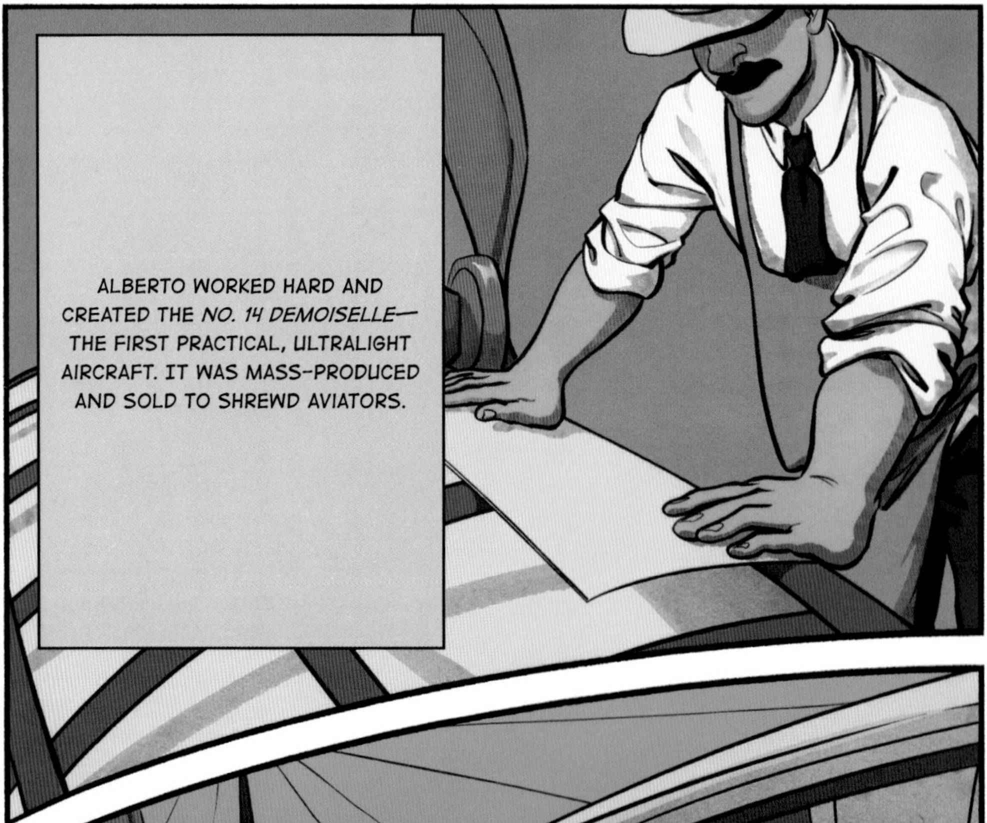
ALBERTO WORKED HARD AND CREATED THE *NO. 14 DEMOISELLE*—THE FIRST PRACTICAL, ULTRALIGHT AIRCRAFT. IT WAS MASS-PRODUCED AND SOLD TO SHREWD AVIATORS.

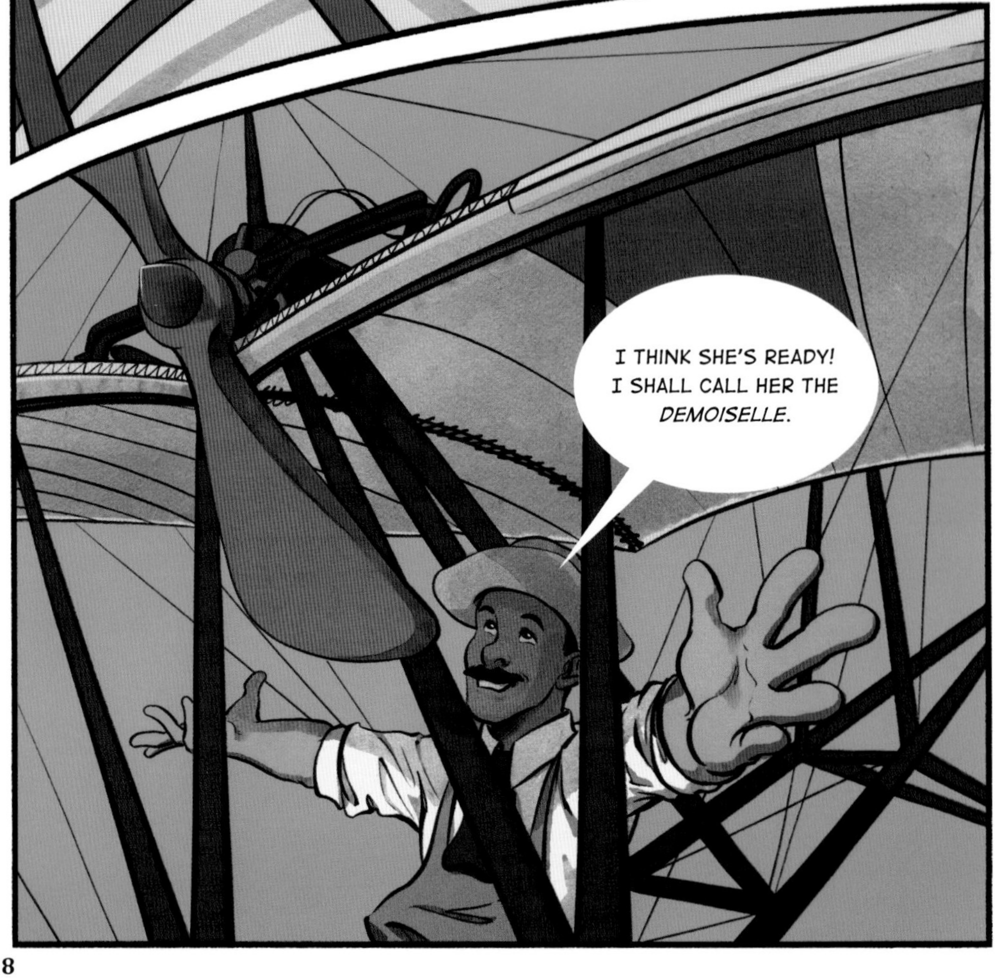
I THINK SHE'S READY! I SHALL CALL HER THE *DEMOISELLE*.

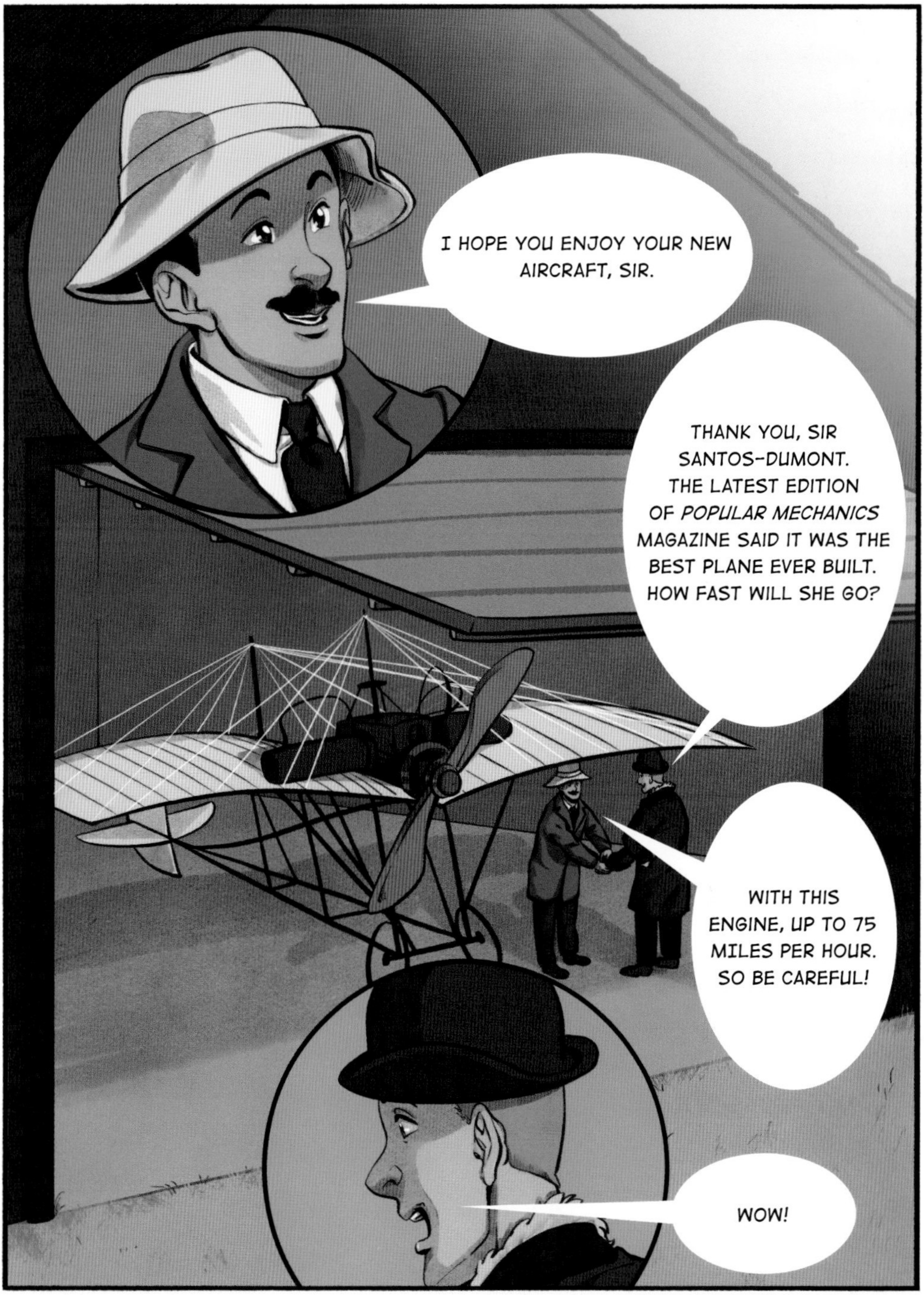

ALMOST PARALLEL TO THE SUCCESSES OF ORVILLE AND WILBUR WRIGHT, ALBERTO PAVED THE WAY FOR OTHER PIONEERS TO CREATE AND FLY THEIR OWN AIRPLANES.

LOUIS BLÉRIOT
(1872–1936)
FLYING BLIND TO VICTORY

ALTHOUGH HE WAS A QUIET, FAMILY MAN, LOUIS FELL IN LOVE WITH THE IDEA OF FLIGHT WHEN WANDERING THE PARIS EXHIBITION HALLS IN FRANCE ONE DAY. HIS PASSION FOR BUILDING AIRCRAFT SOON BECAME AN OBSESSION.

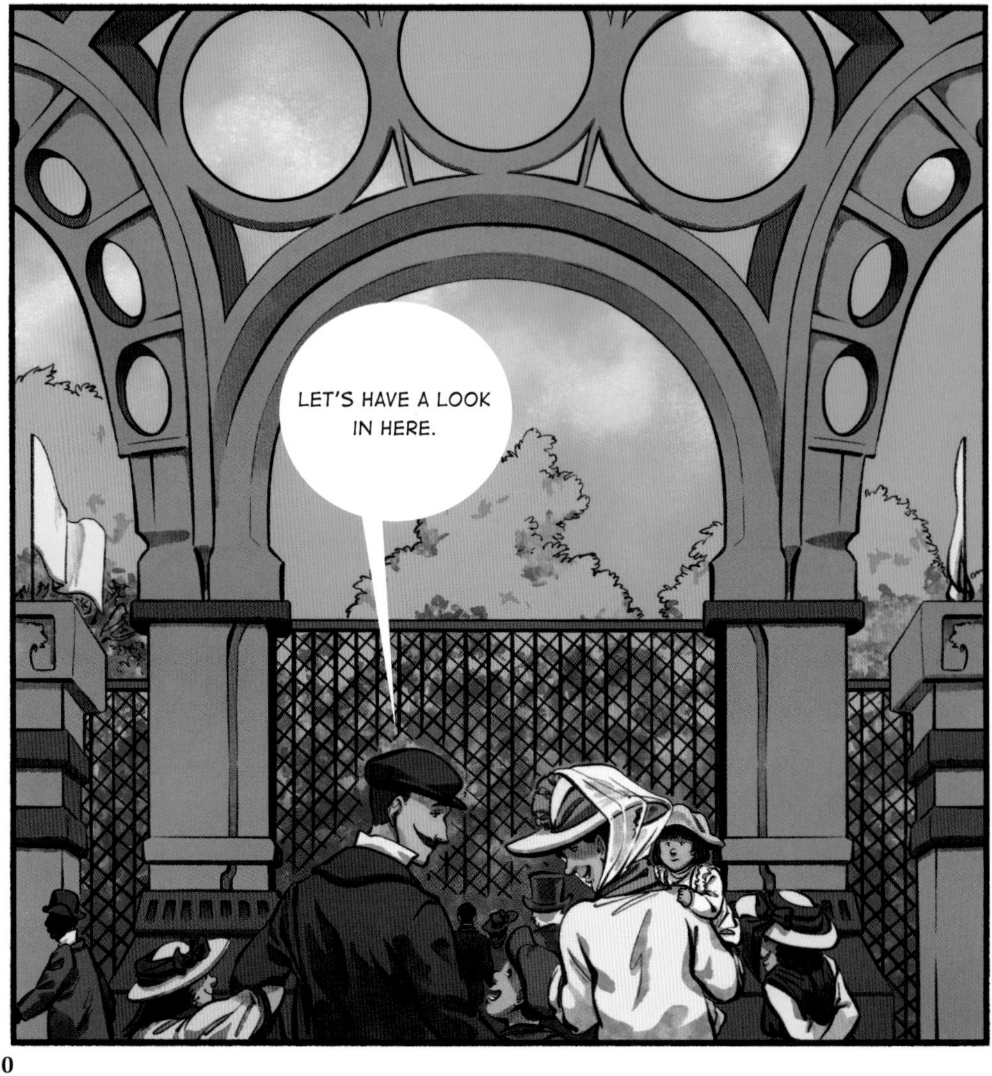

LET'S HAVE A LOOK IN HERE.

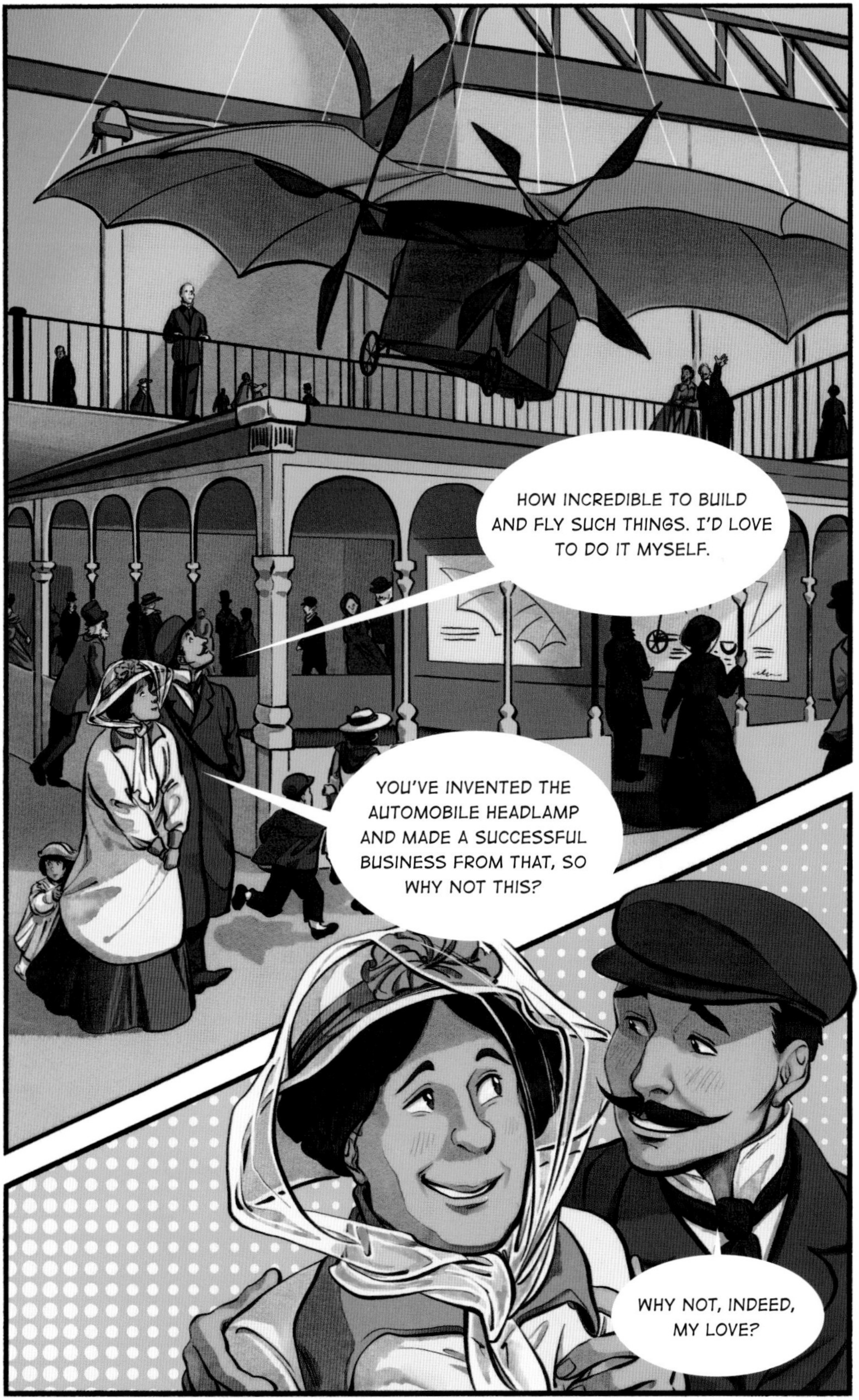
HOW INCREDIBLE TO BUILD AND FLY SUCH THINGS. I'D LOVE TO DO IT MYSELF.
YOU'VE INVENTED THE AUTOMOBILE HEADLAMP AND MADE A SUCCESSFUL BUSINESS FROM THAT, SO WHY NOT THIS?
WHY NOT, INDEED, MY LOVE?

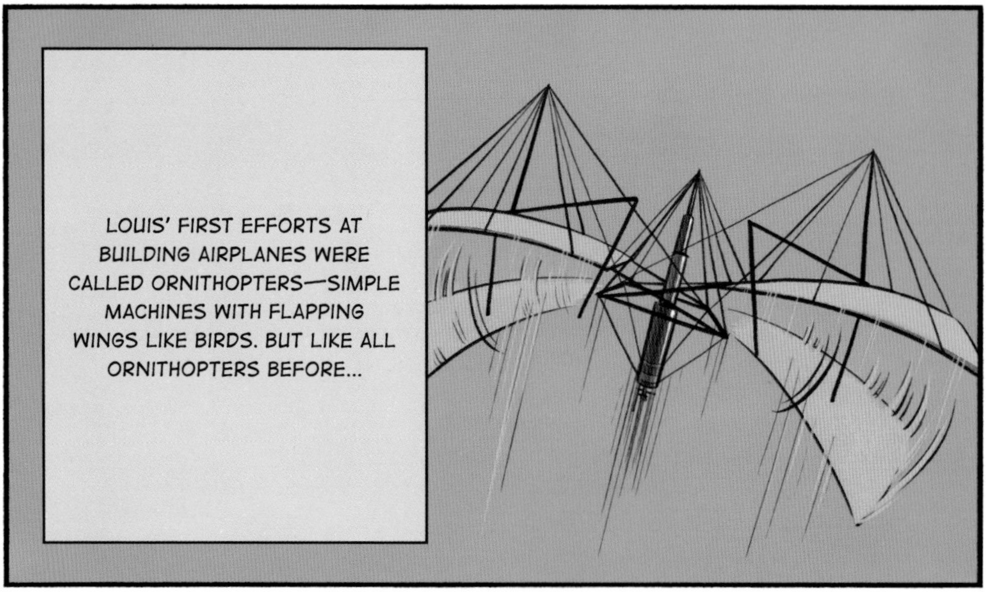
LOUIS' FIRST EFFORTS AT BUILDING AIRPLANES WERE CALLED ORNITHOPTERS—SIMPLE MACHINES WITH FLAPPING WINGS LIKE BIRDS. BUT LIKE ALL ORNITHOPTERS BEFORE...

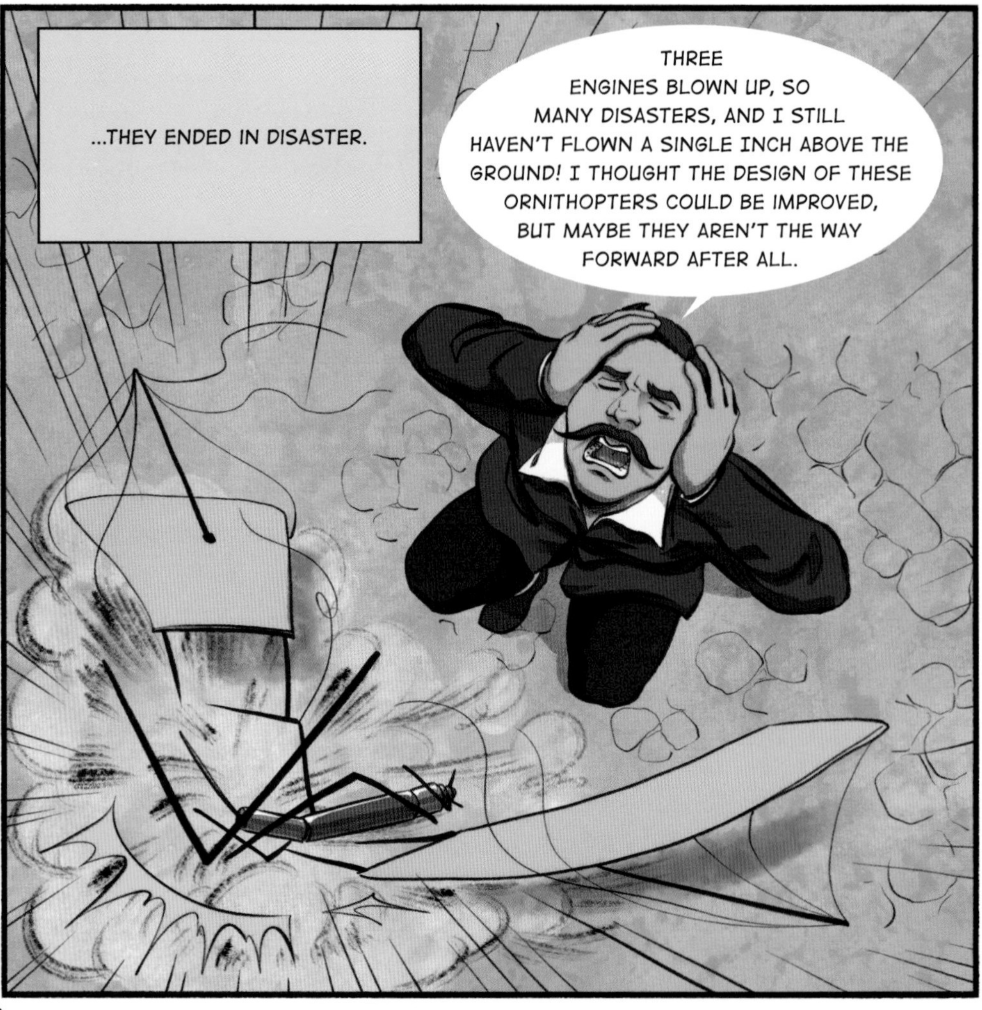
...THEY ENDED IN DISASTER.
THREE ENGINES BLOWN UP, SO MANY DISASTERS, AND I STILL HAVEN'T FLOWN A SINGLE INCH ABOVE THE GROUND! I THOUGHT THE DESIGN OF THESE ORNITHOPTERS COULD BE IMPROVED, BUT MAYBE THEY AREN'T THE WAY FORWARD AFTER ALL.

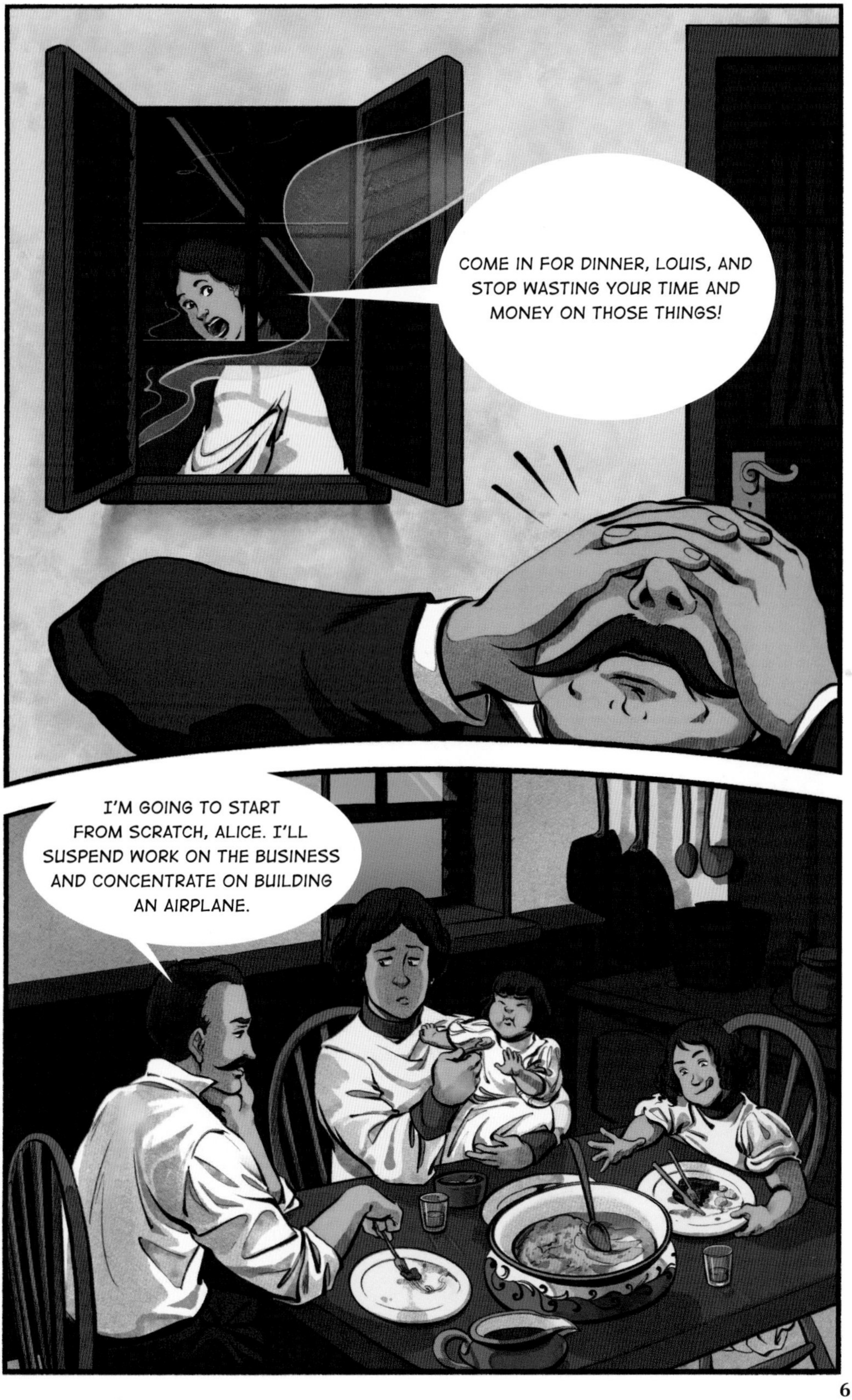
COME IN FOR DINNER, LOUIS, AND STOP WASTING YOUR TIME AND MONEY ON THOSE THINGS!
I'M GOING TO START FROM SCRATCH, ALICE. I'LL SUSPEND WORK ON THE BUSINESS AND CONCENTRATE ON BUILDING AN AIRPLANE.

AFTER TEACHING HIMSELF TO FLY, LOUIS SUCCESSFULLY TOOK TO THE AIR IN HIS FIRST HAND-BUILT AIRPLANE AT AGE 35. HE STARTED ENTERING FLYING COMPETITIONS WITH THE HOPE OF WINNING PRIZE MONEY.

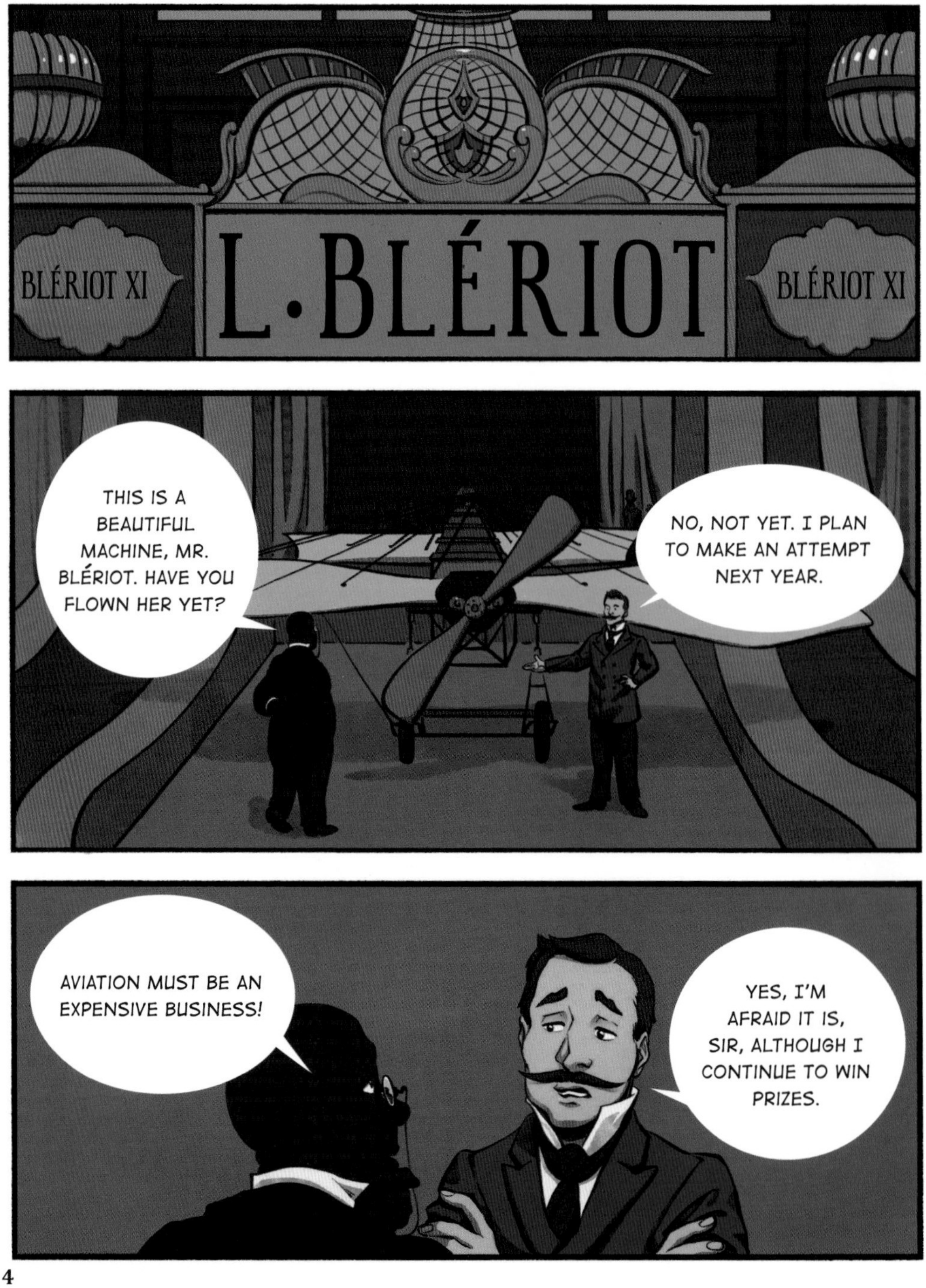
BLÉRIOT XI
L. BLÉRIOT
BLÉRIOT XI
THIS IS A BEAUTIFUL MACHINE, MR. BLÉRIOT. HAVE YOU FLOWN HER YET?
NO, NOT YET. I PLAN TO MAKE AN ATTEMPT NEXT YEAR.
AVIATION MUST BE AN EXPENSIVE BUSINESS!
YES, I'M AFRAID IT IS, SIR, ALTHOUGH I CONTINUE TO WIN PRIZES.

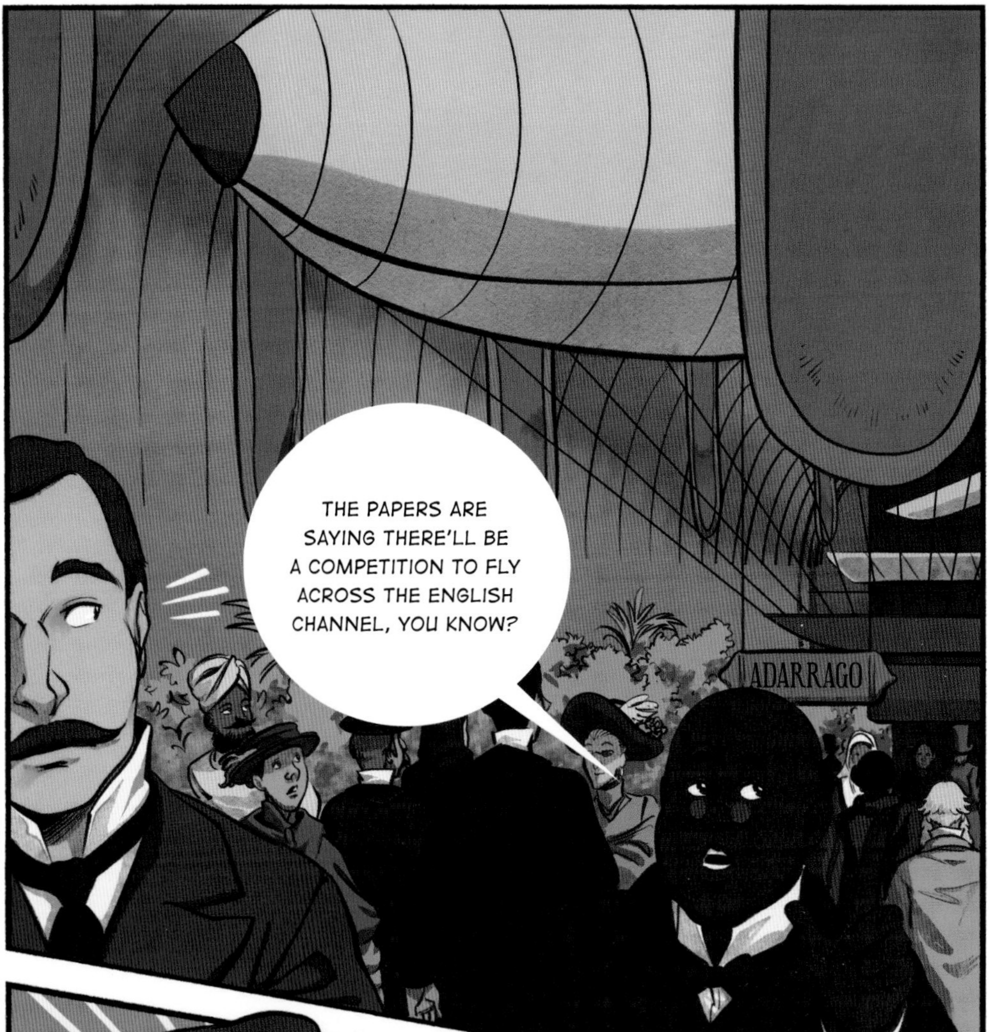
THE PAPERS ARE SAYING THERE'LL BE A COMPETITION TO FLY ACROSS THE ENGLISH CHANNEL, YOU KNOW?
ADARRAGO

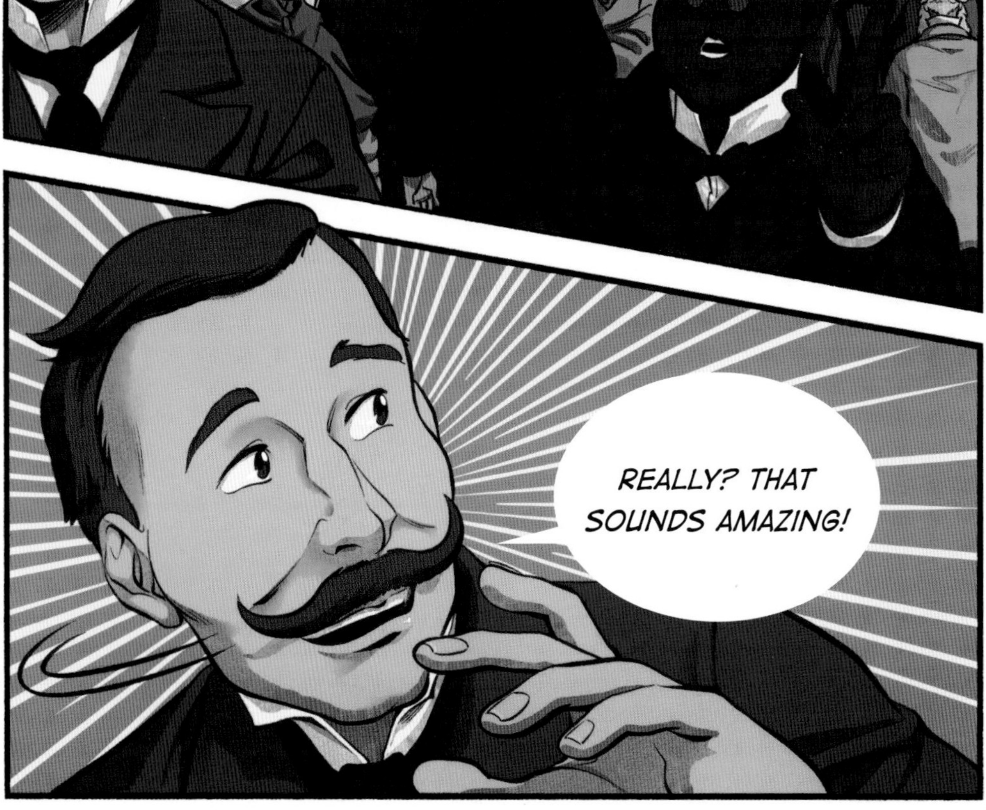
REALLY? THAT SOUNDS AMAZING!

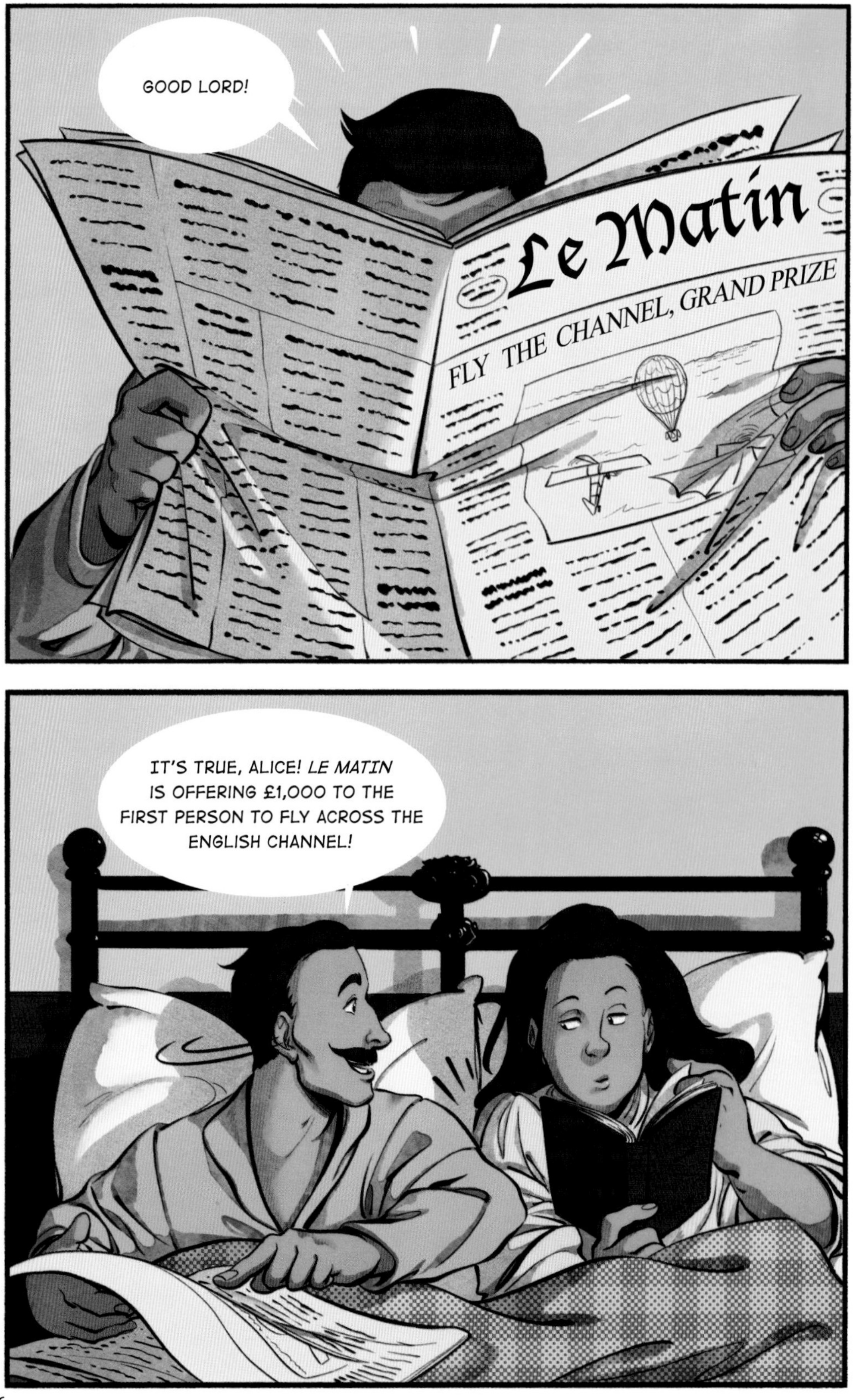
GOOD LORD!
Le Matin
FLY THE CHANNEL, GRAND PRIZE
IT'S TRUE, ALICE! *LE MATIN* IS OFFERING £1,000 TO THE FIRST PERSON TO FLY ACROSS THE ENGLISH CHANNEL!

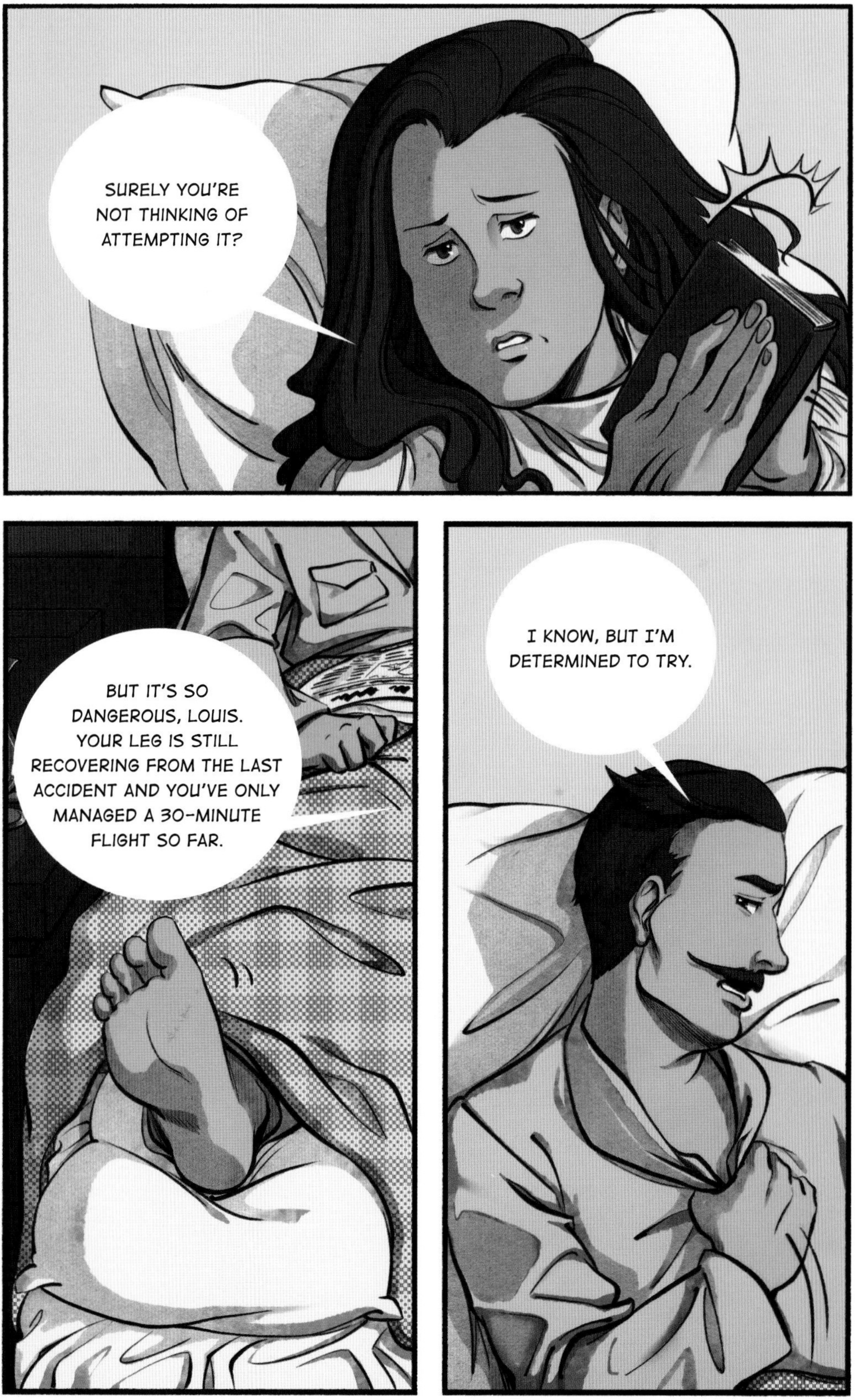
SURELY YOU'RE NOT THINKING OF ATTEMPTING IT?
BUT IT'S SO DANGEROUS, LOUIS. YOUR LEG IS STILL RECOVERING FROM THE LAST ACCIDENT AND YOU'VE ONLY MANAGED A 30-MINUTE FLIGHT SO FAR.
I KNOW, BUT I'M DETERMINED TO TRY.

IN CALAIS, FRANCE, LOUIS WAITED DAYS FOR GOOD WEATHER. NERVOUS THAT SOMEONE ELSE MIGHT MAKE THE CROSSING BEFORE HIM, HE SET OFF EARLY ONE MORNING, AS SOON AS THE WEATHER SEEMED TO BE IMPROVING.

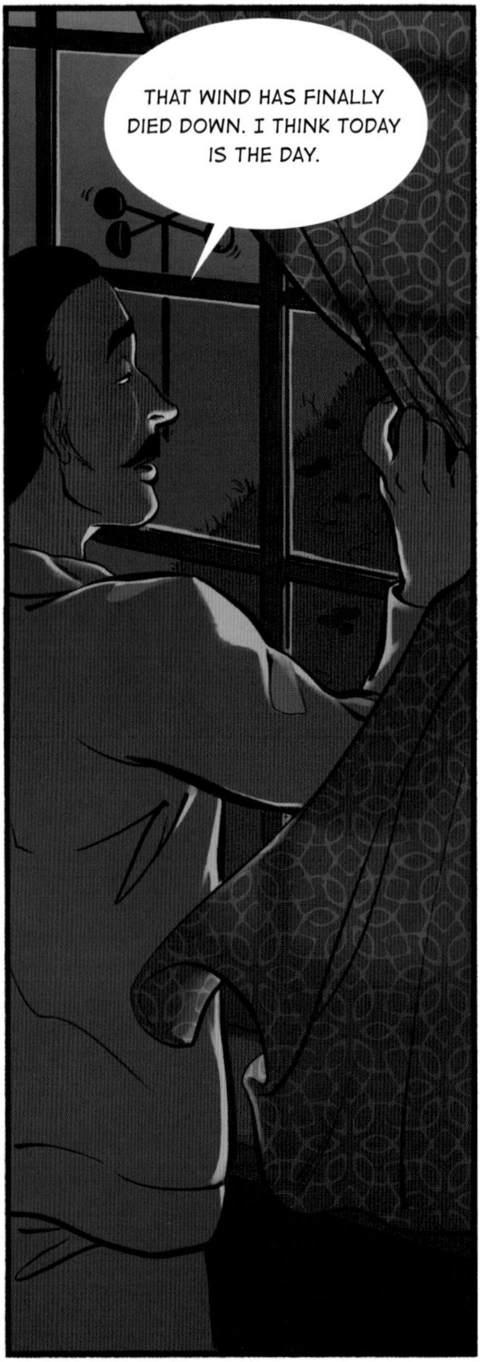
THAT WIND HAS FINALLY DIED DOWN. I THINK TODAY IS THE DAY.

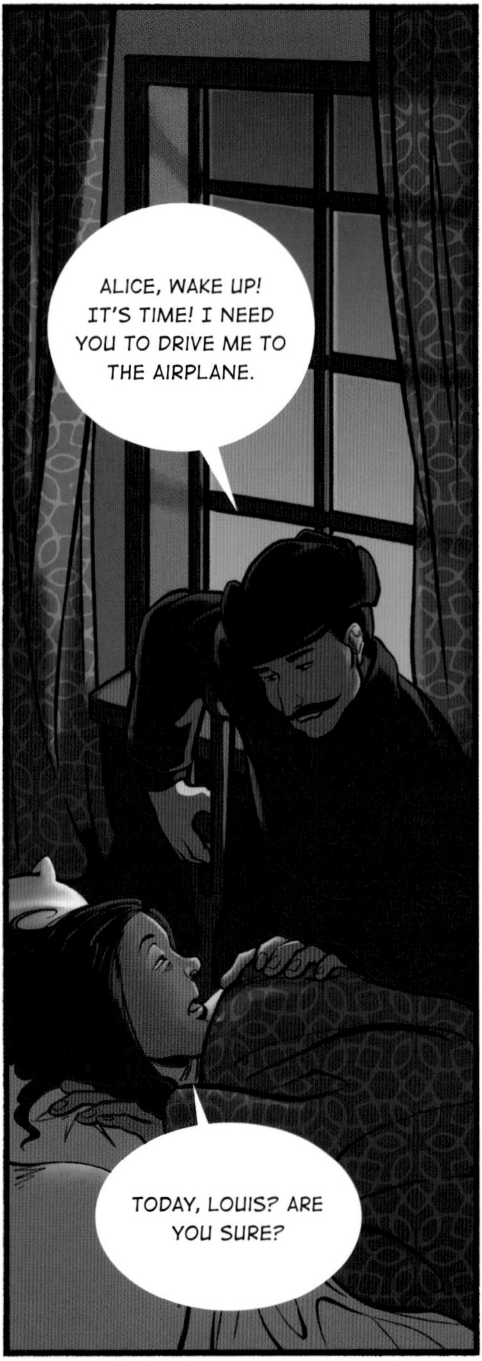
ALICE, WAKE UP! IT'S TIME! I NEED YOU TO DRIVE ME TO THE AIRPLANE.
TODAY, LOUIS? ARE YOU SURE?

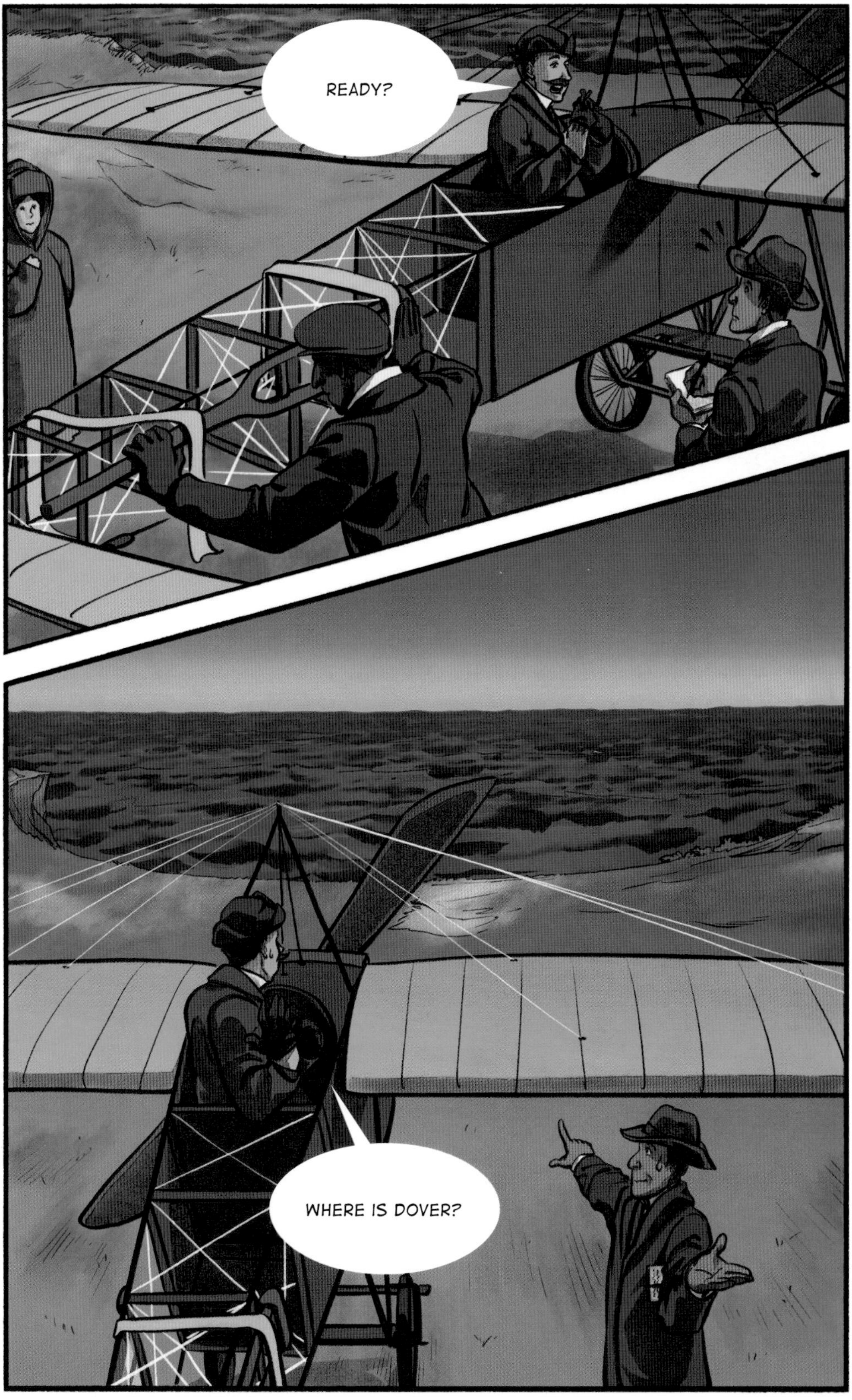
READY?
WHERE IS DOVER?

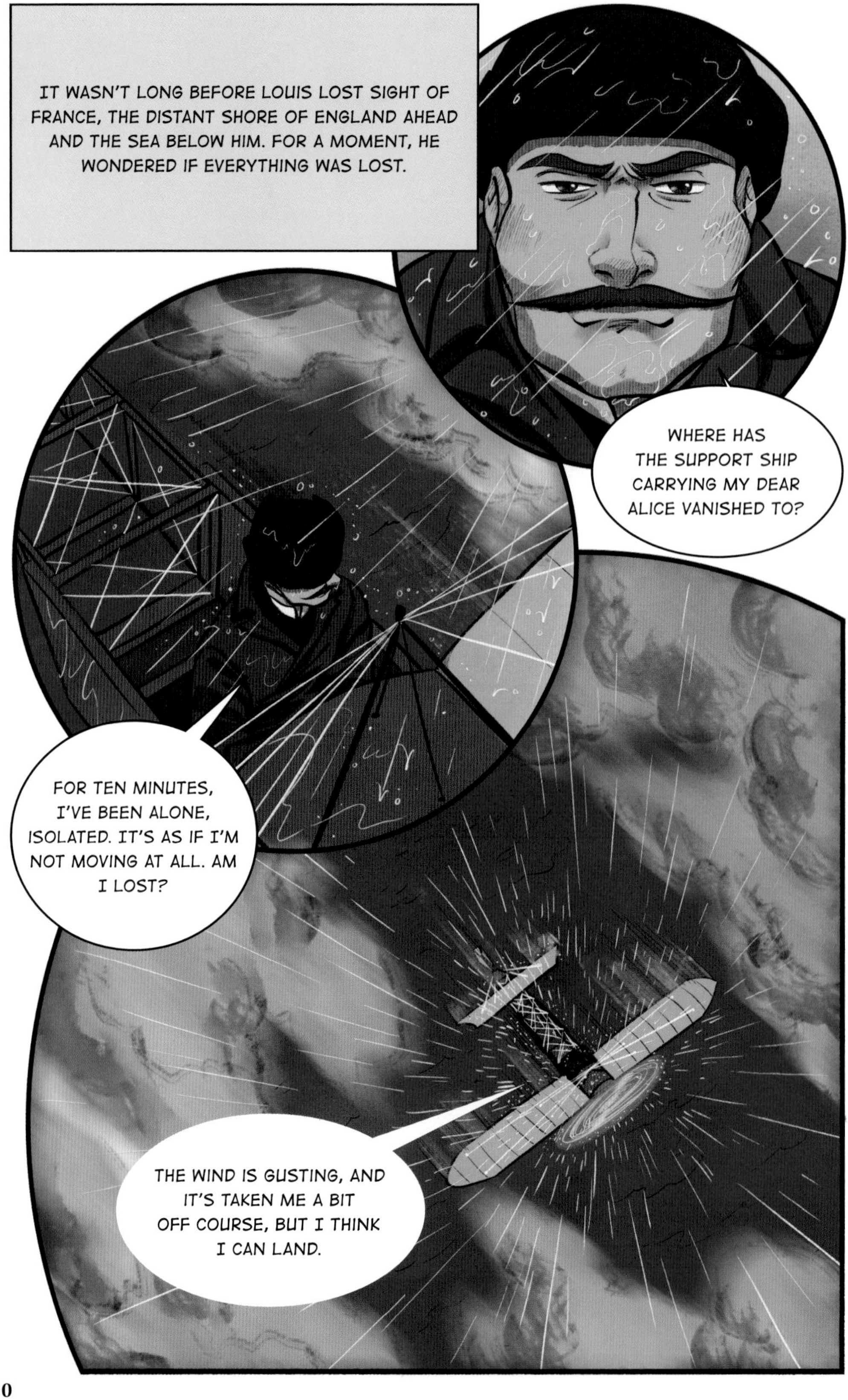
IT WASN'T LONG BEFORE LOUIS LOST SIGHT OF FRANCE, THE DISTANT SHORE OF ENGLAND AHEAD AND THE SEA BELOW HIM. FOR A MOMENT, HE WONDERED IF EVERYTHING WAS LOST.
WHERE HAS THE SUPPORT SHIP CARRYING MY DEAR ALICE VANISHED TO?
FOR TEN MINUTES, I'VE BEEN ALONE, ISOLATED. IT'S AS IF I'M NOT MOVING AT ALL. AM I LOST?
THE WIND IS GUSTING, AND IT'S TAKEN ME A BIT OFF COURSE, BUT I THINK I CAN LAND.

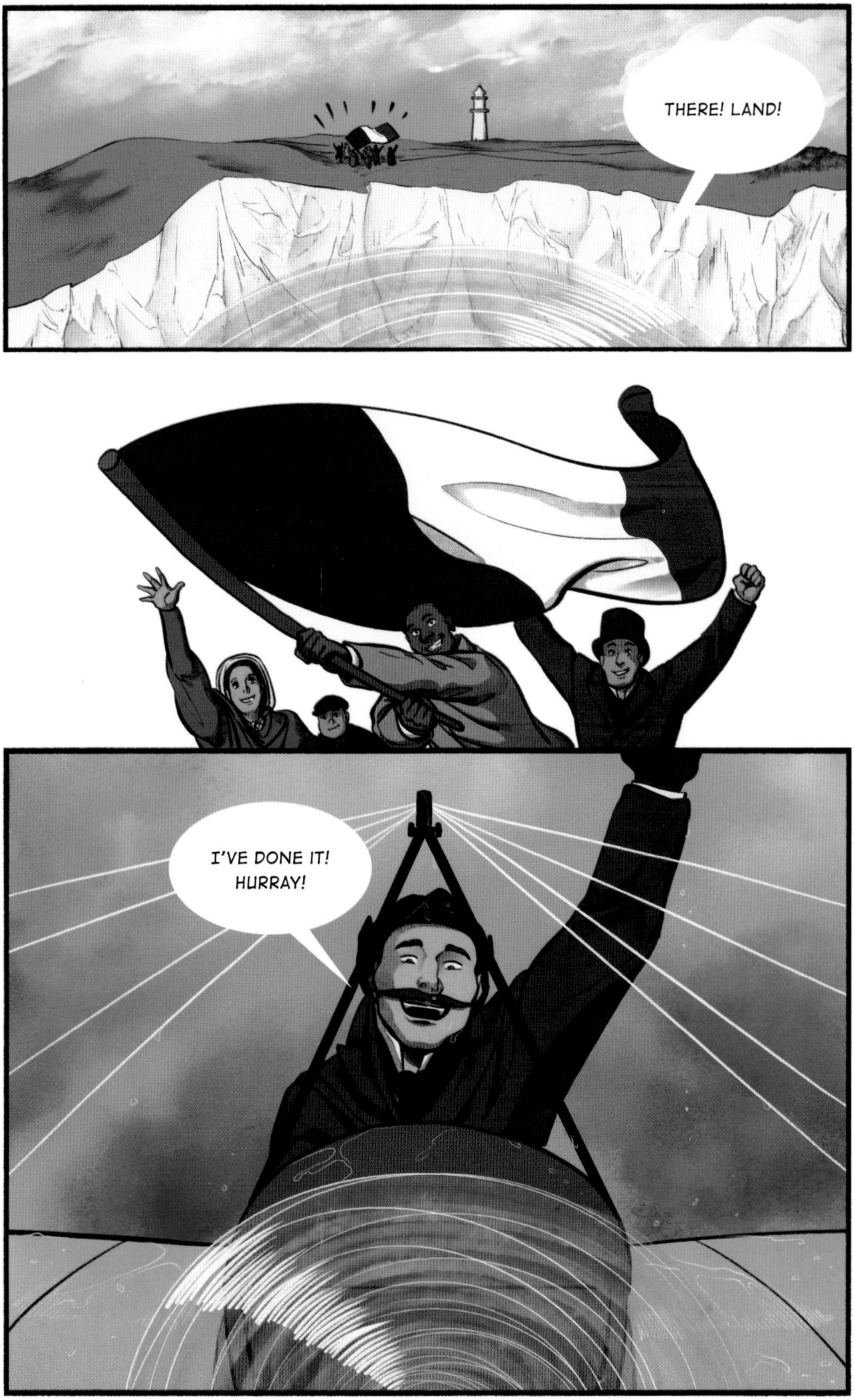
THERE! LAND!
I'VE DONE IT! HURRAY!

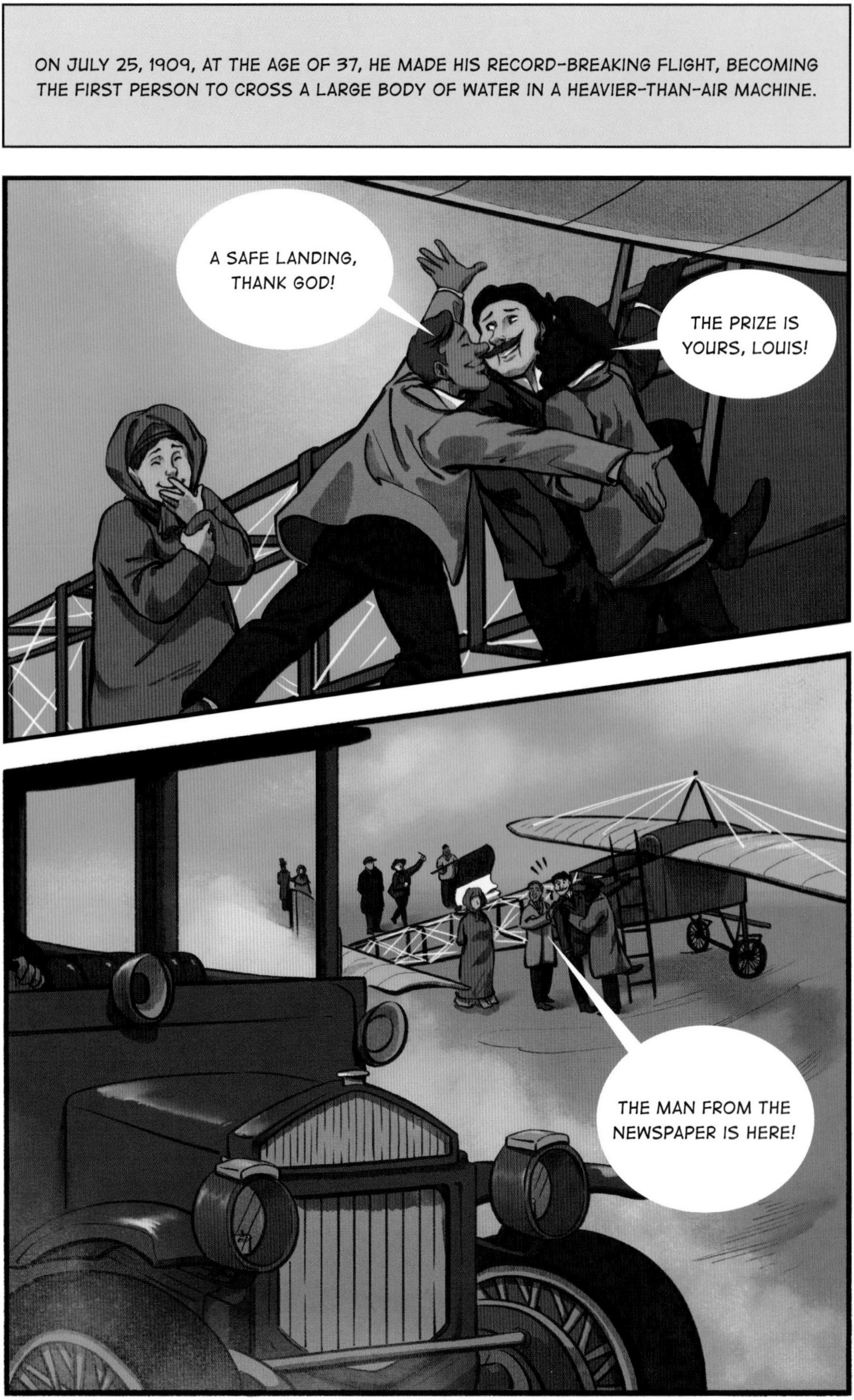
ON JULY 25, 1909, AT THE AGE OF 37, HE MADE HIS RECORD-BREAKING FLIGHT, BECOMING THE FIRST PERSON TO CROSS A LARGE BODY OF WATER IN A HEAVIER-THAN-AIR MACHINE.
A SAFE LANDING, THANK GOD!
THE PRIZE IS YOURS, LOUIS!
THE MAN FROM THE NEWSPAPER IS HERE!

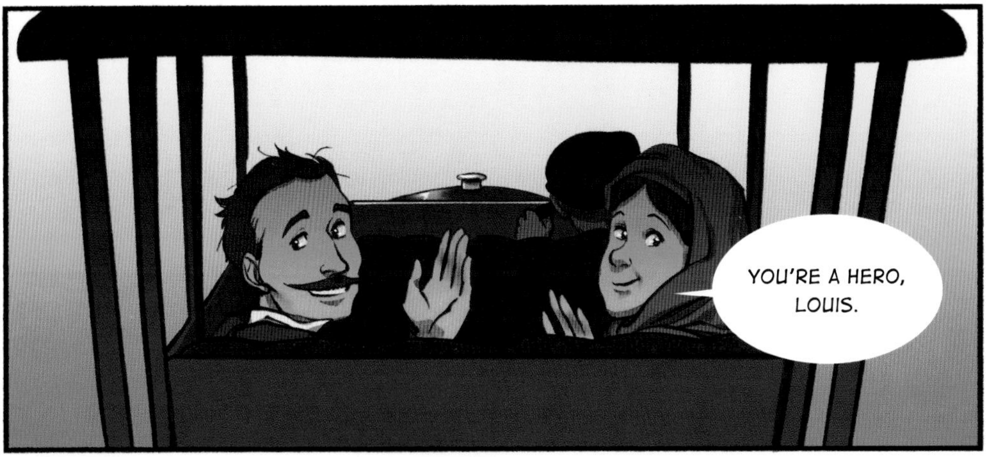
YOU'RE A HERO, LOUIS.

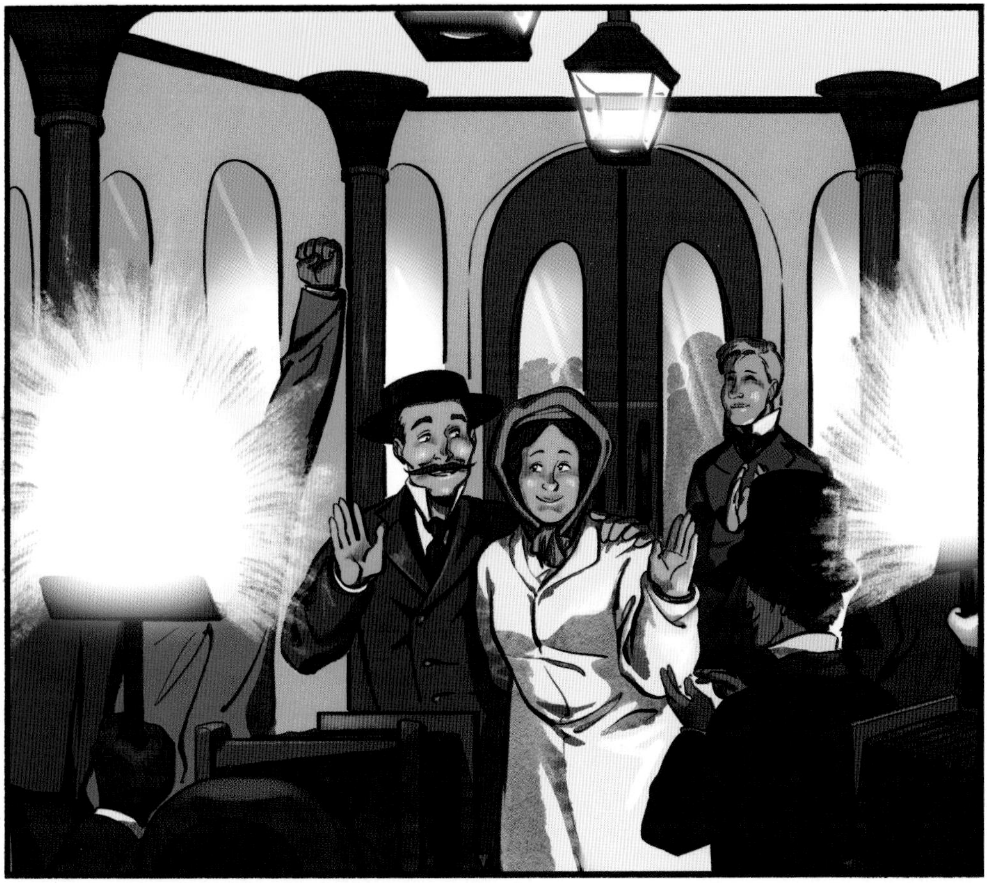

JUST SIX YEARS AFTER THE WRIGHT BROTHERS' FIRST POWERED FLIGHT, LOUIS HAD FLOWN ACROSS AN OPEN BODY OF WATER. HIS FEAT FIRED THE IMAGINATIONS OF MANY OTHER AVIATORS.

AMELIA EARHART
(1897–1937; disappeared)
THE QUEEN OF THE AIR

WHILE TRAINING TO BE A NURSE'S AIDE, AMELIA CARED FOR PILOTS WOUNDED IN WORLD WAR I AND ADMIRED THEIR BRAVERY. SHE SAW NO REASON WHY SHE COULDN'T BE A PILOT HERSELF AND ACHIEVE THE SAME THINGS AS MEN.

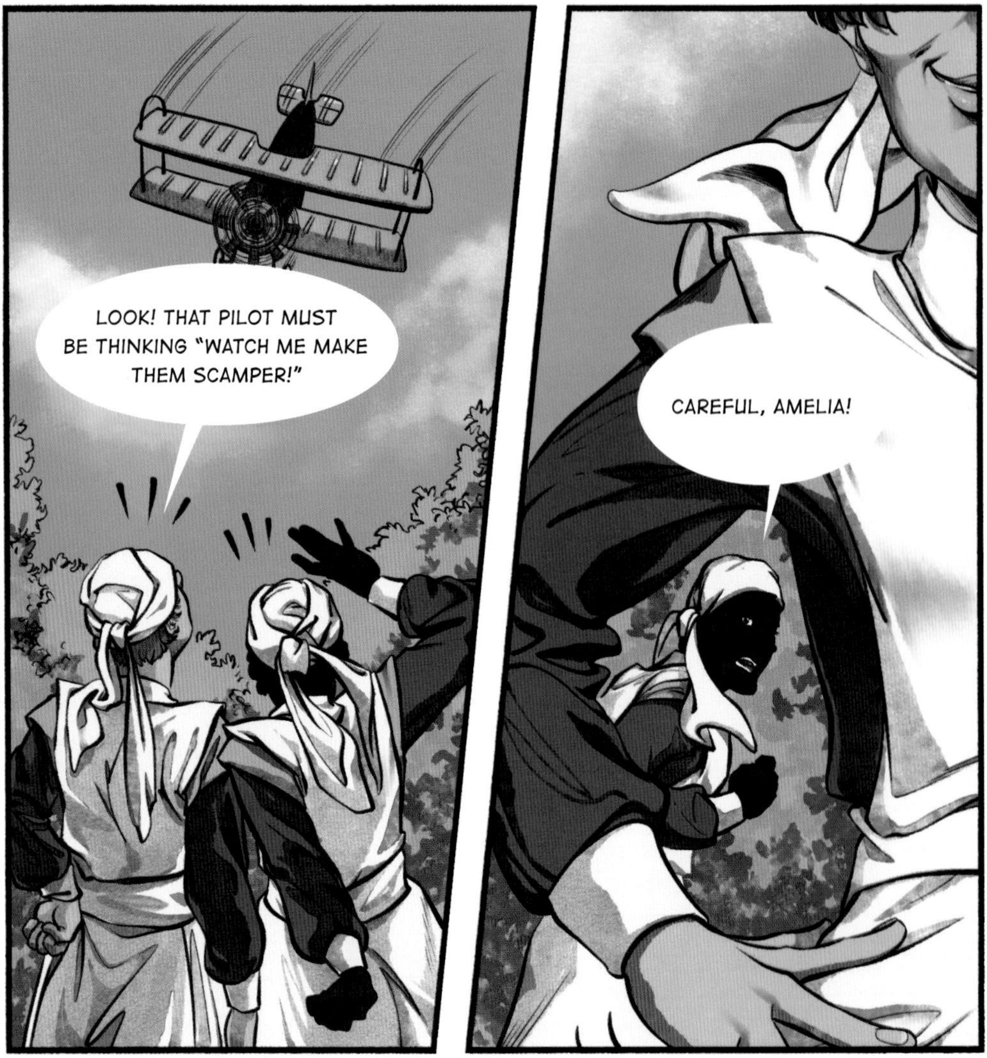

LOOK! THAT PILOT MUST BE THINKING "WATCH ME MAKE THEM SCAMPER!"
CAREFUL, AMELIA!

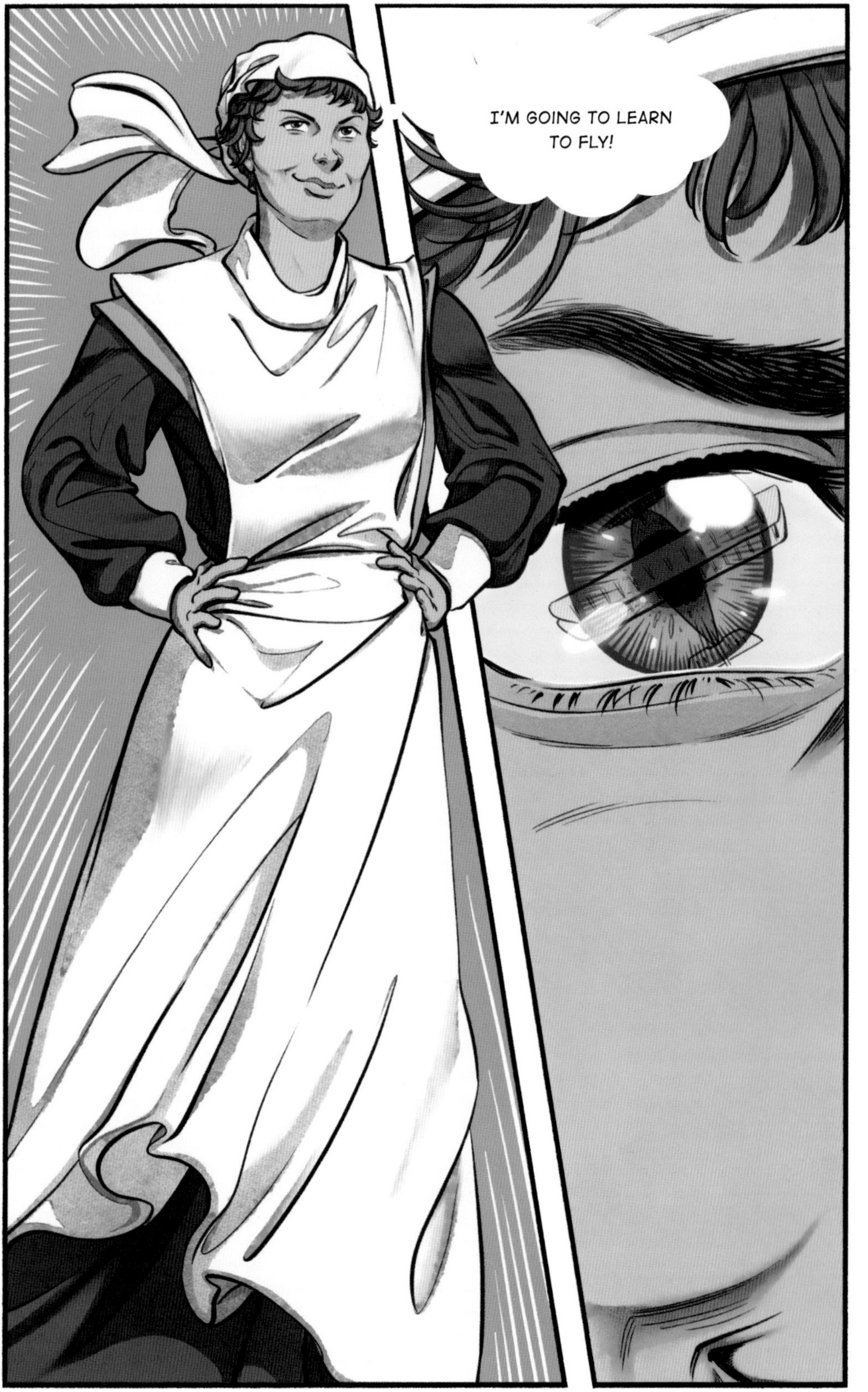
I'M GOING TO LEARN
TO FLY!

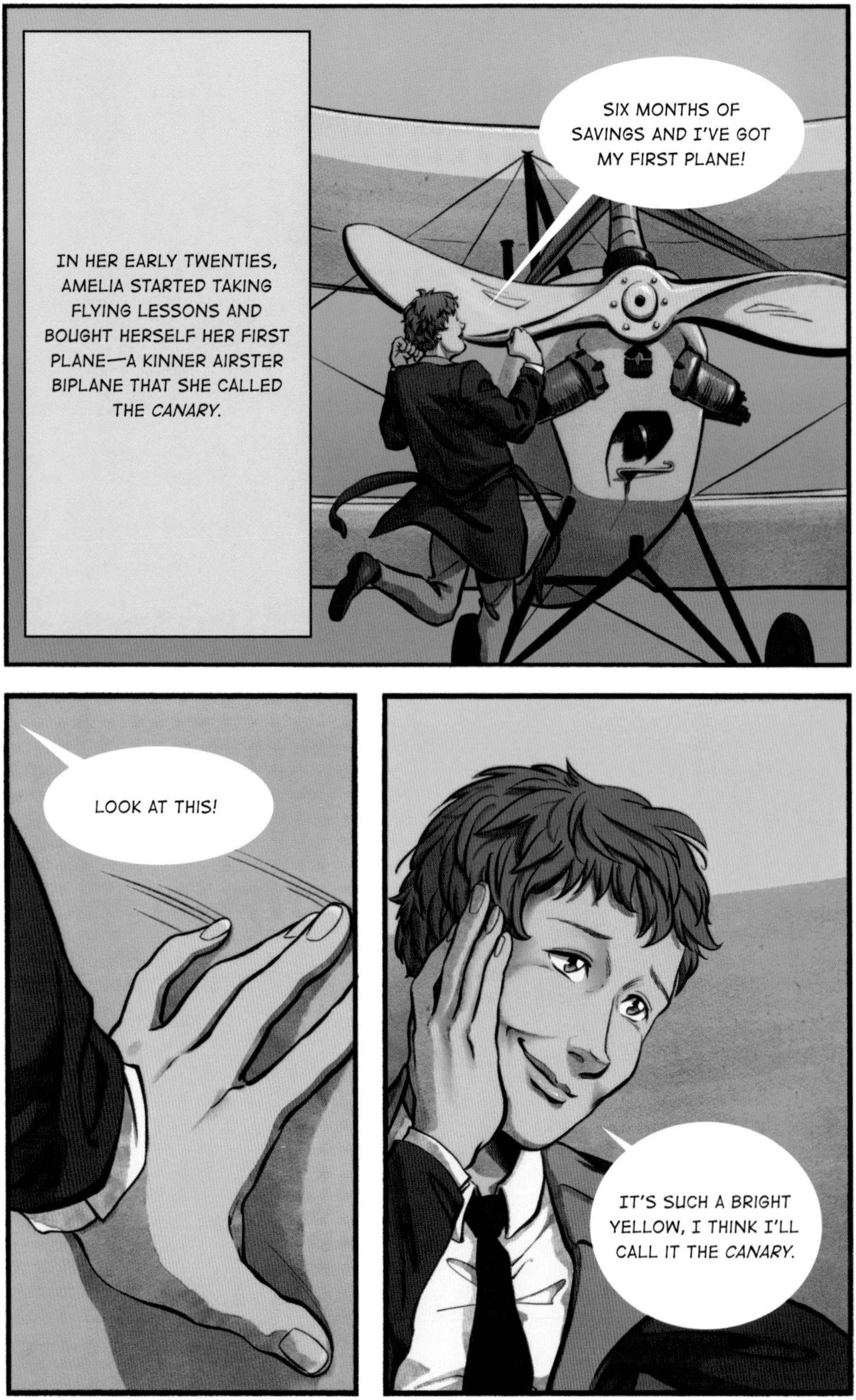
IN HER EARLY TWENTIES, AMELIA STARTED TAKING FLYING LESSONS AND BOUGHT HERSELF HER FIRST PLANE—A KINNER AIRSTER BIPLANE THAT SHE CALLED THE *CANARY*.
SIX MONTHS OF SAVINGS AND I'VE GOT MY FIRST PLANE!
LOOK AT THIS!
IT'S SUCH A BRIGHT YELLOW, I THINK I'LL CALL IT THE *CANARY*.

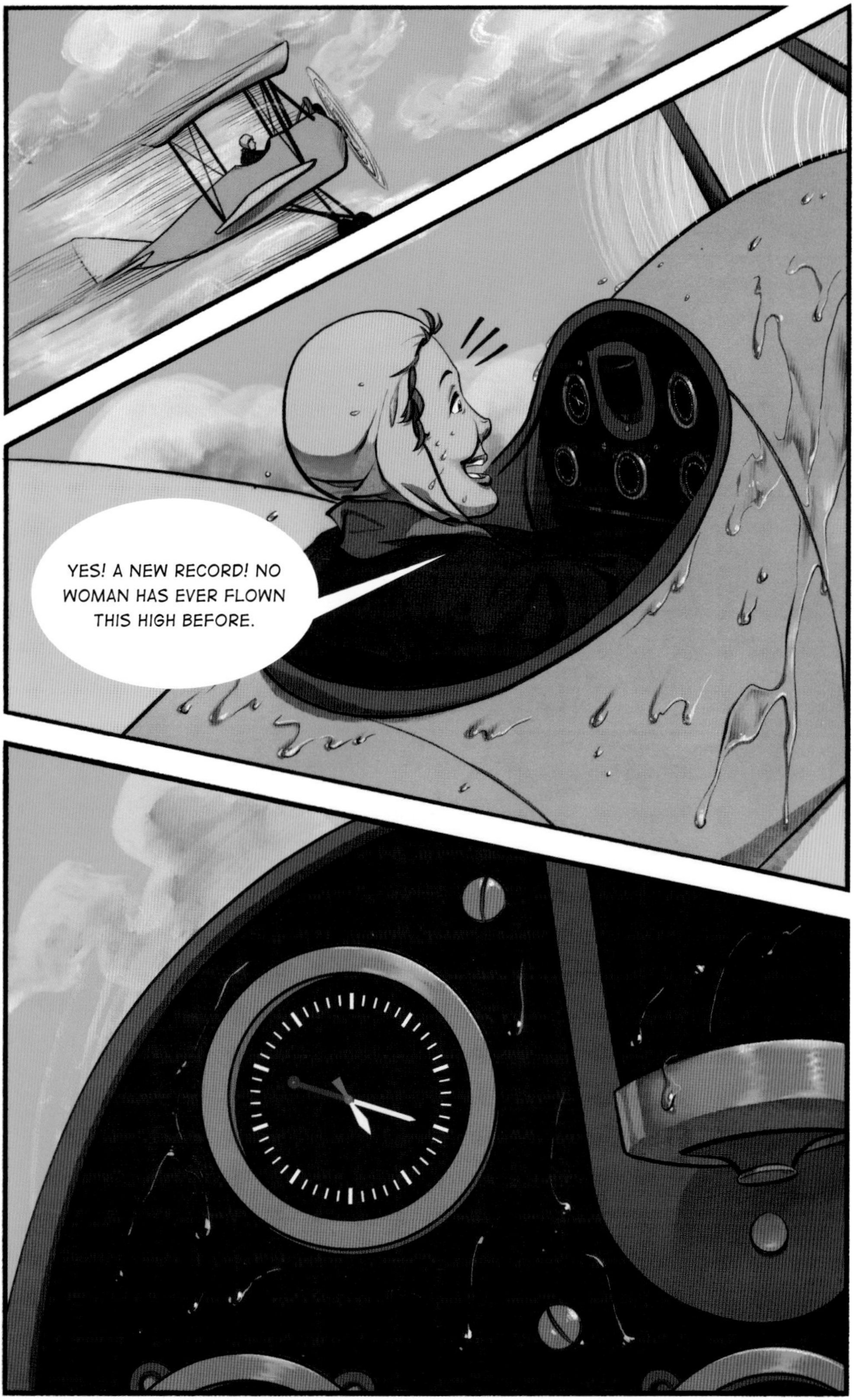
YES! A NEW RECORD! NO WOMAN HAS EVER FLOWN THIS HIGH BEFORE.

NEWS OF CHARLES LINDBERGH'S RECORD-BREAKING SOLO FLIGHT ACROSS THE ATLANTIC IN 1927 FILLED AMELIA WITH LONGING. A YEAR LATER, AN UNEXPECTED PHONE CALL FROM CAPTAIN HILTON H. RAILEY SET AMELIA ON THE PATH TO FAME AND FORTUNE.

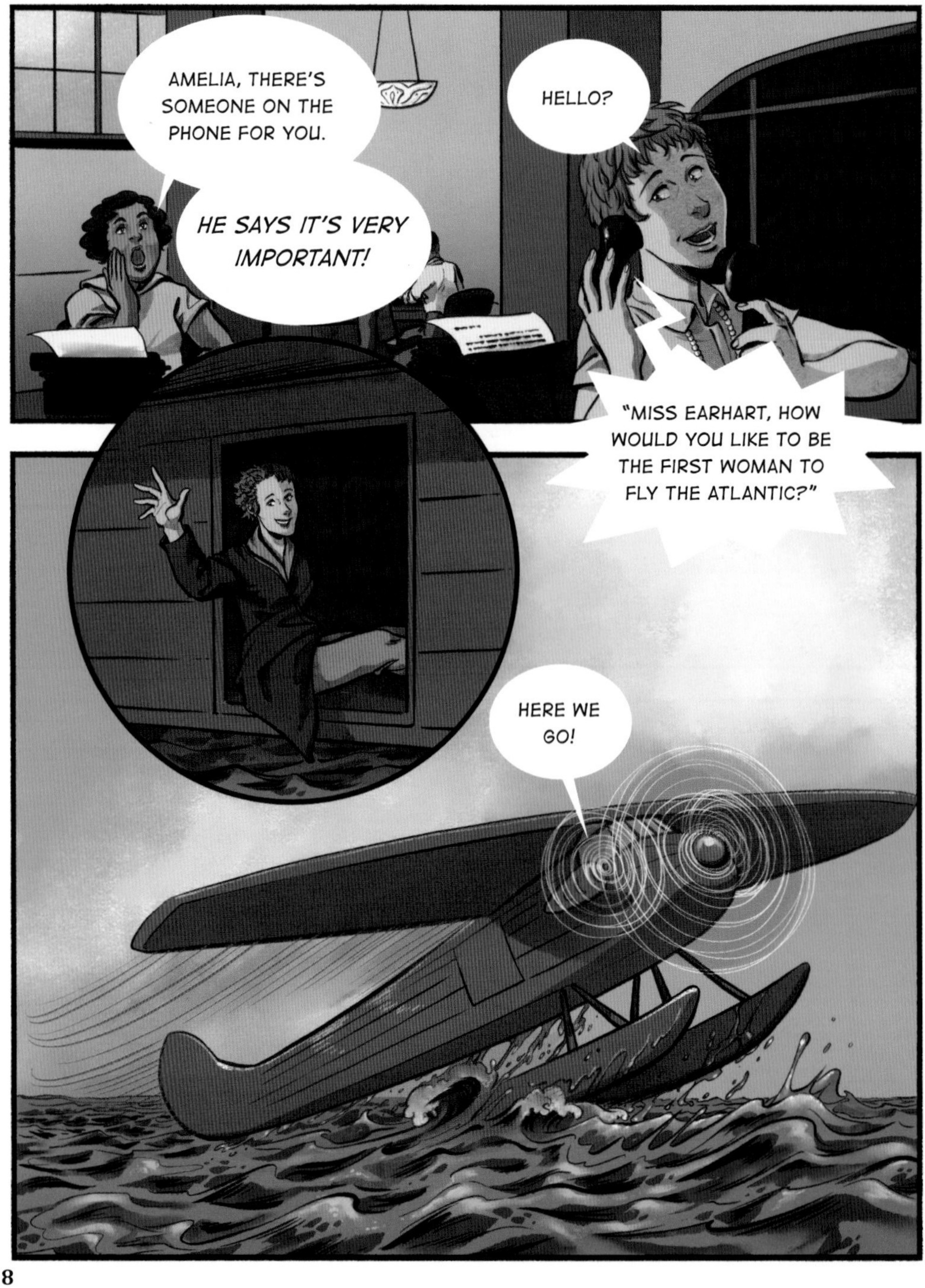
AMELIA, THERE'S SOMEONE ON THE PHONE FOR YOU.
HE SAYS IT'S VERY IMPORTANT!
HELLO?
"MISS EARHART, HOW WOULD YOU LIKE TO BE THE FIRST WOMAN TO FLY THE ATLANTIC?"
HERE WE GO!

ON JUNE 17, 1928, AMELIA TOOK OFF ALONG WITH BILL STULTZ AND LOUIS "SLIM" GORDON ON THE FOKKER TRIPLANE *FRIENDSHIP*.

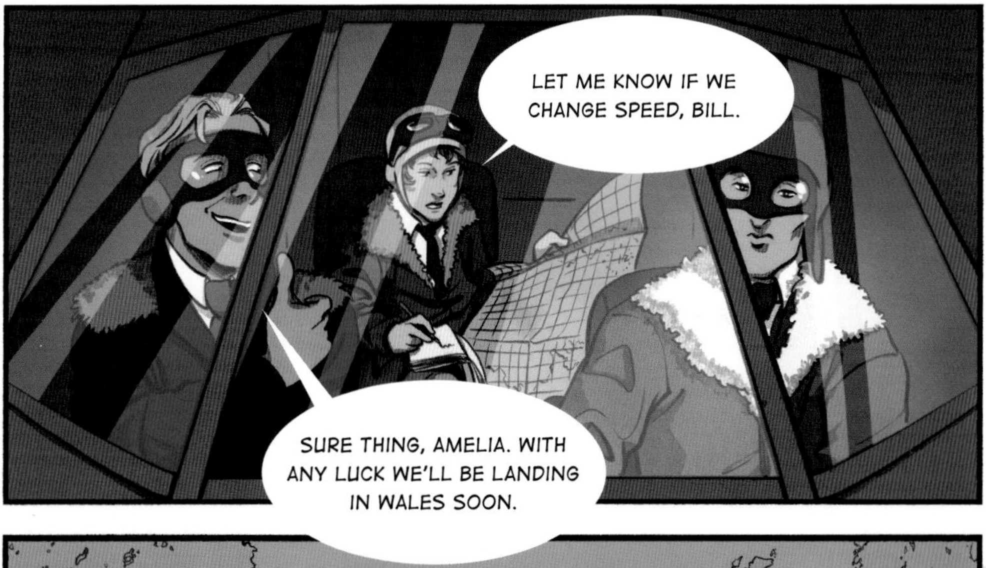
LET ME KNOW IF WE CHANGE SPEED, BILL.
SURE THING, AMELIA. WITH ANY LUCK WE'LL BE LANDING IN WALES SOON.

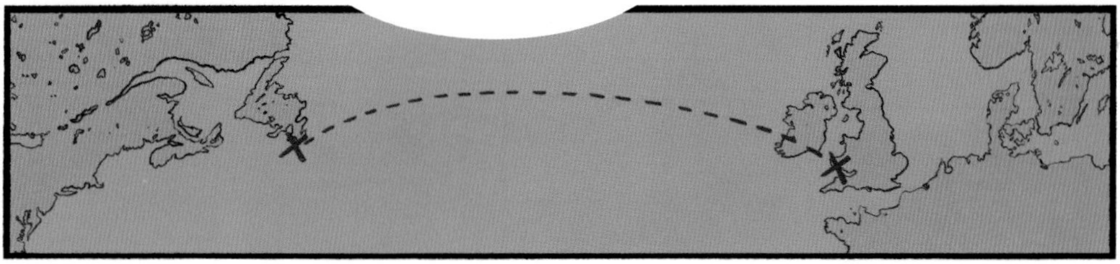

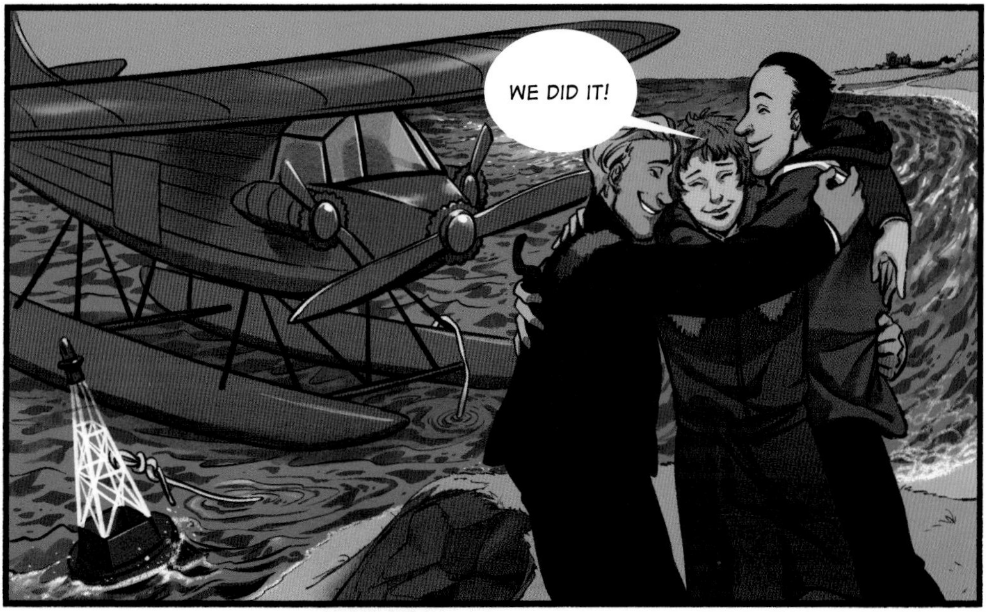
WE DID IT!

IN 1928, AMELIA, BILL, AND LOUIS WERE GREETED WITH A TICKER-TAPE PARADE ON THEIR TRIUMPHANT RETURN TO NEW YORK CITY AFTER THEIR CROSS-ATLANTIC FLIGHT.

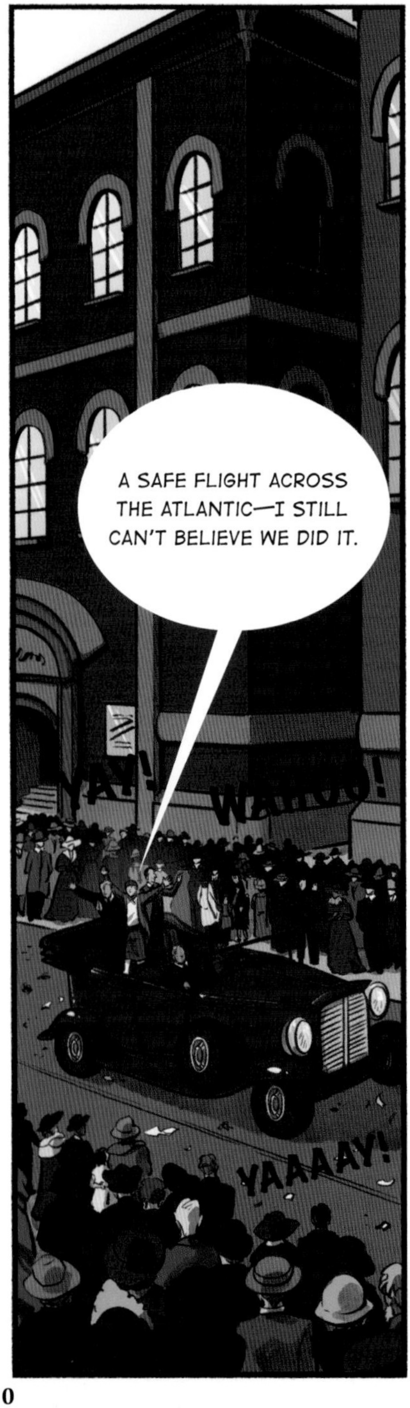
A SAFE FLIGHT ACROSS THE ATLANTIC—I STILL CAN'T BELIEVE WE DID IT.
YAY!
WAHOO!
YAAAAY!

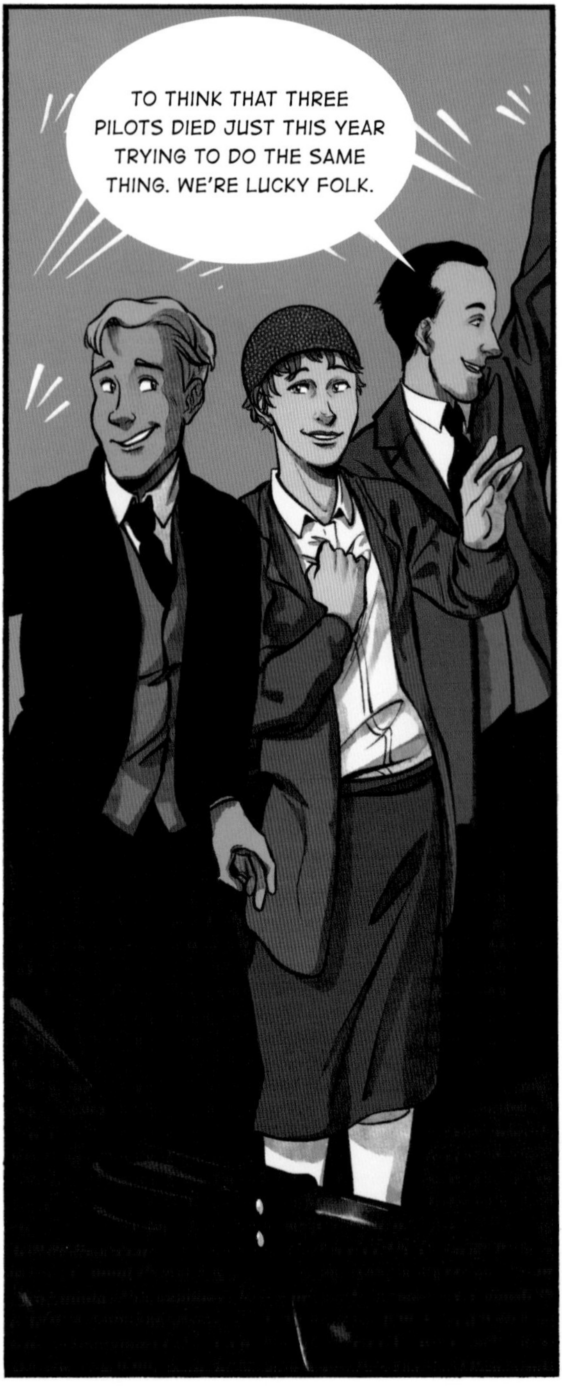
TO THINK THAT THREE PILOTS DIED JUST THIS YEAR TRYING TO DO THE SAME THING. WE'RE LUCKY FOLK.

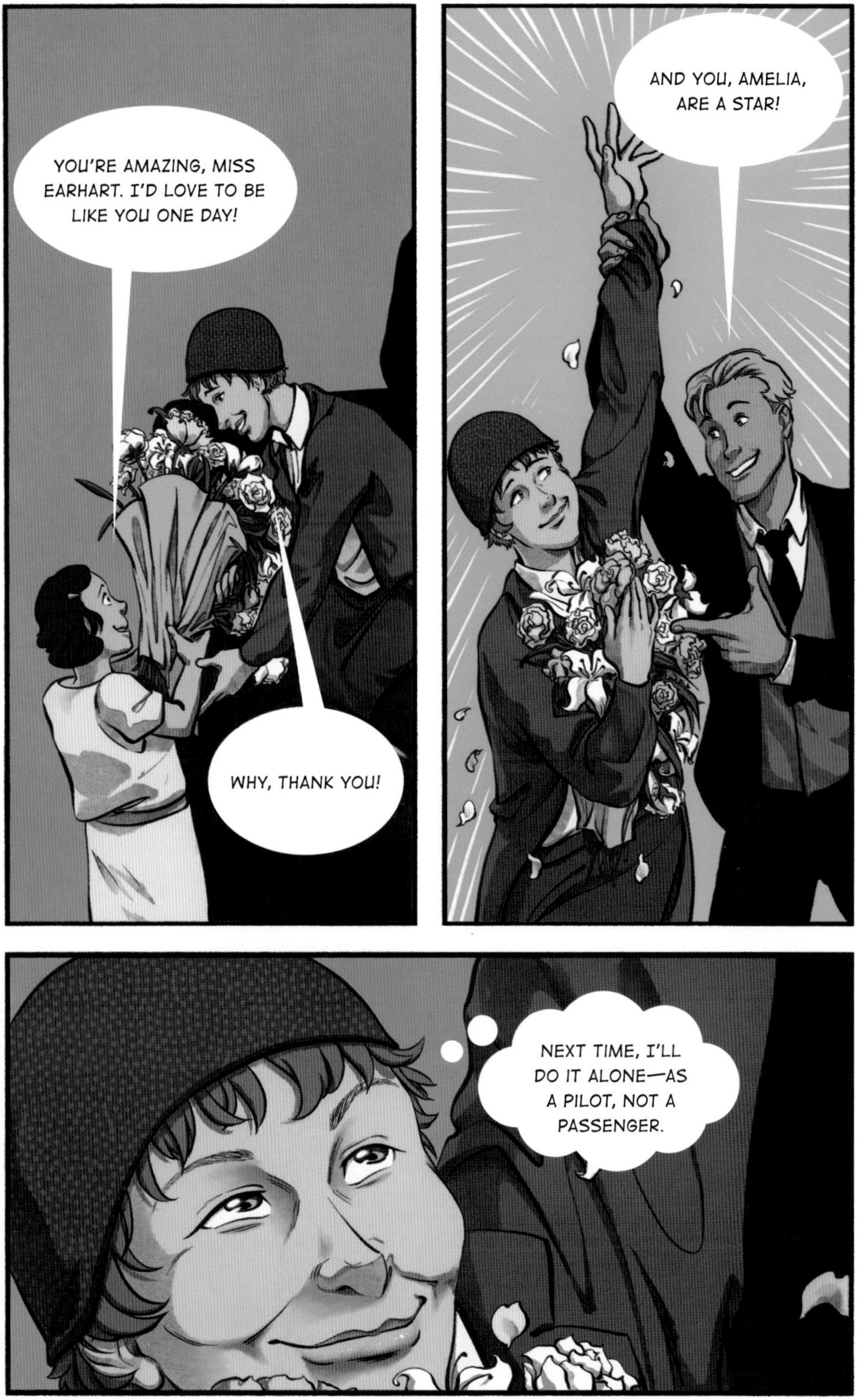
YOU'RE AMAZING, MISS EARHART. I'D LOVE TO BE LIKE YOU ONE DAY!
WHY, THANK YOU!
AND YOU, AMELIA, ARE A STAR!
NEXT TIME, I'LL DO IT ALONE—AS A PILOT, NOT A PASSENGER.

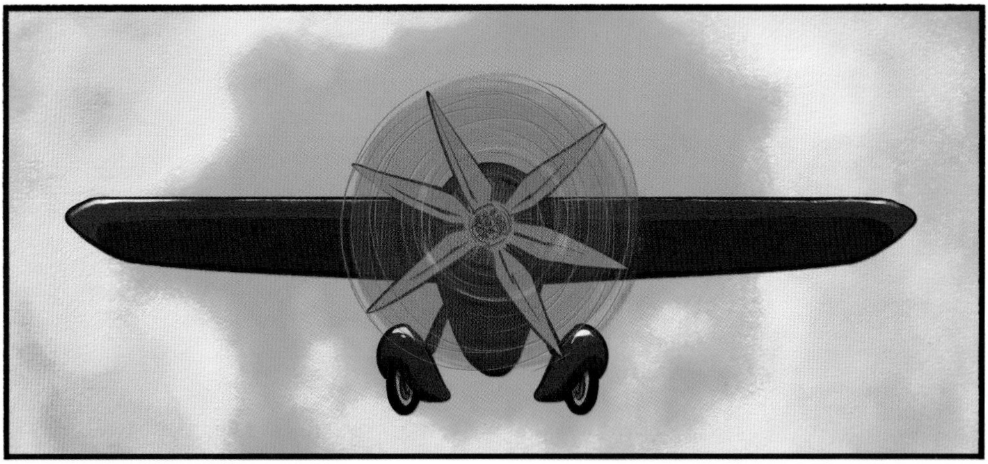

IN 1932, AT AGE 35, AMELIA'S DREAM CAME TRUE AND SHE FLEW SOLO ALL THE WAY ACROSS THE ATLANTIC OCEAN IN A LOCKHEED VEGA PLANE THAT SHE CALLED HER "LITTLE RED BUS."

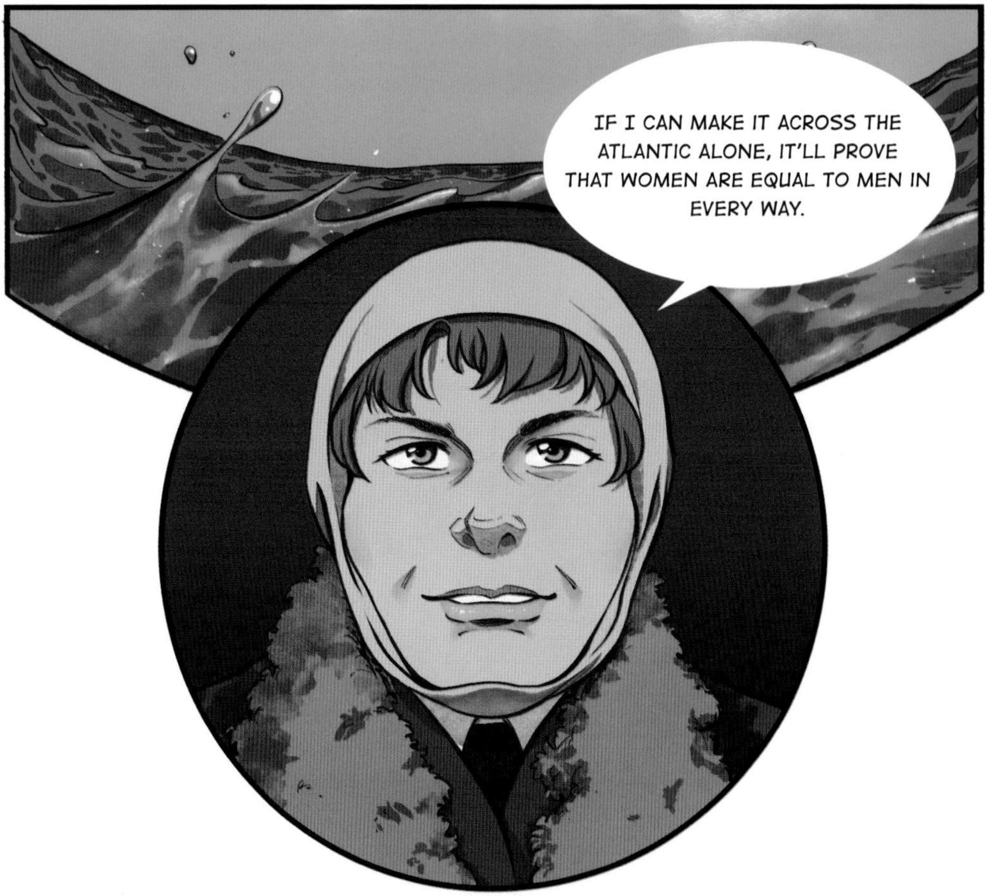
IF I CAN MAKE IT ACROSS THE ATLANTIC ALONE, IT'LL PROVE THAT WOMEN ARE EQUAL TO MEN IN EVERY WAY.

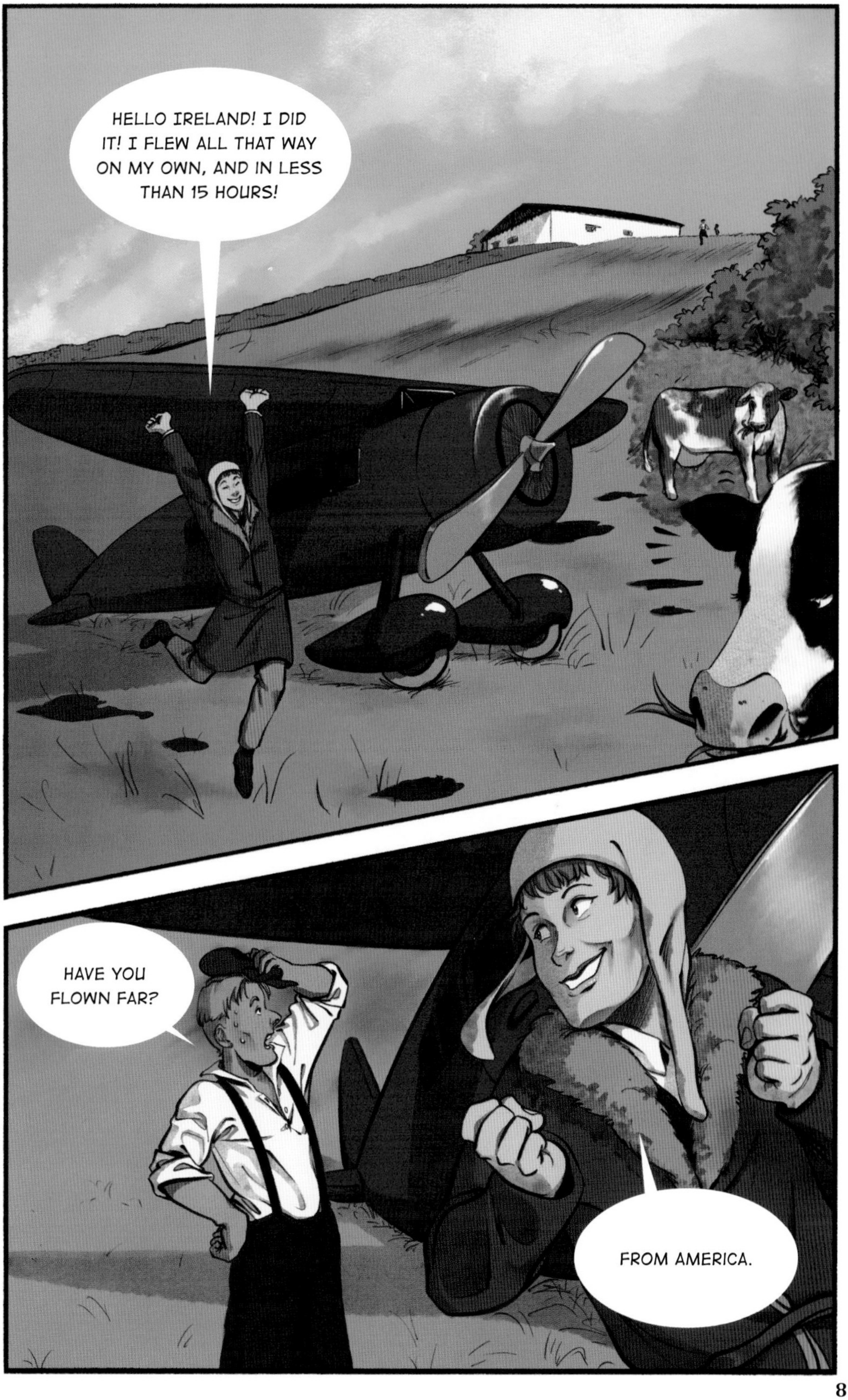
HELLO IRELAND! I DID IT! I FLEW ALL THAT WAY ON MY OWN, AND IN LESS THAN 15 HOURS!
HAVE YOU FLOWN FAR?
FROM AMERICA.

IN THE YEARS THAT FOLLOWED HER SOLO ATLANTIC FLIGHT, AMELIA CONTINUED TO REACH NEW HEIGHTS AND SMASH RECORDS AS A PILOT. BETWEEN 1930 AND 1935, SHE SET SEVEN NEW WOMEN'S SPEED AND DISTANCE AVIATION RECORDS.

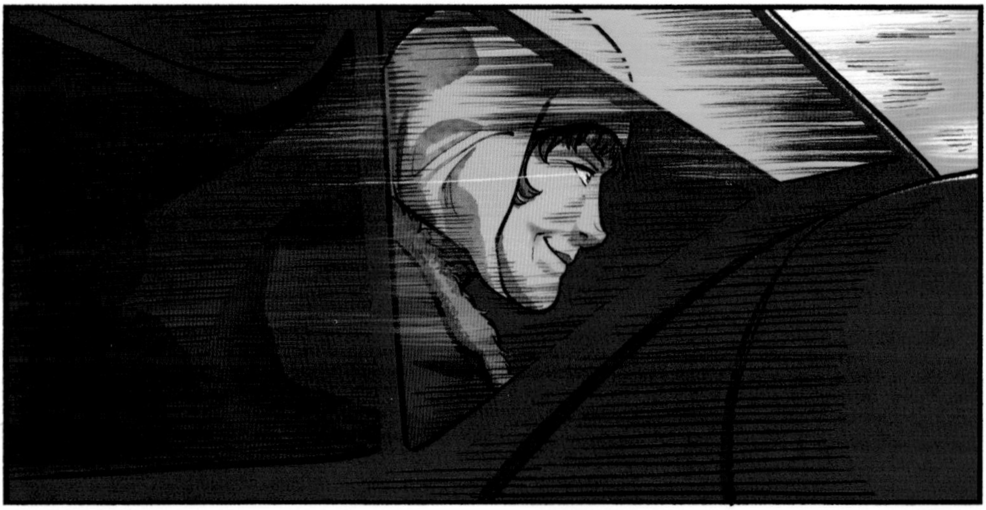

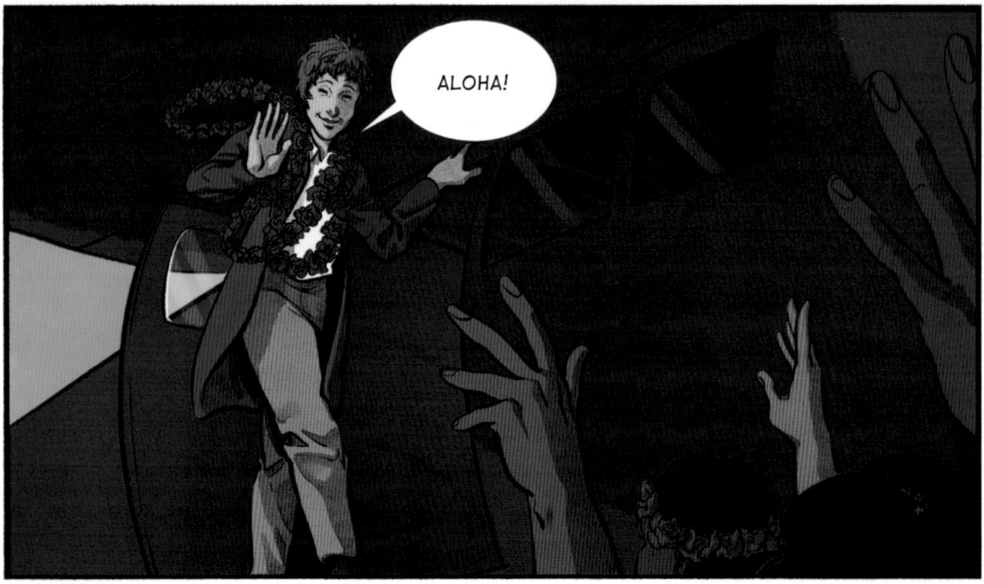
ALOHA!

JANUARY 11, 1935: AMELIA BECAME THE FIRST PERSON TO FLY SOLO ACROSS THE PACIFIC FROM HONOLULU, HAWAII, TO OAKLAND, CALIFORNIA.

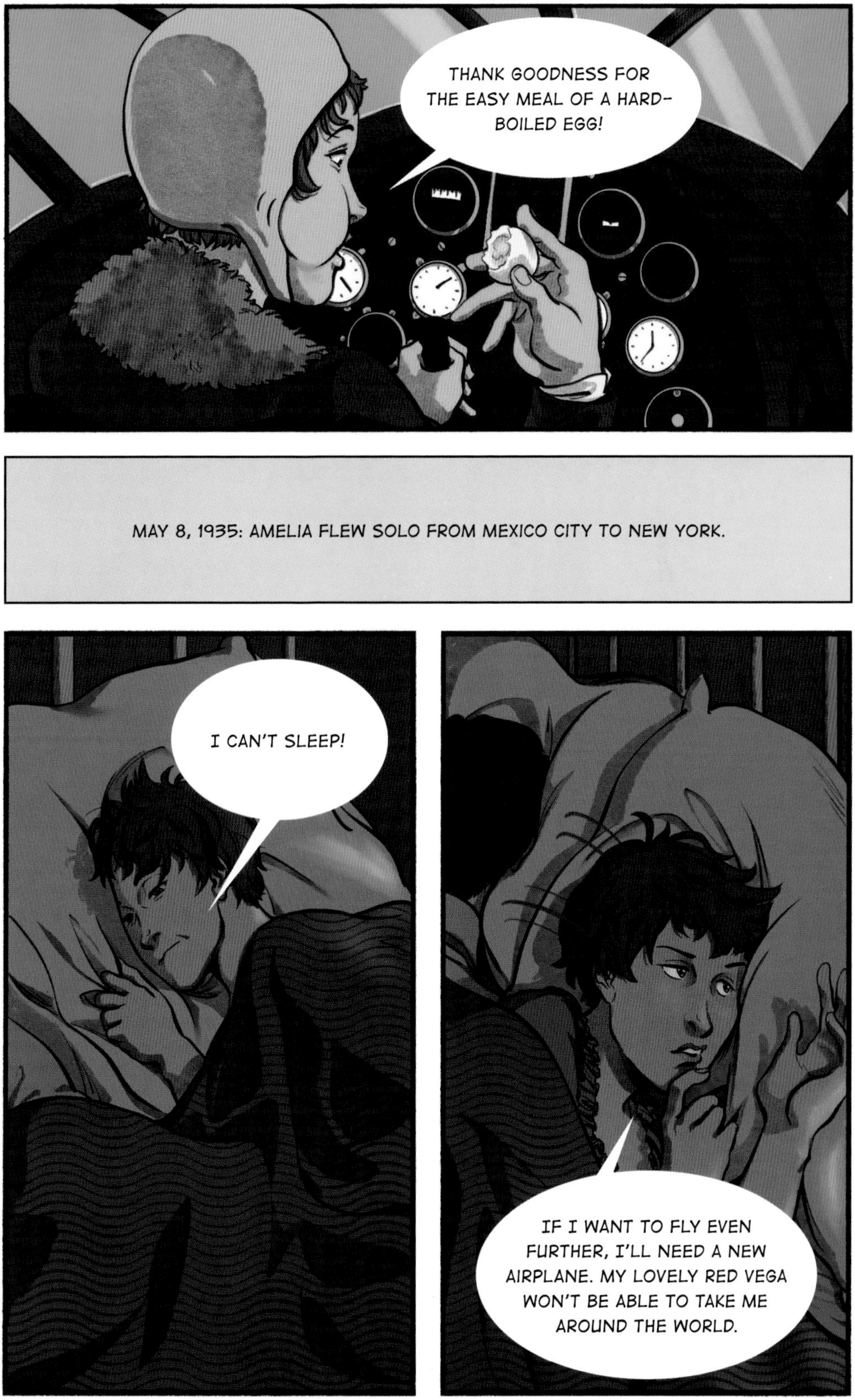
THANK GOODNESS FOR THE EASY MEAL OF A HARD-BOILED EGG!
MAY 8, 1935: AMELIA FLEW SOLO FROM MEXICO CITY TO NEW YORK.
I CAN'T SLEEP!
IF I WANT TO FLY EVEN FURTHER, I'LL NEED A NEW AIRPLANE. MY LOVELY RED VEGA WON'T BE ABLE TO TAKE ME AROUND THE WORLD.

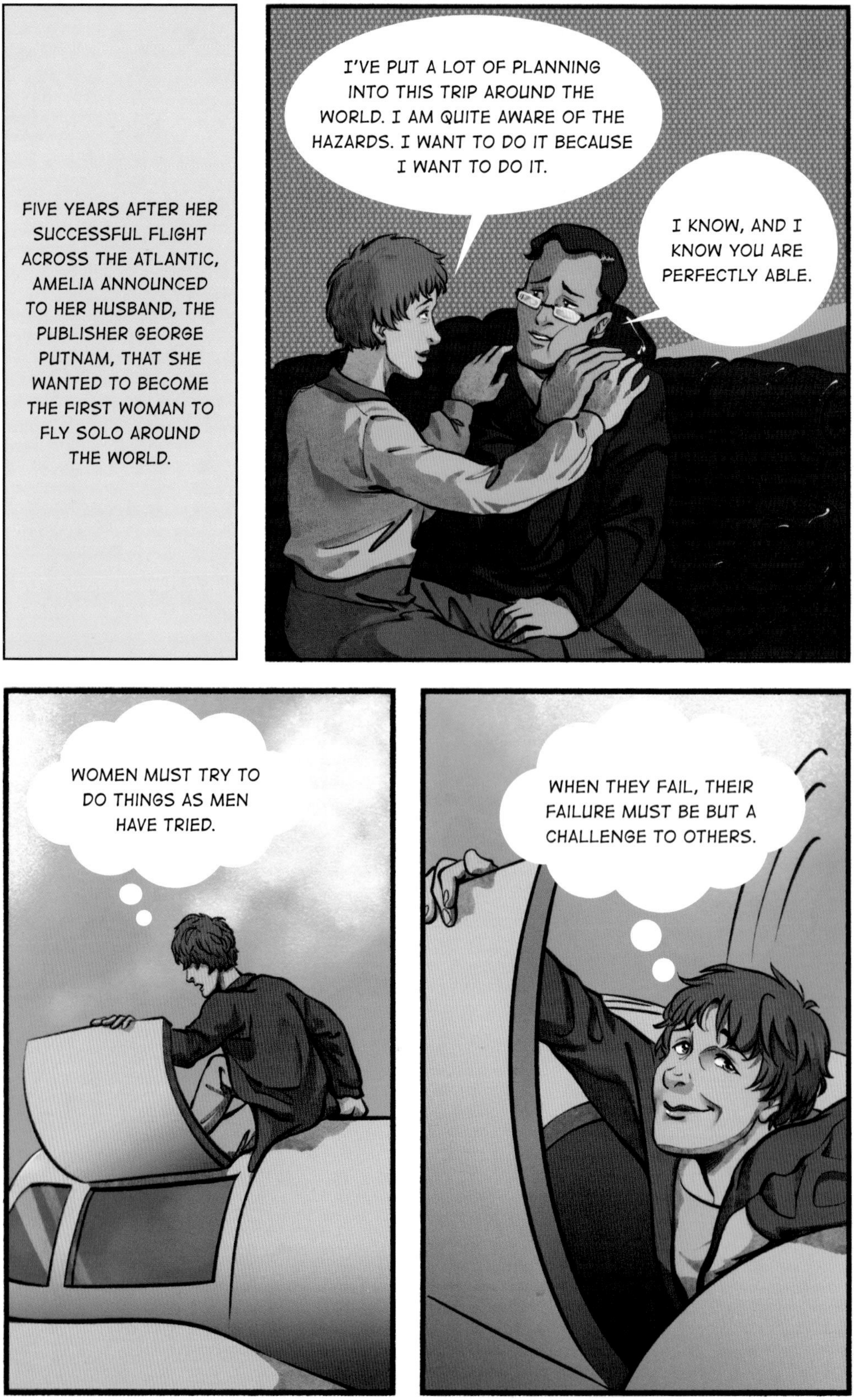
FIVE YEARS AFTER HER SUCCESSFUL FLIGHT ACROSS THE ATLANTIC, AMELIA ANNOUNCED TO HER HUSBAND, THE PUBLISHER GEORGE PUTNAM, THAT SHE WANTED TO BECOME THE FIRST WOMAN TO FLY SOLO AROUND THE WORLD.
I'VE PUT A LOT OF PLANNING INTO THIS TRIP AROUND THE WORLD. I AM QUITE AWARE OF THE HAZARDS. I WANT TO DO IT BECAUSE I WANT TO DO IT.
I KNOW, AND I KNOW YOU ARE PERFECTLY ABLE.
WOMEN MUST TRY TO DO THINGS AS MEN HAVE TRIED.
WHEN THEY FAIL, THEIR FAILURE MUST BE BUT A CHALLENGE TO OTHERS.

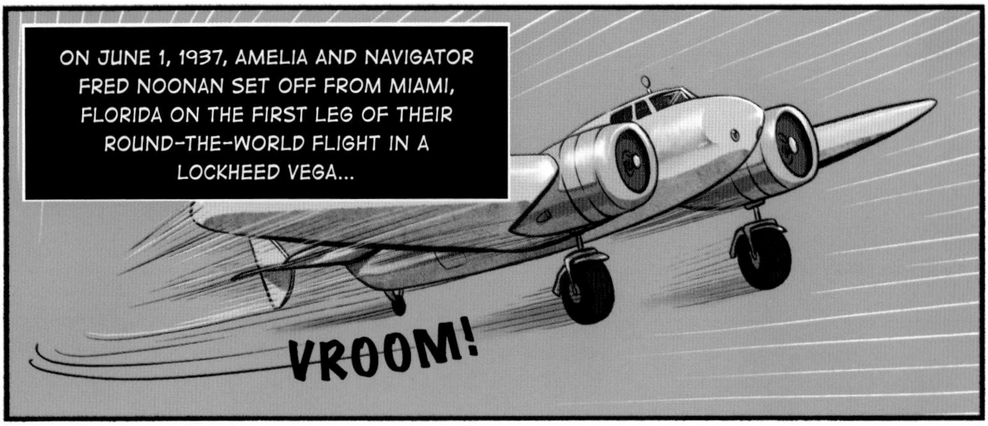
ON JUNE 1, 1937, AMELIA AND NAVIGATOR FRED NOONAN SET OFF FROM MIAMI, FLORIDA ON THE FIRST LEG OF THEIR ROUND-THE-WORLD FLIGHT IN A LOCKHEED VEGA...
VROOM!

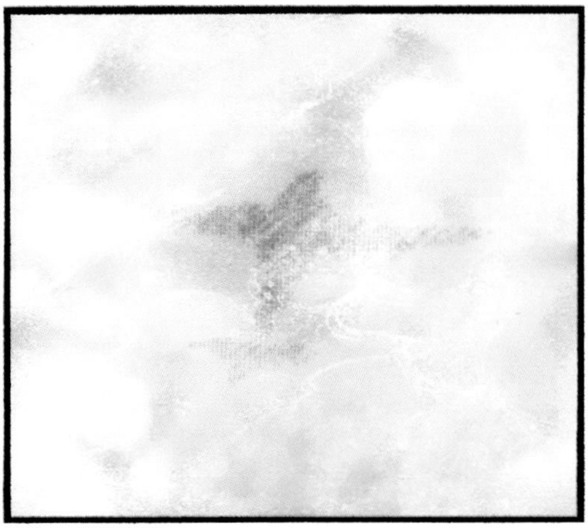

SADLY, THE TRIP ENDED IN TRAGEDY, AS HER PLANE WAS LOST IN THE PACIFIC OCEAN ON THE FINAL LEG OF THE JOURNEY. THE WRECKAGE WAS NEVER FOUND, AND MANY PEOPLE BELIEVED SHE MAY HAVE SURVIVED. AMELIA'S BRAVERY INSPIRED WOMEN AROUND THE WORLD—NOT JUST AVIATORS—TO PURSUE THEIR DREAMS.

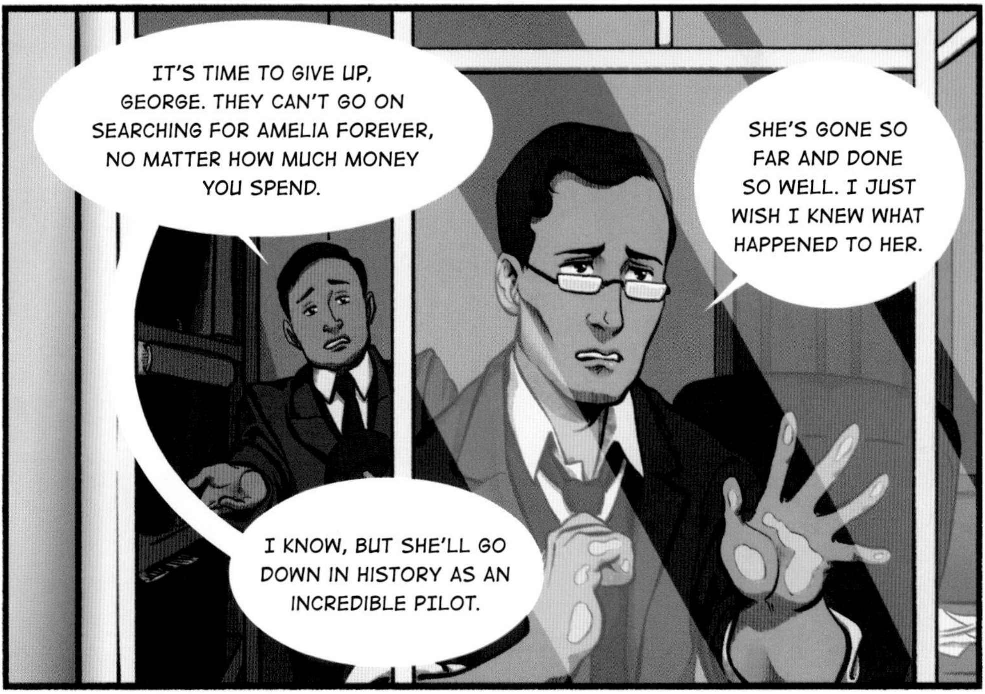
IT'S TIME TO GIVE UP, GEORGE. THEY CAN'T GO ON SEARCHING FOR AMELIA FOREVER, NO MATTER HOW MUCH MONEY YOU SPEND.
SHE'S GONE SO FAR AND DONE SO WELL. I JUST WISH I KNEW WHAT HAPPENED TO HER.
I KNOW, BUT SHE'LL GO DOWN IN HISTORY AS AN INCREDIBLE PILOT.

IGOR SIKORSKY
(1889–1972)
BUILDING A LIFESAVER

AT AGE 20, YOUNG IGOR TRAVELED FROM HIS HOME IN KIEV, RUSSIA TO PARIS, FRANCE—THE CENTER OF THE AVIATION WORLD. HE RETURNED WITH DREAMS OF BUILDING A HELICOPTER.

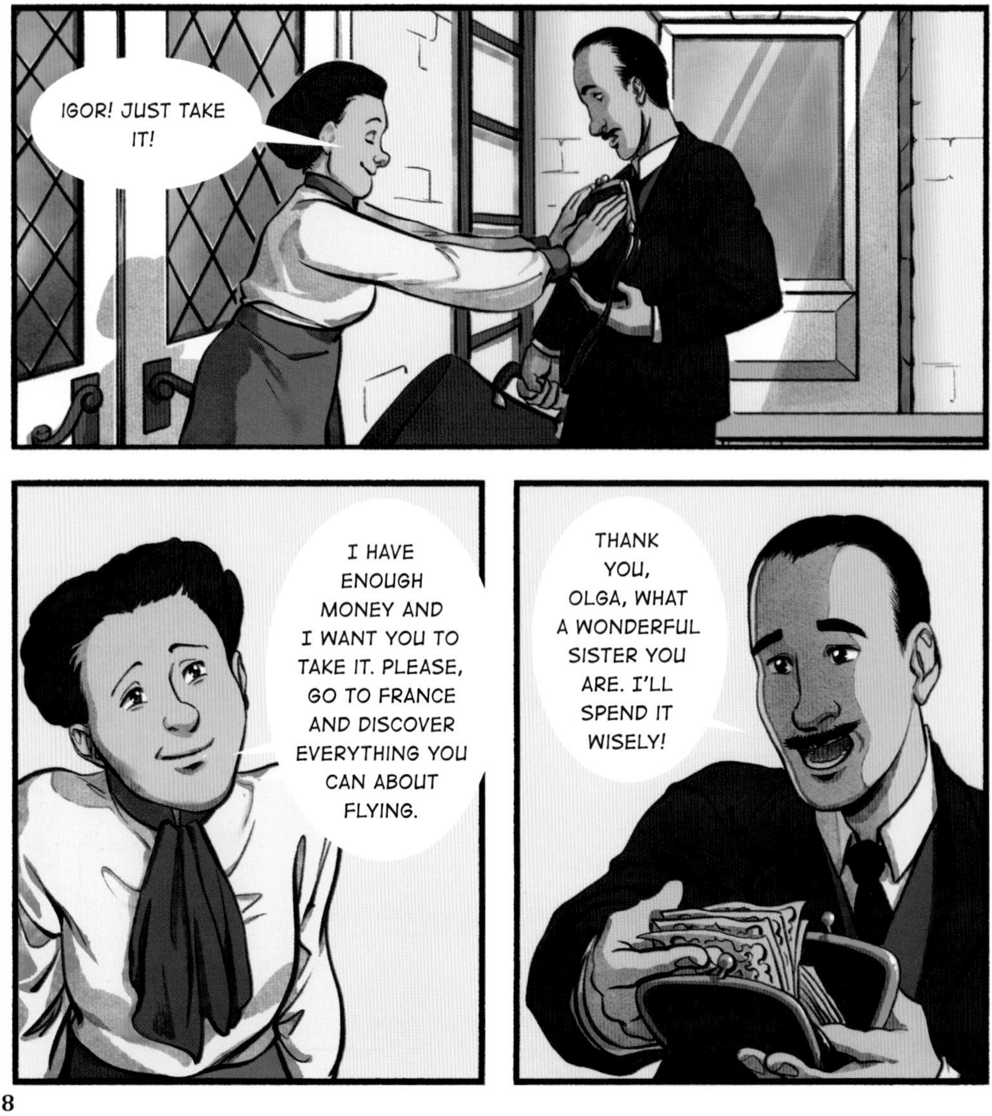
IGOR! JUST TAKE IT!
I HAVE ENOUGH MONEY AND I WANT YOU TO TAKE IT. PLEASE, GO TO FRANCE AND DISCOVER EVERYTHING YOU CAN ABOUT FLYING.
THANK YOU, OLGA, WHAT A WONDERFUL SISTER YOU ARE. I'LL SPEND IT WISELY!

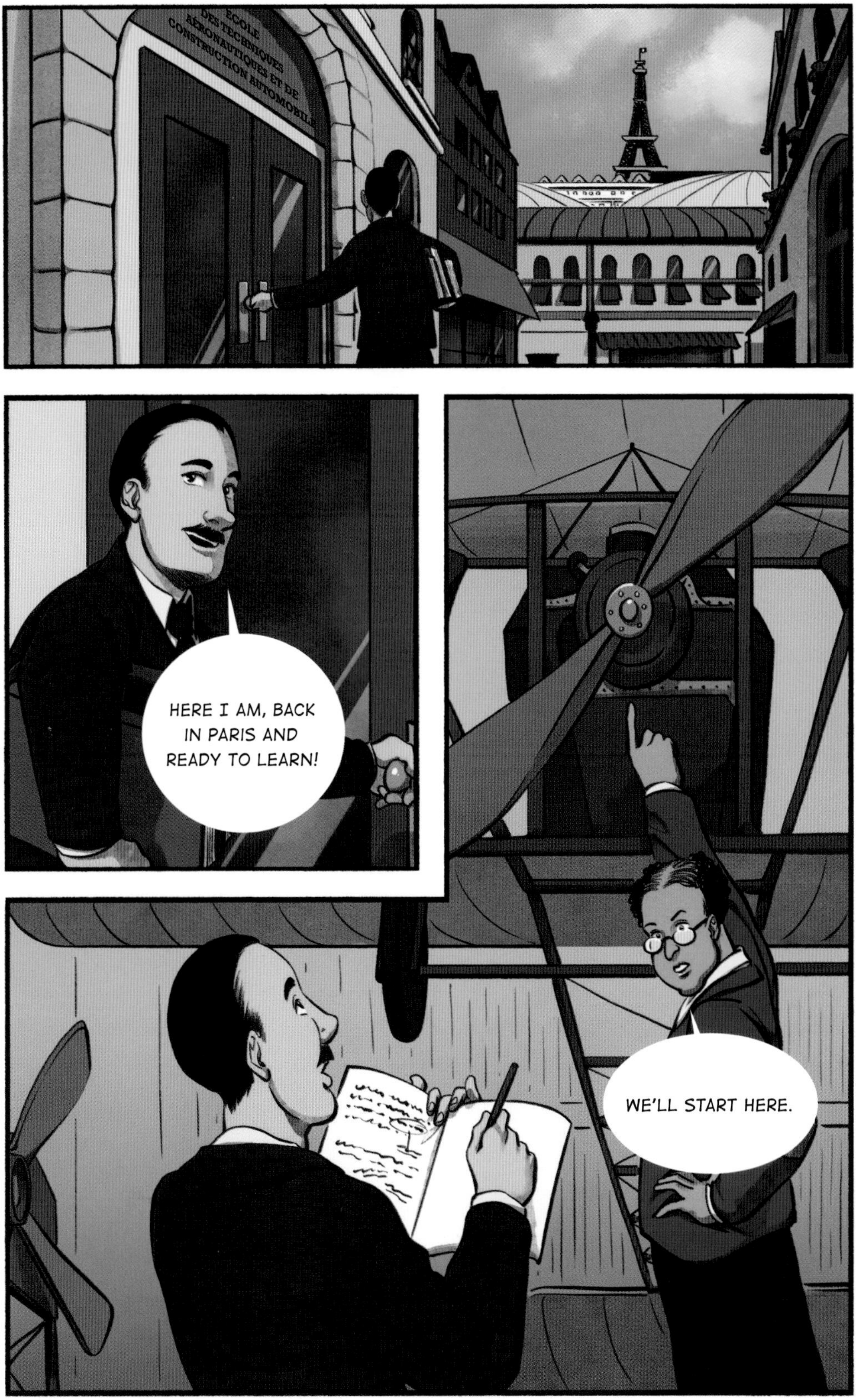
ECOLE DES TECHNIQUES AÉRONAUTIQUES ET DE CONSTRUCTION AUTOMOBILE
HERE I AM, BACK IN PARIS AND READY TO LEARN!
WE'LL START HERE.

AFTER RETURNING TO KIEV FROM PARIS IN 1909, IGOR BEGAN TO DESIGN HIS FIRST HELICOPTER, BUT THE ORIGINAL PROTOTYPES COULDN'T LIFT THEIR OWN WEIGHT OFF THE GROUND.

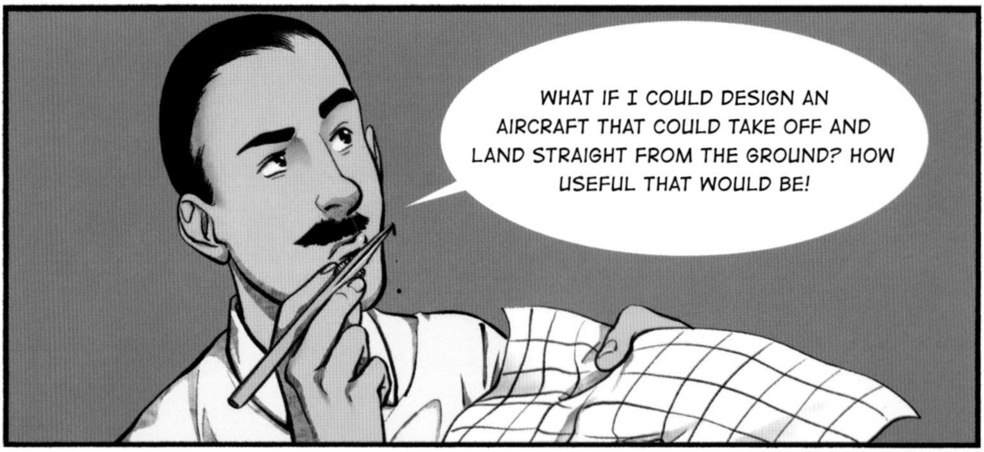
WHAT IF I COULD DESIGN AN AIRCRAFT THAT COULD TAKE OFF AND LAND STRAIGHT FROM THE GROUND? HOW USEFUL THAT WOULD BE!

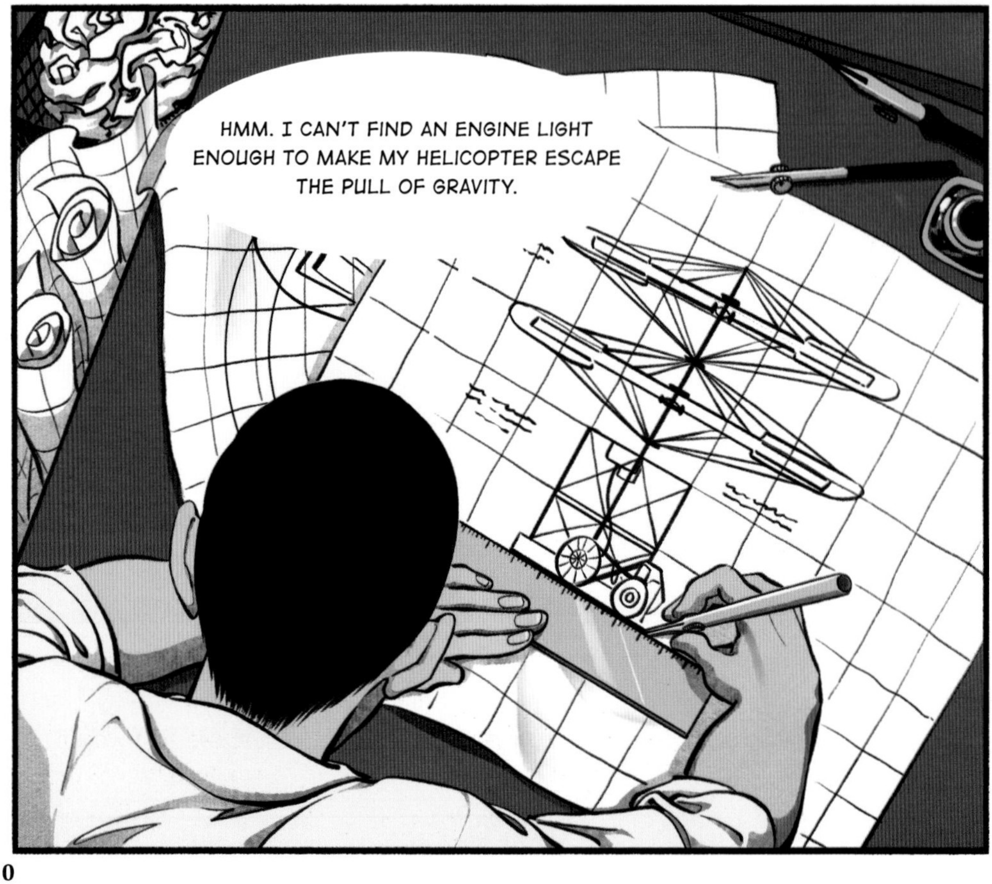
HMM. I CAN'T FIND AN ENGINE LIGHT ENOUGH TO MAKE MY HELICOPTER ESCAPE THE PULL OF GRAVITY.

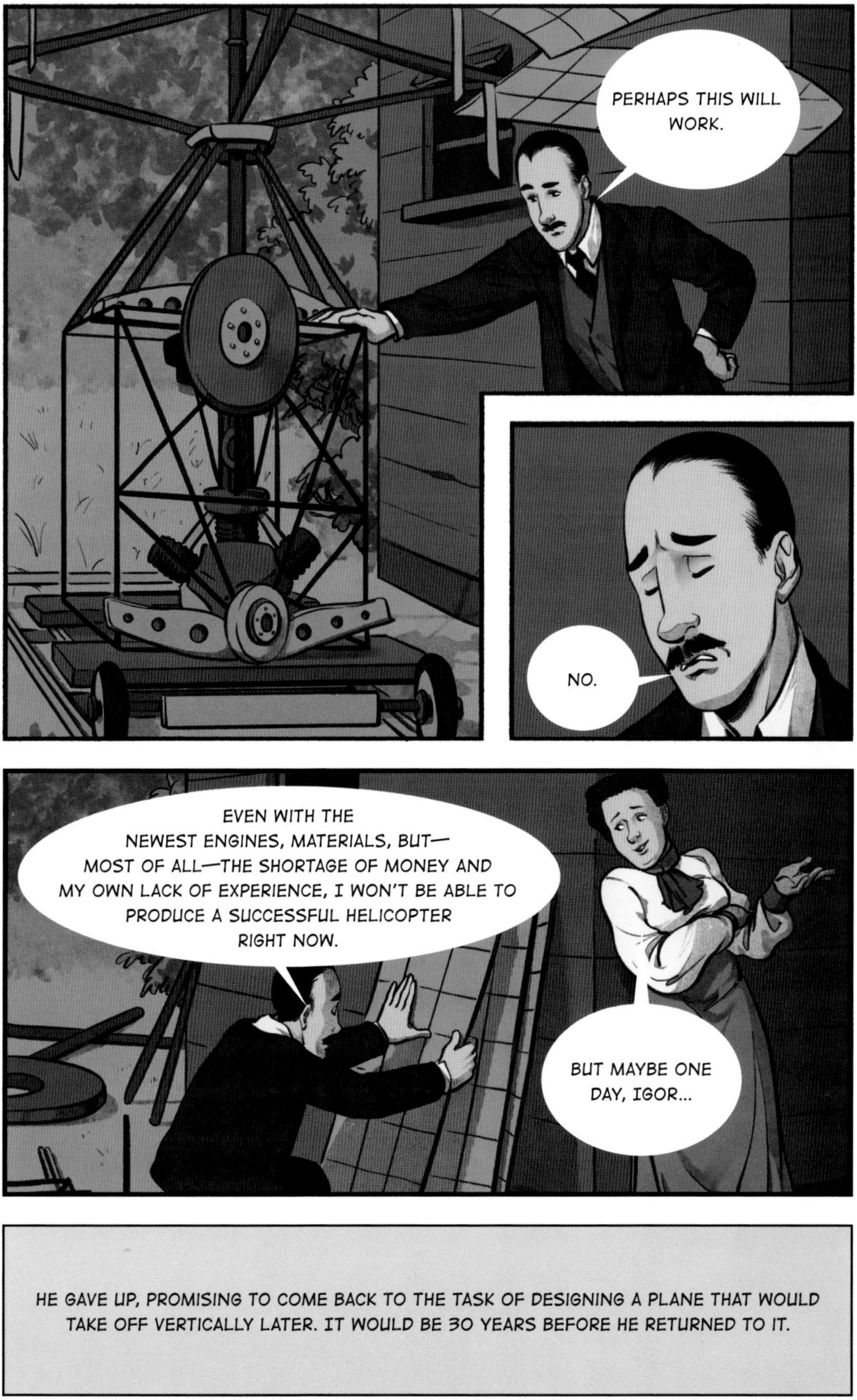
PERHAPS THIS WILL WORK.
NO.
EVEN WITH THE NEWEST ENGINES, MATERIALS, BUT—MOST OF ALL—THE SHORTAGE OF MONEY AND MY OWN LACK OF EXPERIENCE, I WON'T BE ABLE TO PRODUCE A SUCCESSFUL HELICOPTER RIGHT NOW.
BUT MAYBE ONE DAY, IGOR...
HE GAVE UP, PROMISING TO COME BACK TO THE TASK OF DESIGNING A PLANE THAT WOULD TAKE OFF VERTICALLY LATER. IT WOULD BE 30 YEARS BEFORE HE RETURNED TO IT.

FOR SEVERAL YEARS, IGOR BUILT AND FLEW PLANE AFTER PLANE, FIRST FOR HIMSELF, THEN AS CHIEF ENGINEER FOR THE RUSSIAN BALTIC RAILROAD CAR WORKS. HE LATER RAN HIS OWN FACTORY.

S-1 BIPLANE, 1910

THE ENGINE'S JUST NOT POWERFUL ENOUGH TO LIFT IT UNLESS THE WIND BLOWS IN MY FAVOR.

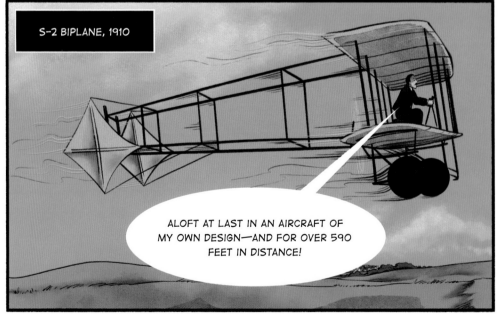

S-2 BIPLANE, 1910

ALOFT AT LAST IN AN AIRCRAFT OF MY OWN DESIGN—AND FOR OVER 590 FEET IN DISTANCE!

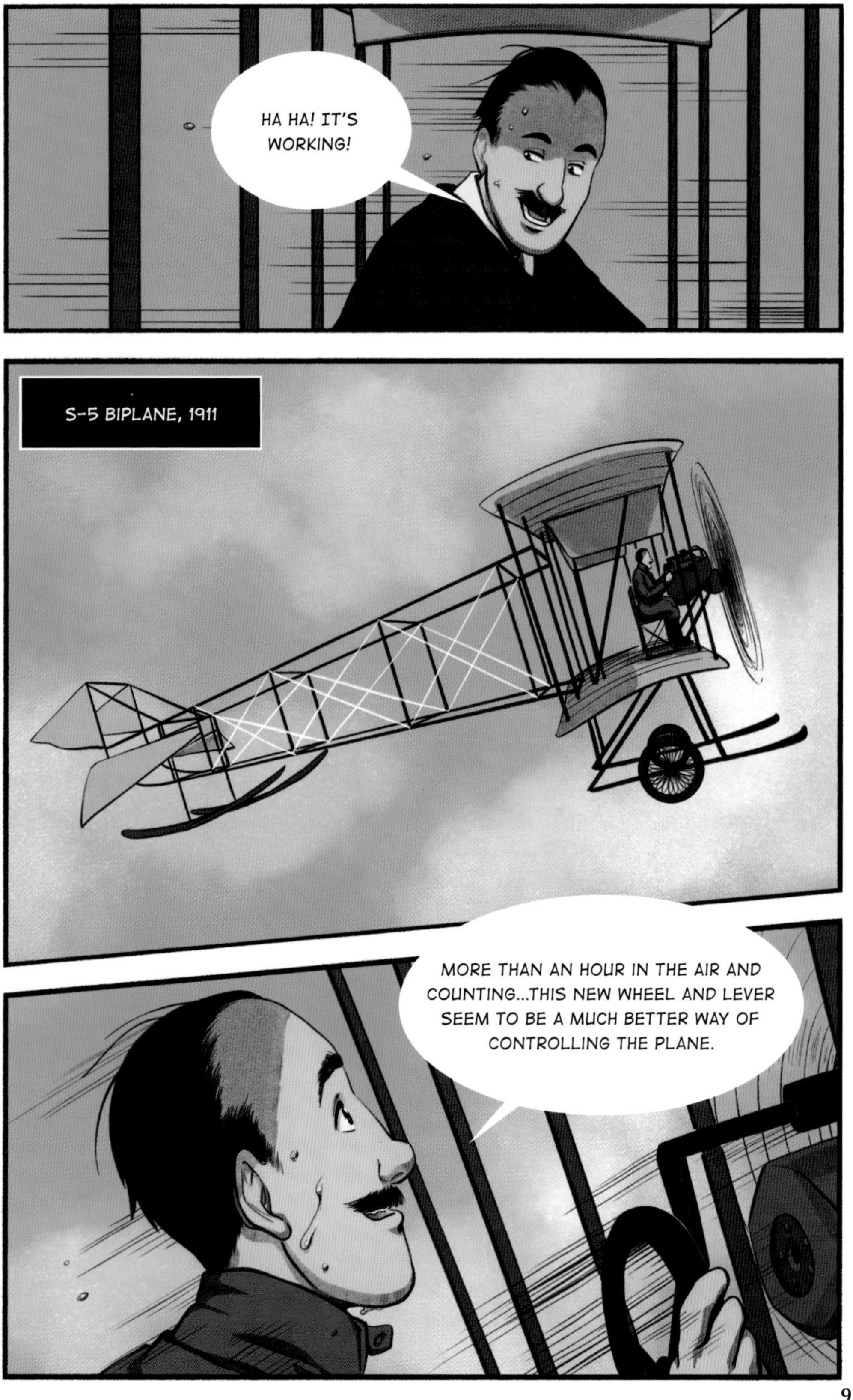
HA HA! IT'S WORKING!
S-5 BIPLANE, 1911
MORE THAN AN HOUR IN THE AIR AND COUNTING...THIS NEW WHEEL AND LEVER SEEM TO BE A MUCH BETTER WAY OF CONTROLLING THE PLANE.

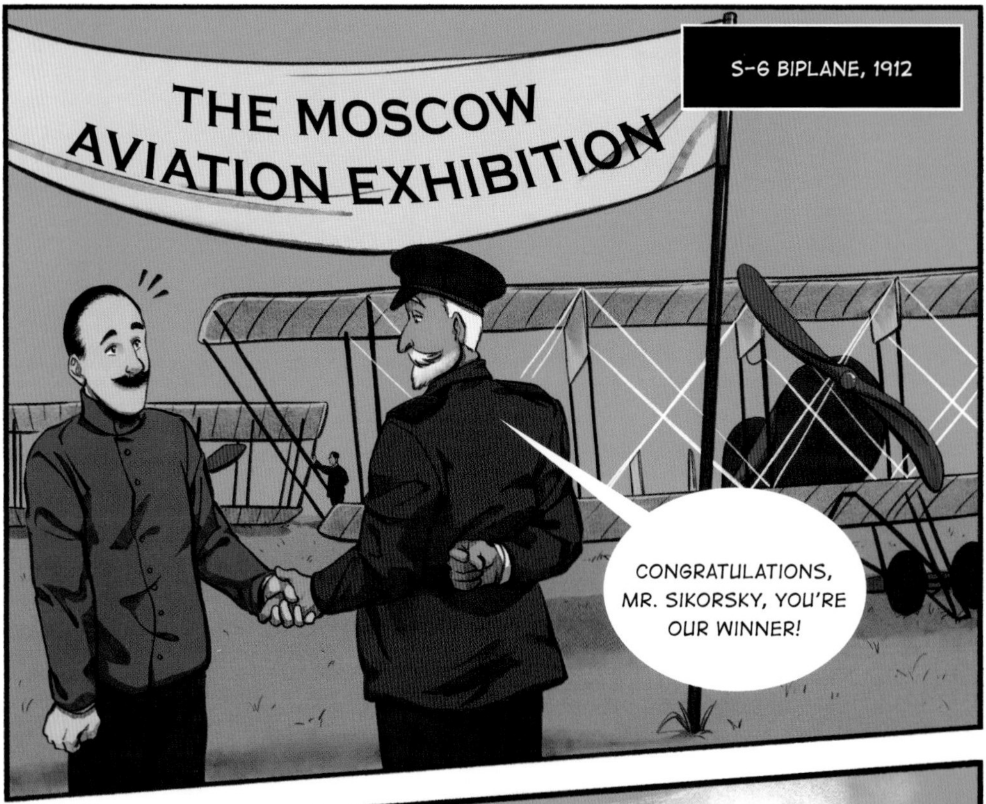
THE MOSCOW AVIATION EXHIBITION
S-6 BIPLANE, 1912
CONGRATULATIONS, MR. SIKORSKY, YOU'RE OUR WINNER!

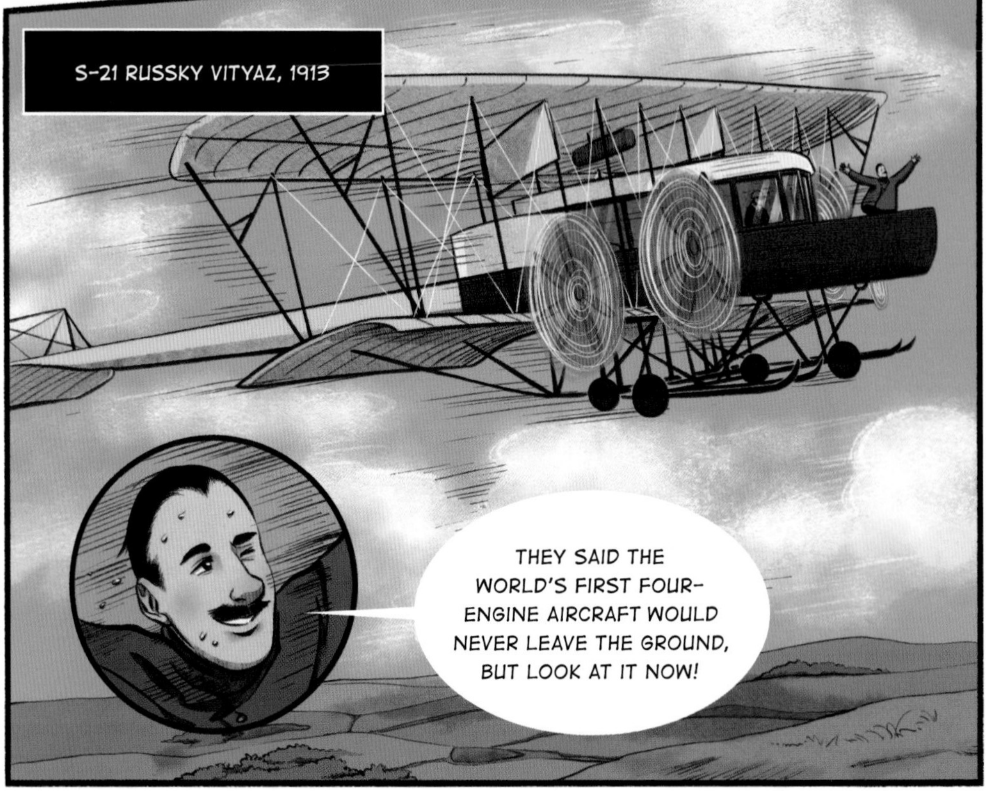
S-21 RUSSKY VITYAZ, 1913
THEY SAID THE WORLD'S FIRST FOUR-ENGINE AIRCRAFT WOULD NEVER LEAVE THE GROUND, BUT LOOK AT IT NOW!

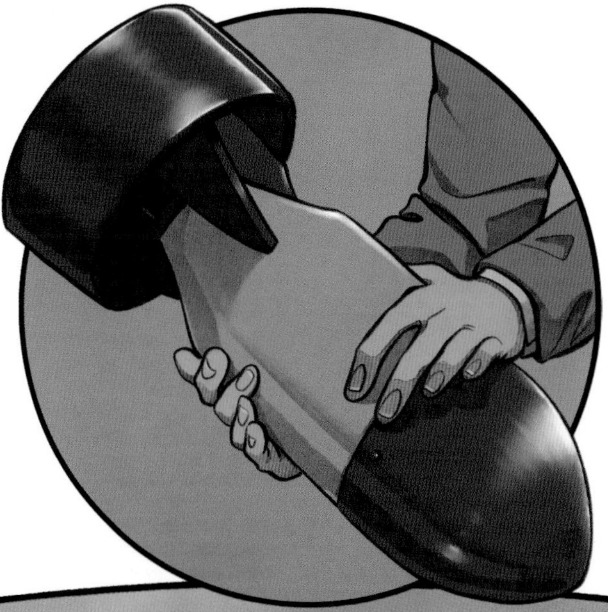

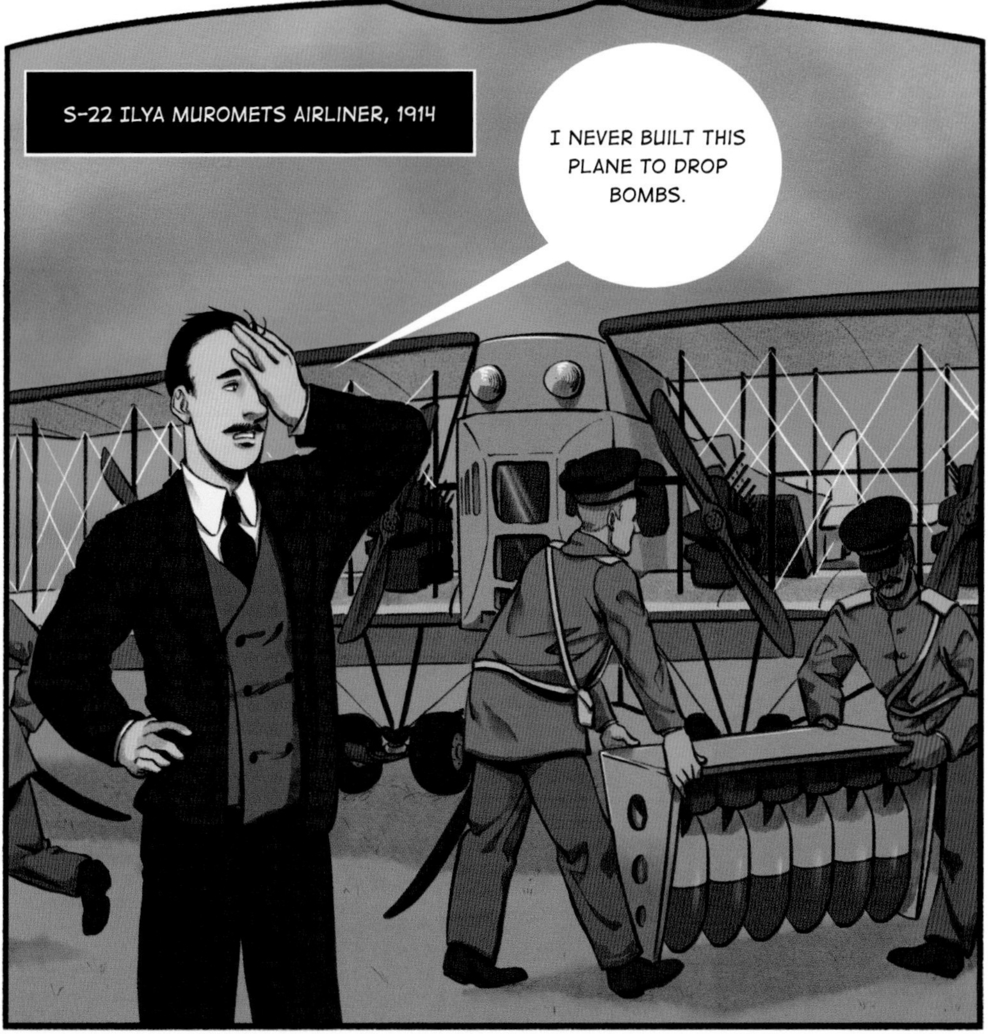
S-22 ILYA MUROMETS AIRLINER, 1914
I NEVER BUILT THIS PLANE TO DROP BOMBS.

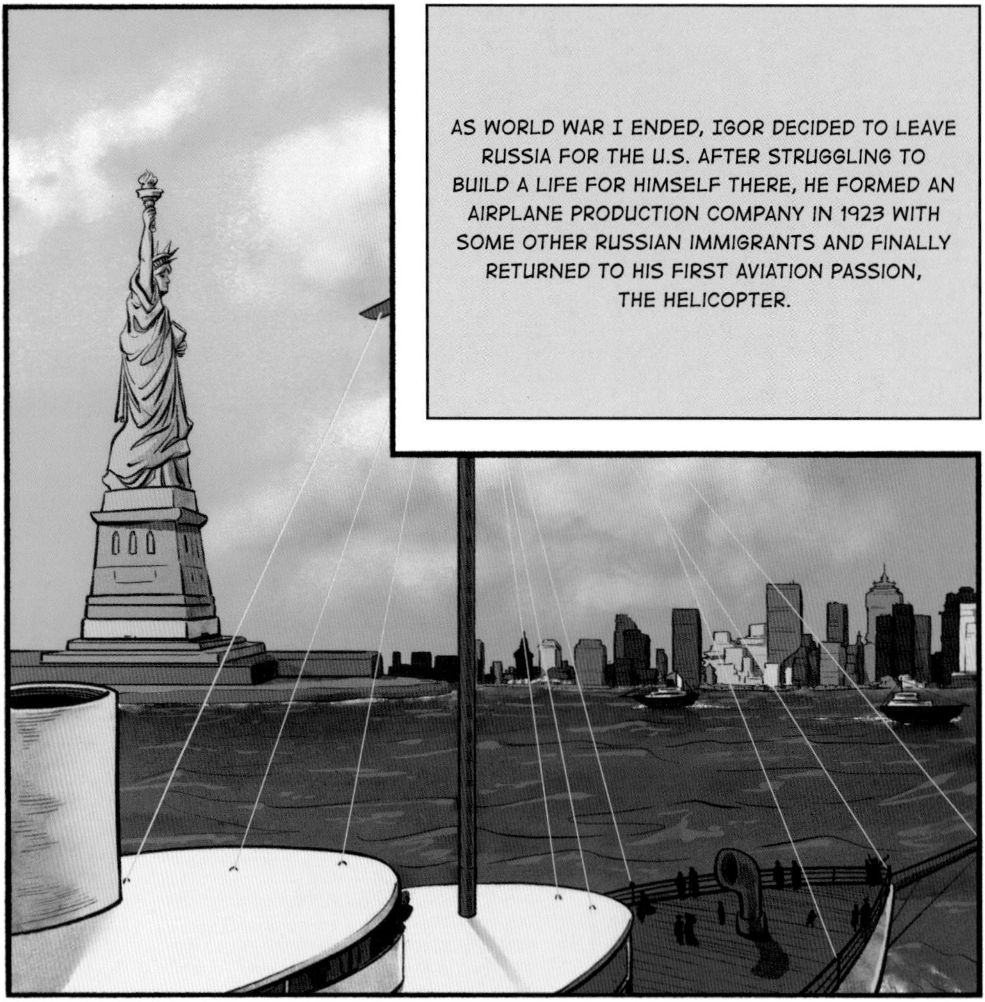
AS WORLD WAR I ENDED, IGOR DECIDED TO LEAVE RUSSIA FOR THE U.S. AFTER STRUGGLING TO BUILD A LIFE FOR HIMSELF THERE, HE FORMED AN AIRPLANE PRODUCTION COMPANY IN 1923 WITH SOME OTHER RUSSIAN IMMIGRANTS AND FINALLY RETURNED TO HIS FIRST AVIATION PASSION, THE HELICOPTER.

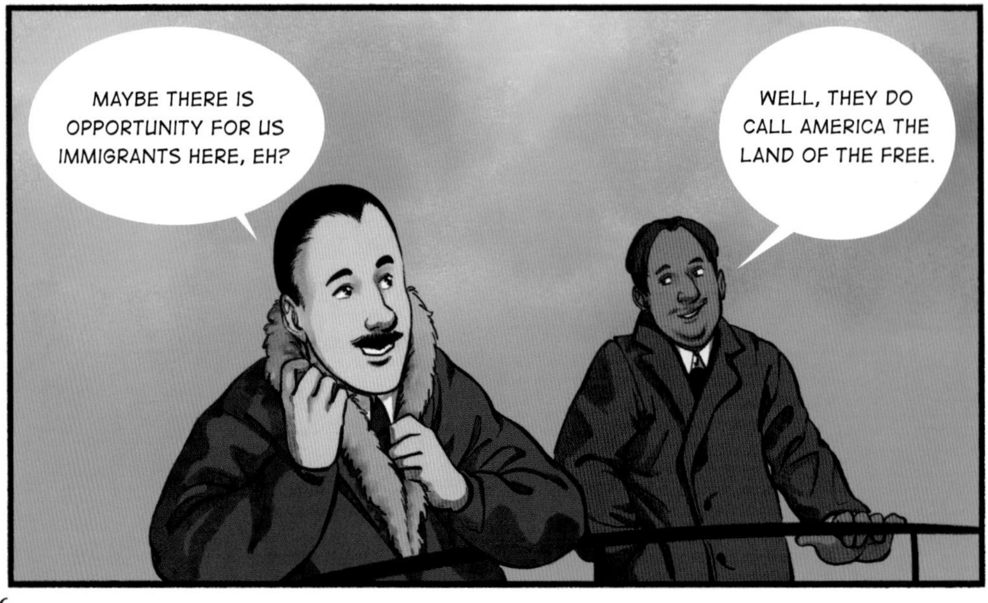
MAYBE THERE IS OPPORTUNITY FOR US IMMIGRANTS HERE, EH?
WELL, THEY DO CALL AMERICA THE LAND OF THE FREE.

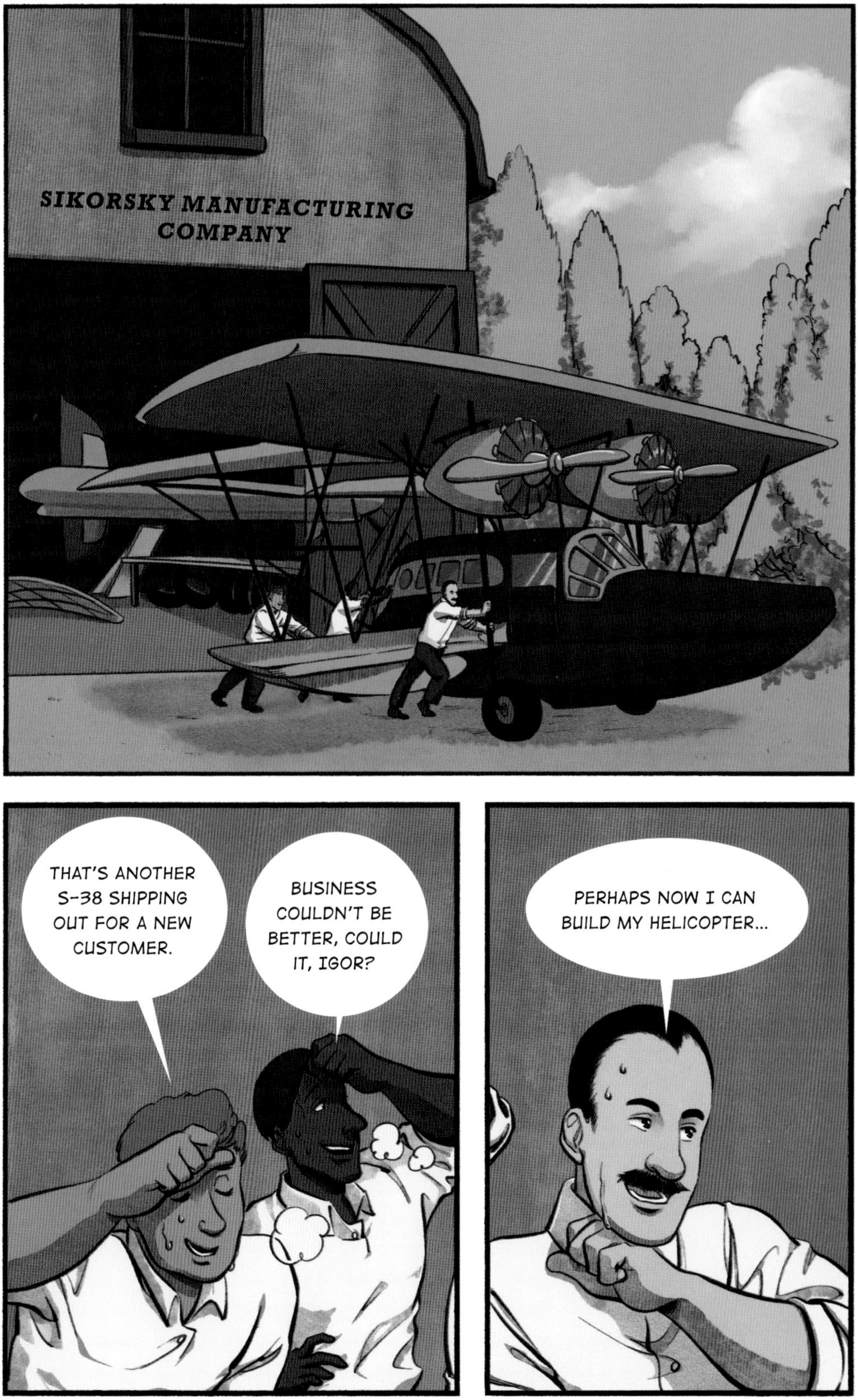
SIKORSKY MANUFACTURING COMPANY
THAT'S ANOTHER S-38 SHIPPING OUT FOR A NEW CUSTOMER.
BUSINESS COULDN'T BE BETTER, COULD IT, IGOR?
PERHAPS NOW I CAN BUILD MY HELICOPTER...

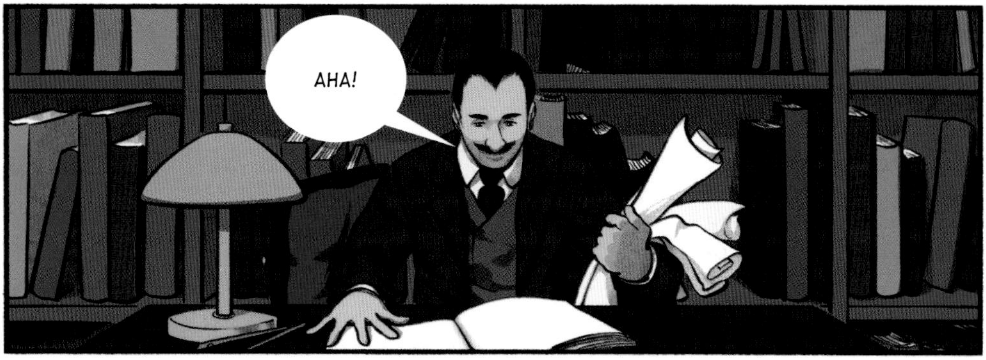
AHA!

BY THE LATE 1930s, THE TECHNOLOGY FOR MAKING HELICOPTERS POSSIBLE WAS FINALLY AVAILABLE.

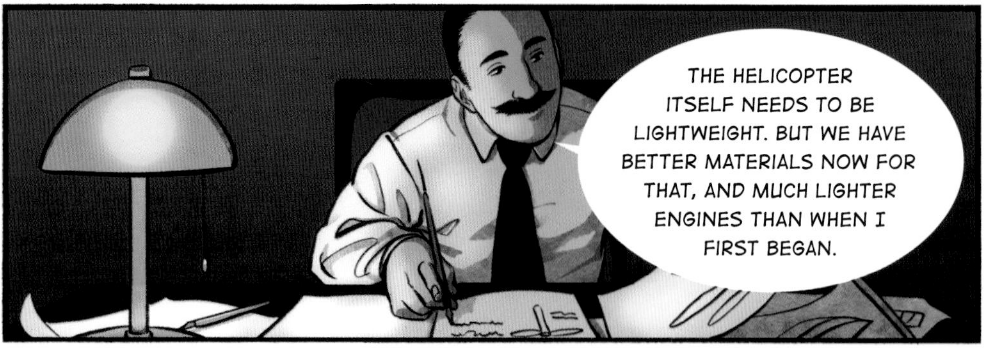
THE HELICOPTER ITSELF NEEDS TO BE LIGHTWEIGHT. BUT WE HAVE BETTER MATERIALS NOW FOR THAT, AND MUCH LIGHTER ENGINES THAN WHEN I FIRST BEGAN.

IGOR STARTED FOCUSING ON HIS LIFELONG DREAM.

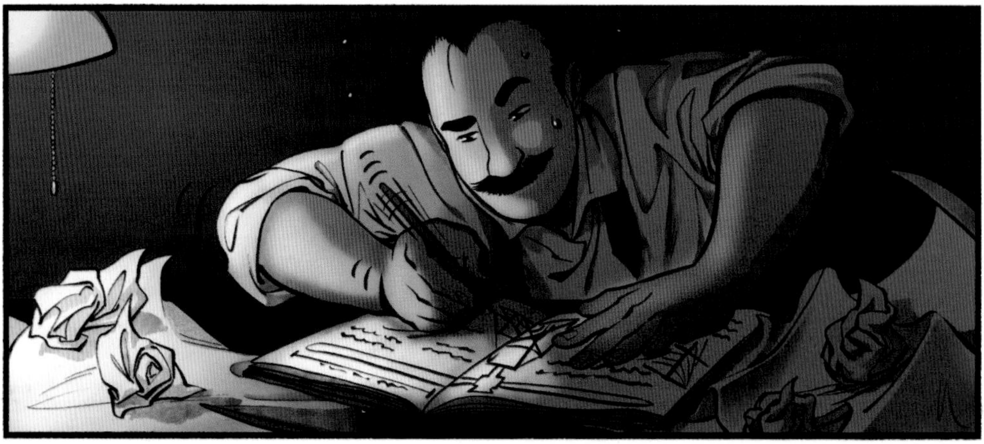

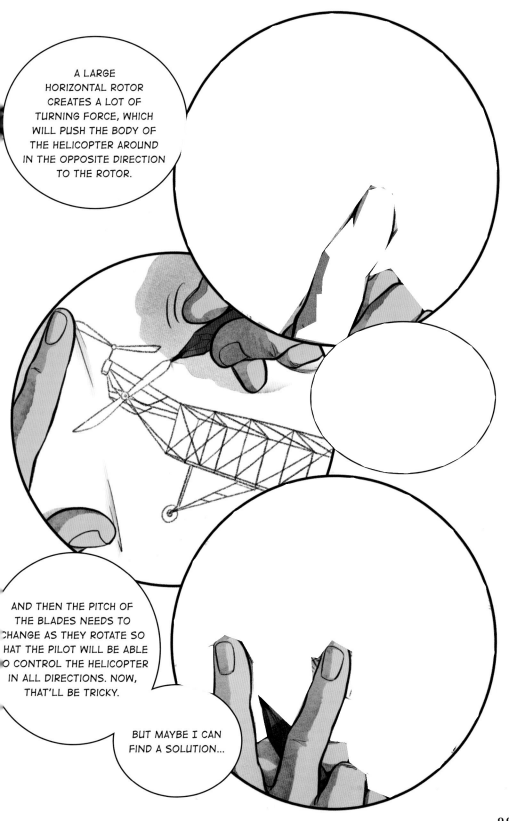

A LARGE HORIZONTAL ROTOR CREATES A LOT OF TURNING FORCE, WHICH WILL PUSH THE BODY OF THE HELICOPTER AROUND IN THE OPPOSITE DIRECTION TO THE ROTOR.

AND THEN THE PITCH OF THE BLADES NEEDS TO CHANGE AS THEY ROTATE SO THAT THE PILOT WILL BE ABLE TO CONTROL THE HELICOPTER IN ALL DIRECTIONS. NOW, THAT'LL BE TRICKY.

BUT MAYBE I CAN FIND A SOLUTION...

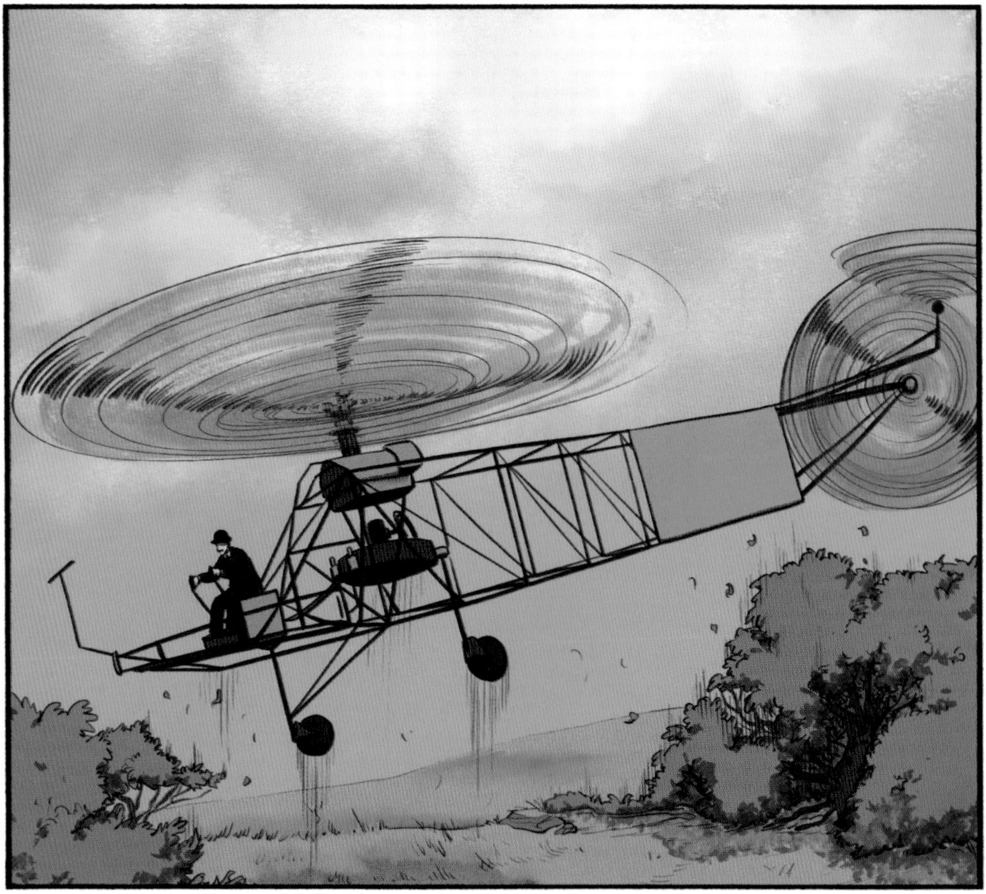

THE VS-300 MADE THE FIRST MODERN HELICOPTER FLIGHT ON SEPTEMBER 14, 1939, WITH IGOR IN THE PILOT'S SEAT. IT WAS THE ACHIEVEMENT OF HIS LIFELONG DREAM.

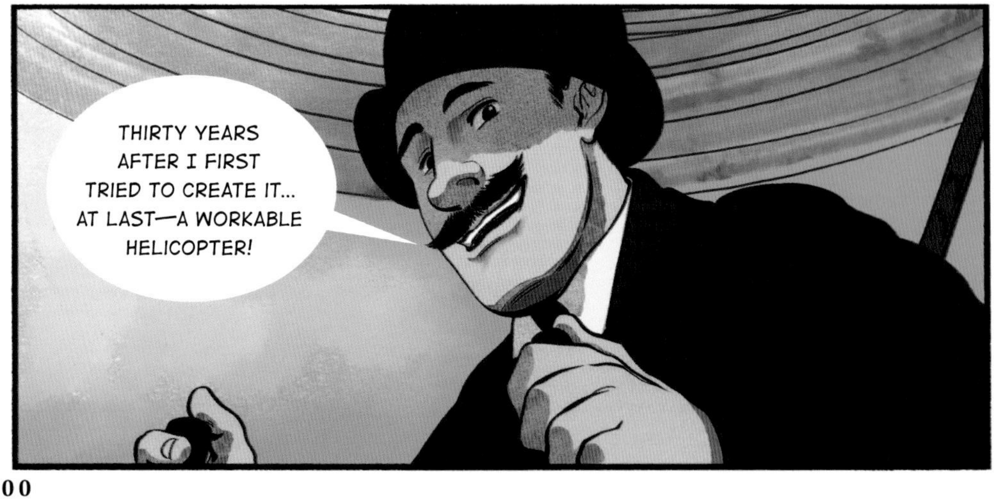
THIRTY YEARS AFTER I FIRST TRIED TO CREATE IT... AT LAST—A WORKABLE HELICOPTER!

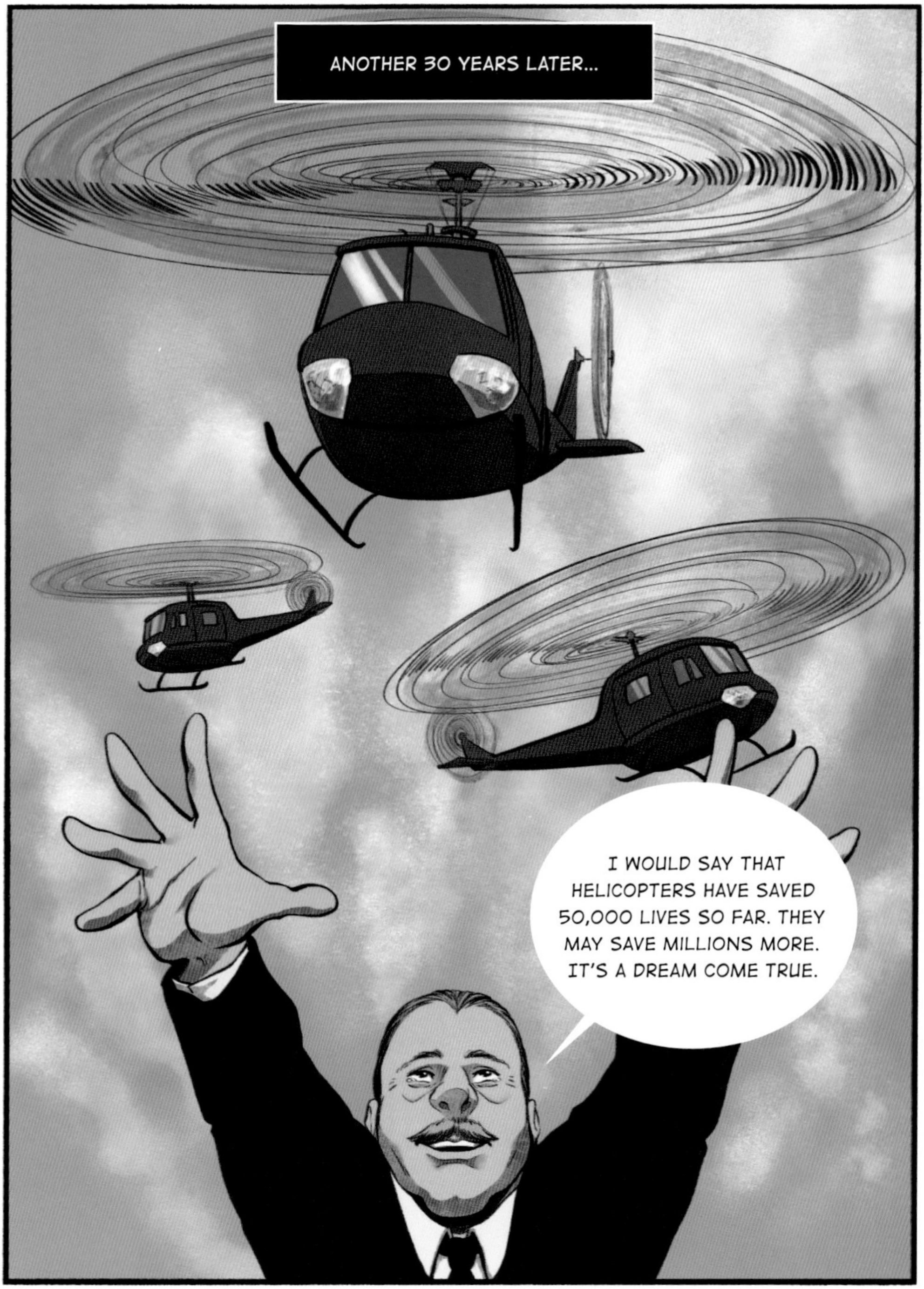
ANOTHER 30 YEARS LATER...
I WOULD SAY THAT HELICOPTERS HAVE SAVED 50,000 LIVES SO FAR. THEY MAY SAVE MILLIONS MORE. IT'S A DREAM COME TRUE.

AT THE END OF IGOR'S LIFE, HE OFTEN REFLECTED ON HOW PROUD HE WAS THAT HIS INVENTION HAD SAVED SO MANY LIVES, AS HE HAD HOPED IT WOULD.

FRANK WHITTLE
(1907–1996)
JET ENGINE GENIUS

FRANK'S DREAM OF JOINING THE BRITISH ROYAL AIR FORCE (RAF) DIDN'T COME EASY. AT THE AGE OF 15, HE WAS REJECTED FOR BEING TOO SMALL, BUT AFTER REAPPLYING, HE BECAME A SUCCESSFUL CADET WITH PLENTY OF BRIGHT IDEAS.

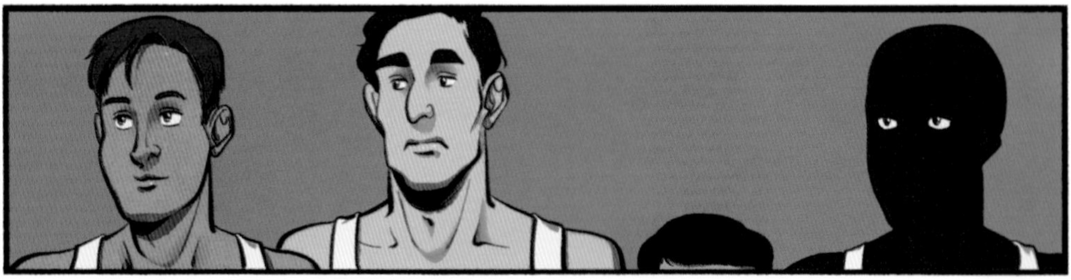

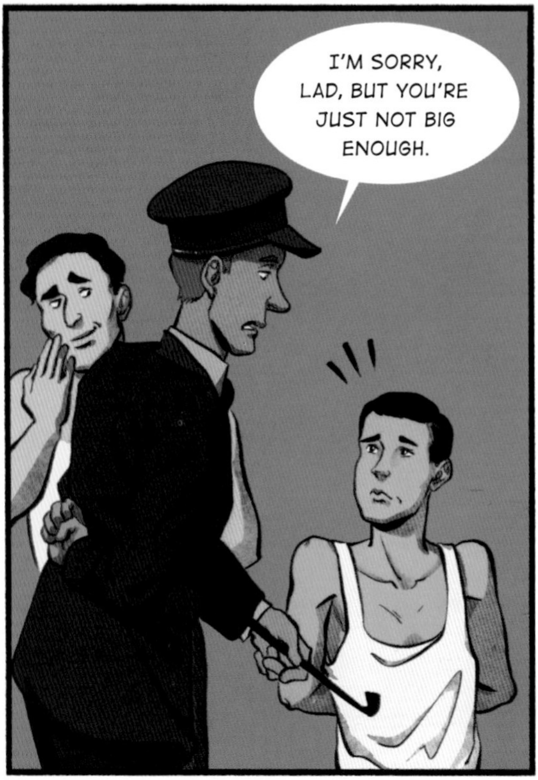
I'M SORRY, LAD, BUT YOU'RE JUST NOT BIG ENOUGH.

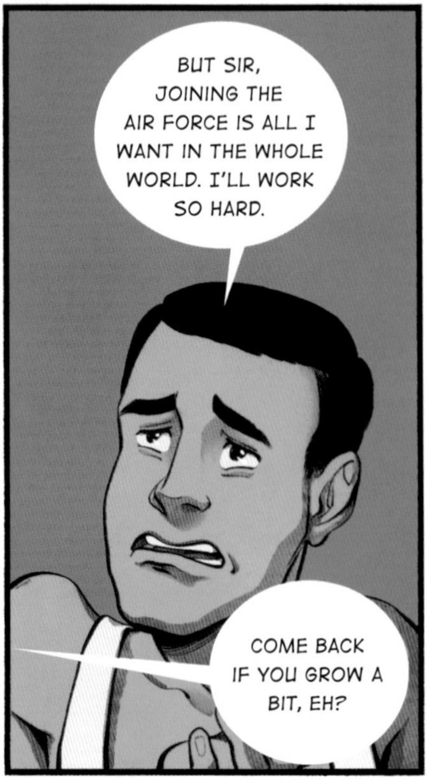
BUT SIR, JOINING THE AIR FORCE IS ALL I WANT IN THE WHOLE WORLD. I'LL WORK SO HARD.
COME BACK IF YOU GROW A BIT, EH?

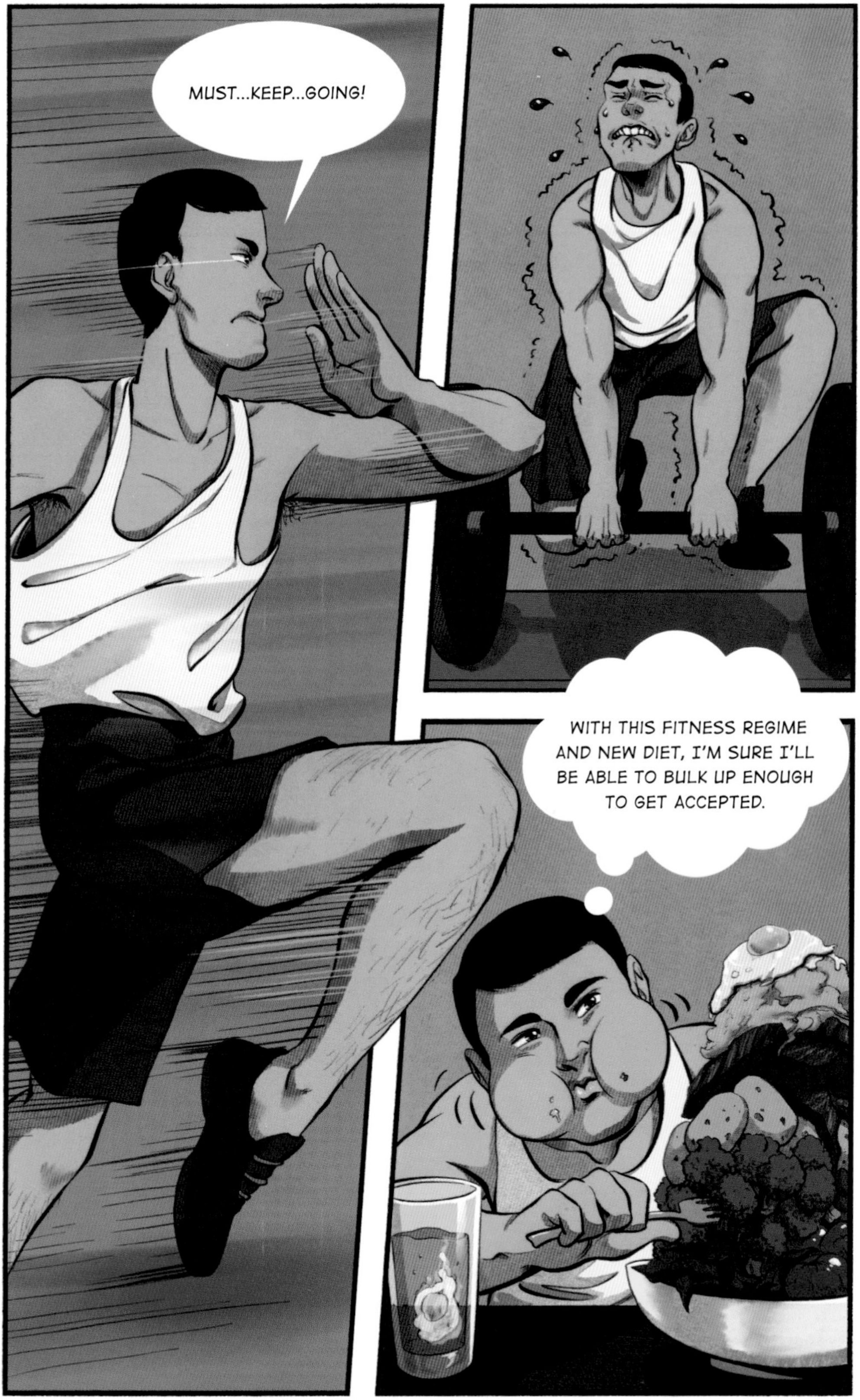
MUST...KEEP...GOING!
WITH THIS FITNESS REGIME AND NEW DIET, I'M SURE I'LL BE ABLE TO BULK UP ENOUGH TO GET ACCEPTED.

FRANK'S FITNESS REGIME HAD ADDED SOME STRENGTH TO HIS SMALL BODY. AFTER BEING REJECTED ONCE MORE AND APPLYING UNDER A DIFFERENT NAME, FRANK WAS FINALLY ACCEPTED FOR A CADETSHIP AT RAF CRANWELL, ENGLAND.

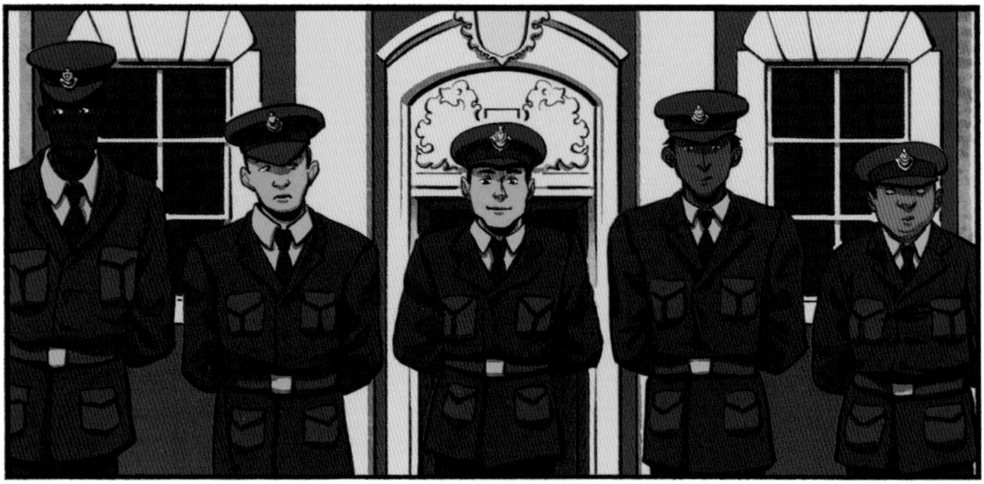

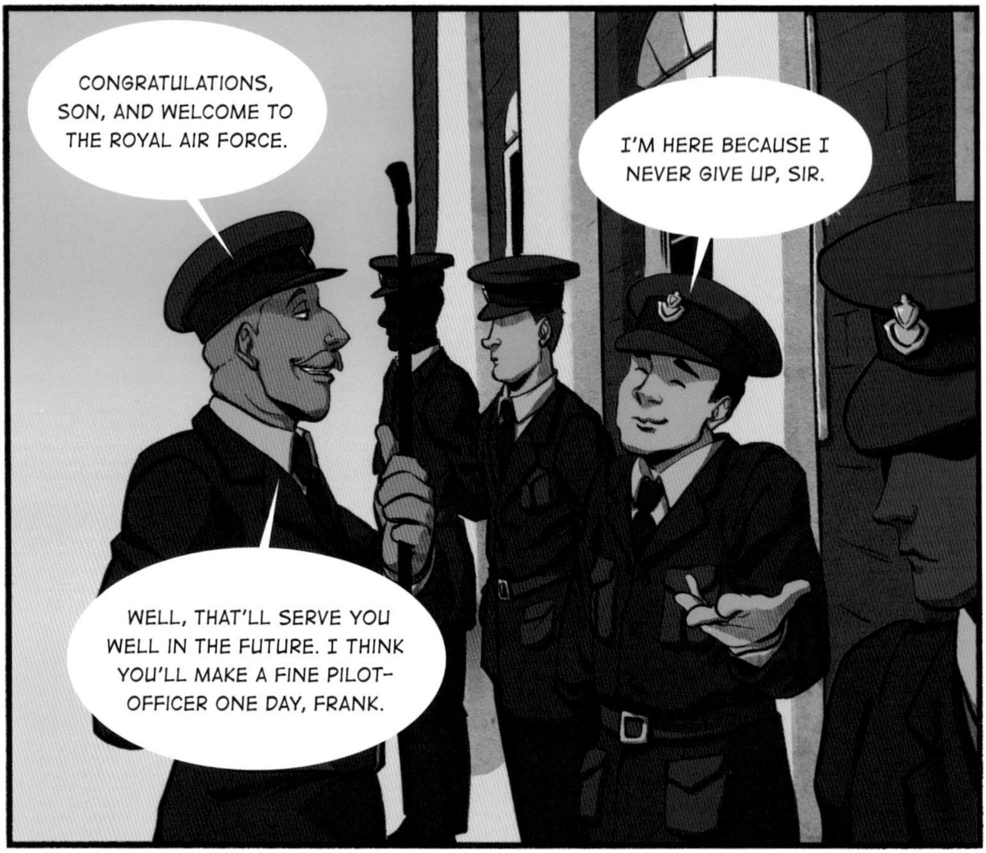
CONGRATULATIONS, SON, AND WELCOME TO THE ROYAL AIR FORCE.
I'M HERE BECAUSE I NEVER GIVE UP, SIR.
WELL, THAT'LL SERVE YOU WELL IN THE FUTURE. I THINK YOU'LL MAKE A FINE PILOT-OFFICER ONE DAY, FRANK.

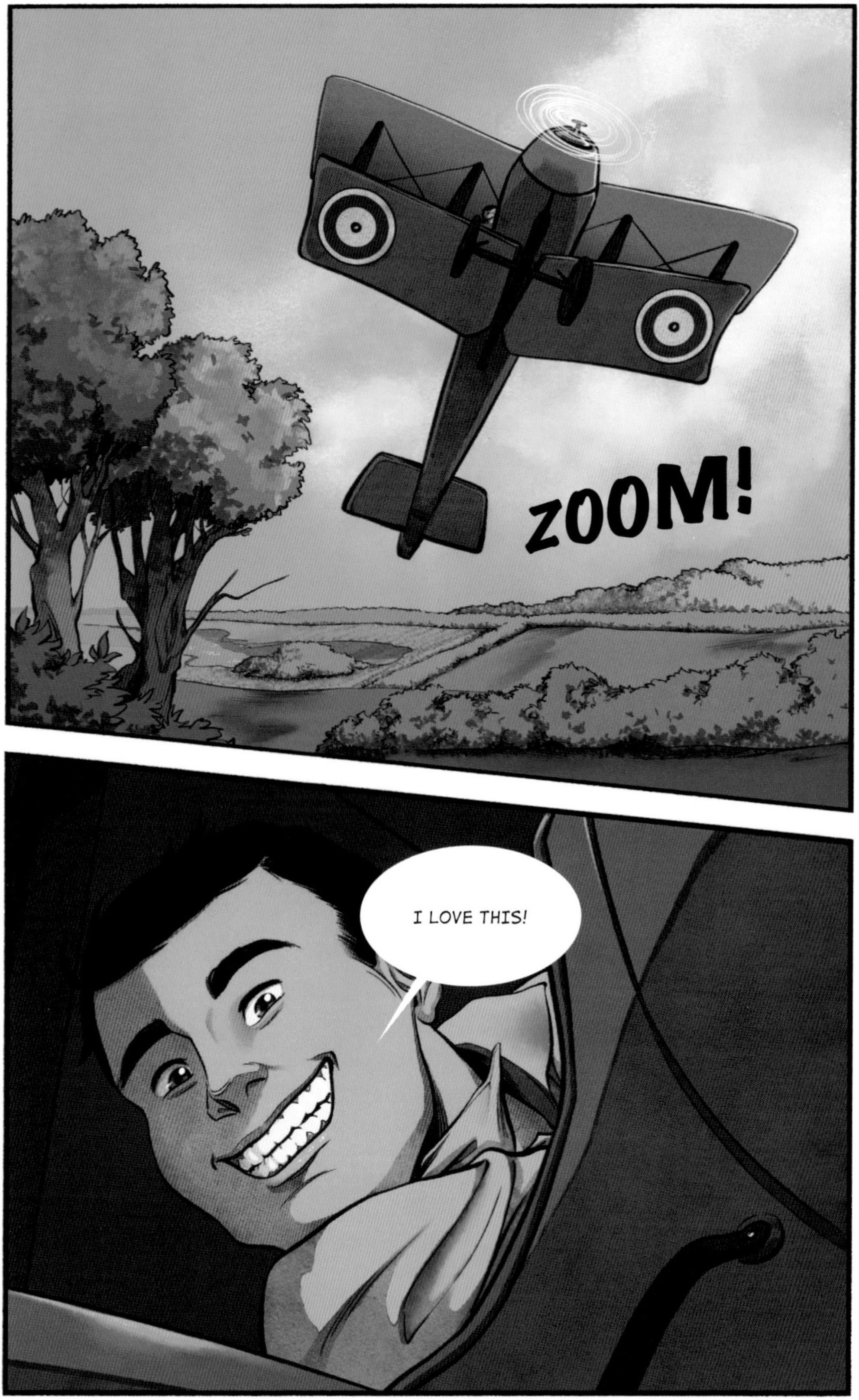
ZOOM!
I LOVE THIS!

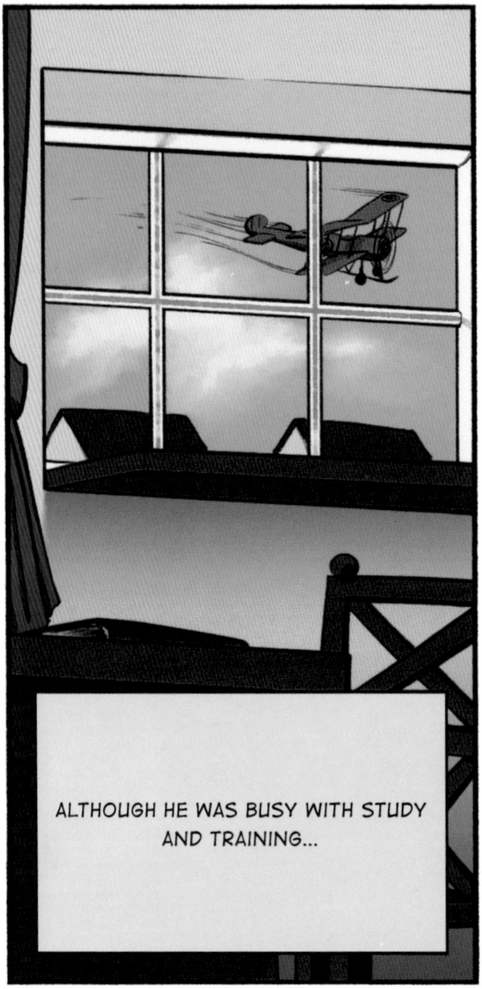
ALTHOUGH HE WAS BUSY WITH STUDY AND TRAINING...

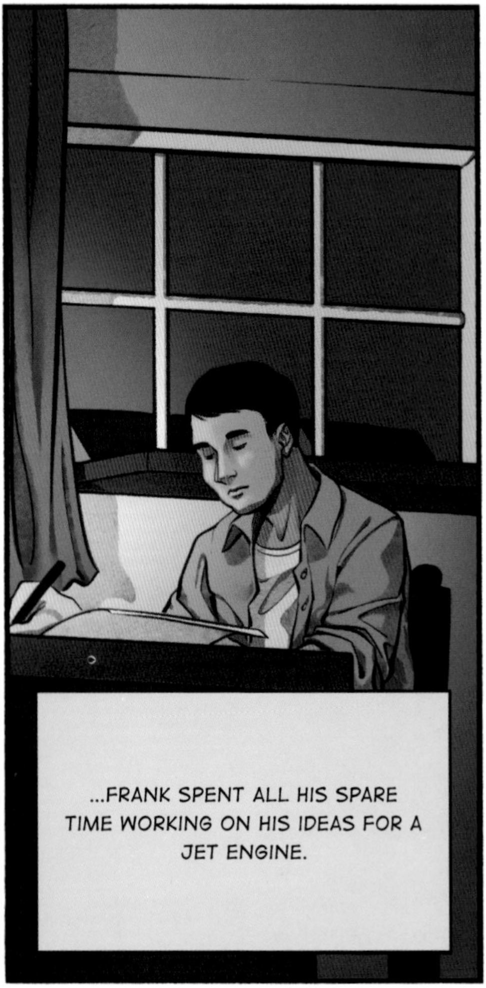
...FRANK SPENT ALL HIS SPARE TIME WORKING ON HIS IDEAS FOR A JET ENGINE.

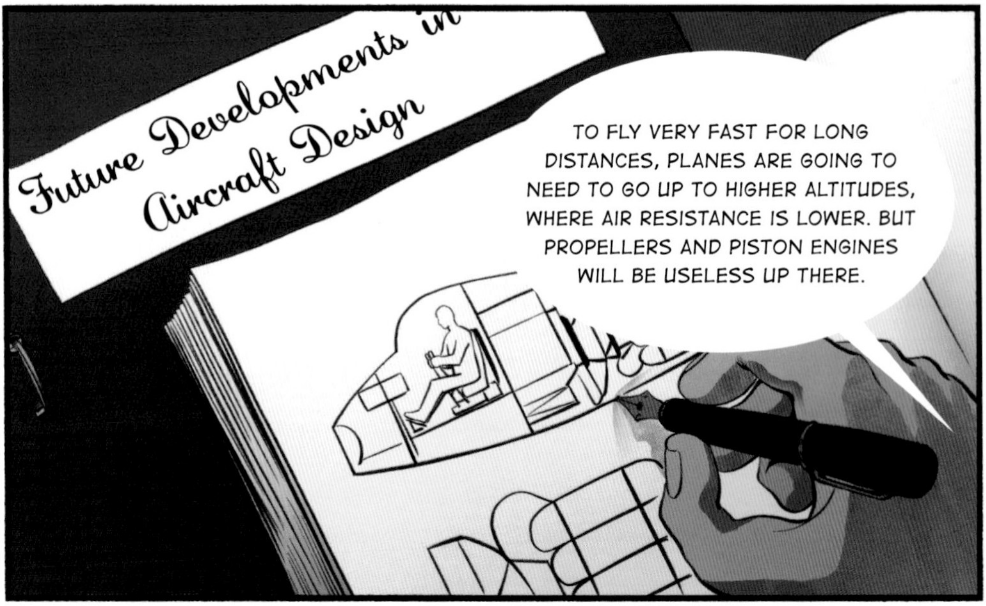
Future Developments in Aircraft Design
TO FLY VERY FAST FOR LONG DISTANCES, PLANES ARE GOING TO NEED TO GO UP TO HIGHER ALTITUDES, WHERE AIR RESISTANCE IS LOWER. BUT PROPELLERS AND PISTON ENGINES WILL BE USELESS UP THERE.

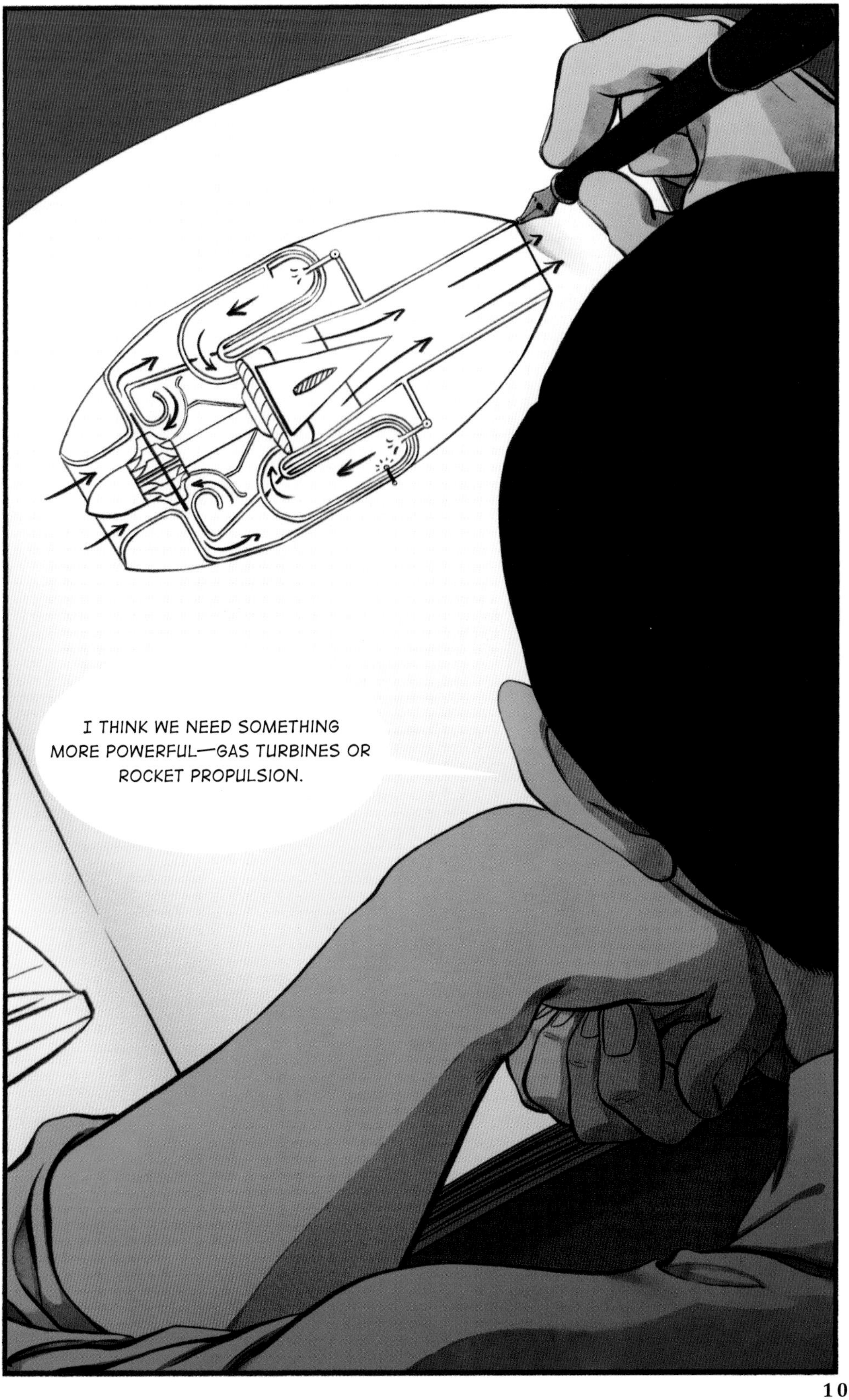
I THINK WE NEED SOMETHING MORE POWERFUL—GAS TURBINES OR ROCKET PROPULSION.

FRANK'S GRAND PLAN FOR AN ENGINE THAT COULD POWER A PLANE TO FLY HUNDREDS OF MILES PER HOUR WAS REPEATEDLY DISMISSED BY SENIOR RAF ENGINEERS. BUT HE HAD A PATENT, MEANING HIS DESIGN COULDN'T BE COPIED, AND HE STILL BELIEVED IN HIS IDEA.

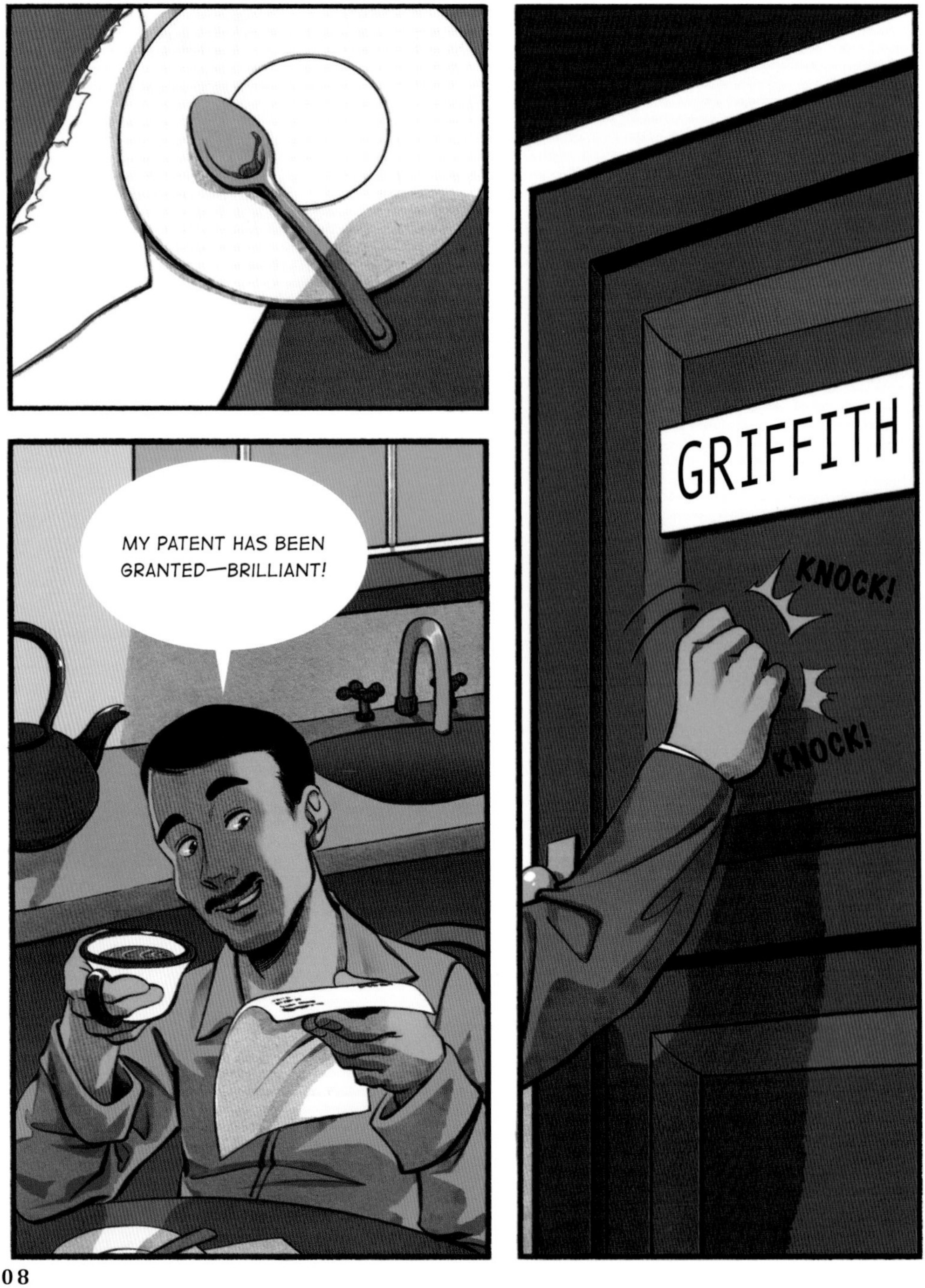
MY PATENT HAS BEEN GRANTED—BRILLIANT!
GRIFFITH
KNOCK!
KNOCK!

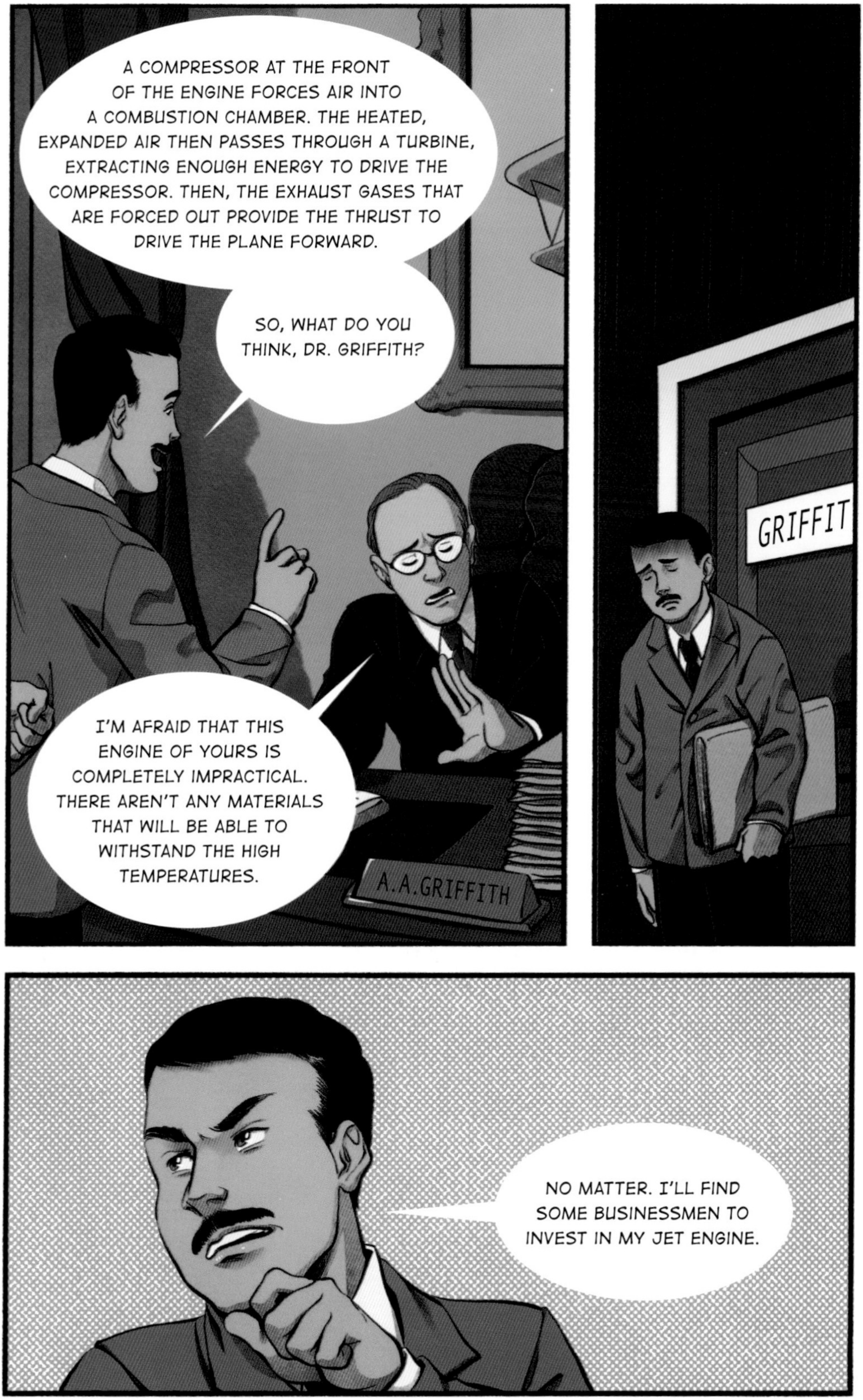
A COMPRESSOR AT THE FRONT OF THE ENGINE FORCES AIR INTO A COMBUSTION CHAMBER. THE HEATED, EXPANDED AIR THEN PASSES THROUGH A TURBINE, EXTRACTING ENOUGH ENERGY TO DRIVE THE COMPRESSOR. THEN, THE EXHAUST GASES THAT ARE FORCED OUT PROVIDE THE THRUST TO DRIVE THE PLANE FORWARD.
SO, WHAT DO YOU THINK, DR. GRIFFITH?
I'M AFRAID THAT THIS ENGINE OF YOURS IS COMPLETELY IMPRACTICAL. THERE AREN'T ANY MATERIALS THAT WILL BE ABLE TO WITHSTAND THE HIGH TEMPERATURES.
A.A.GRIFFITH
GRIFFIT
NO MATTER. I'LL FIND SOME BUSINESSMEN TO INVEST IN MY JET ENGINE.

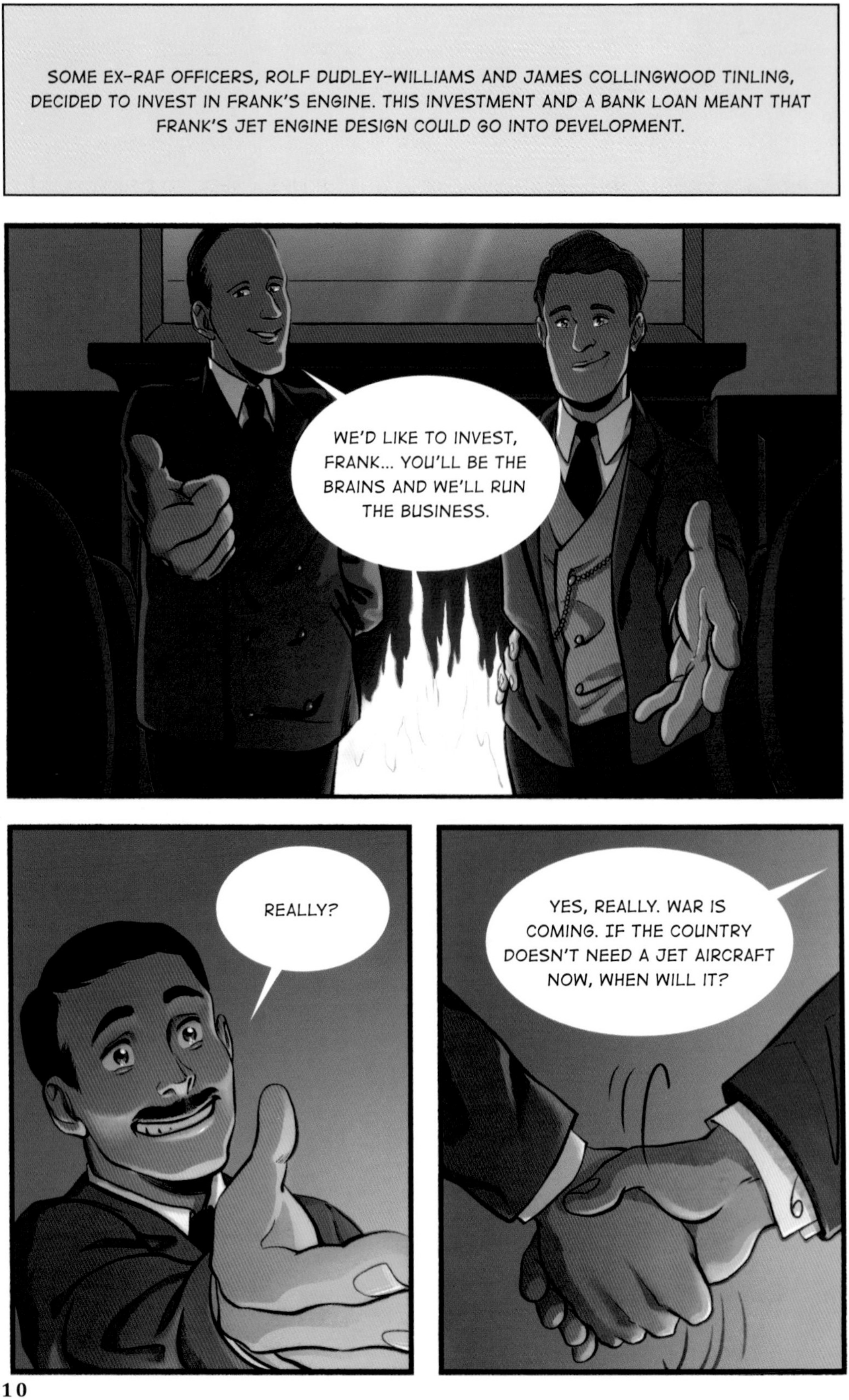
SOME EX-RAF OFFICERS, ROLF DUDLEY-WILLIAMS AND JAMES COLLINGWOOD TINLING, DECIDED TO INVEST IN FRANK'S ENGINE. THIS INVESTMENT AND A BANK LOAN MEANT THAT FRANK'S JET ENGINE DESIGN COULD GO INTO DEVELOPMENT.
WE'D LIKE TO INVEST, FRANK... YOU'LL BE THE BRAINS AND WE'LL RUN THE BUSINESS.
REALLY?
YES, REALLY. WAR IS COMING. IF THE COUNTRY DOESN'T NEED A JET AIRCRAFT NOW, WHEN WILL IT?

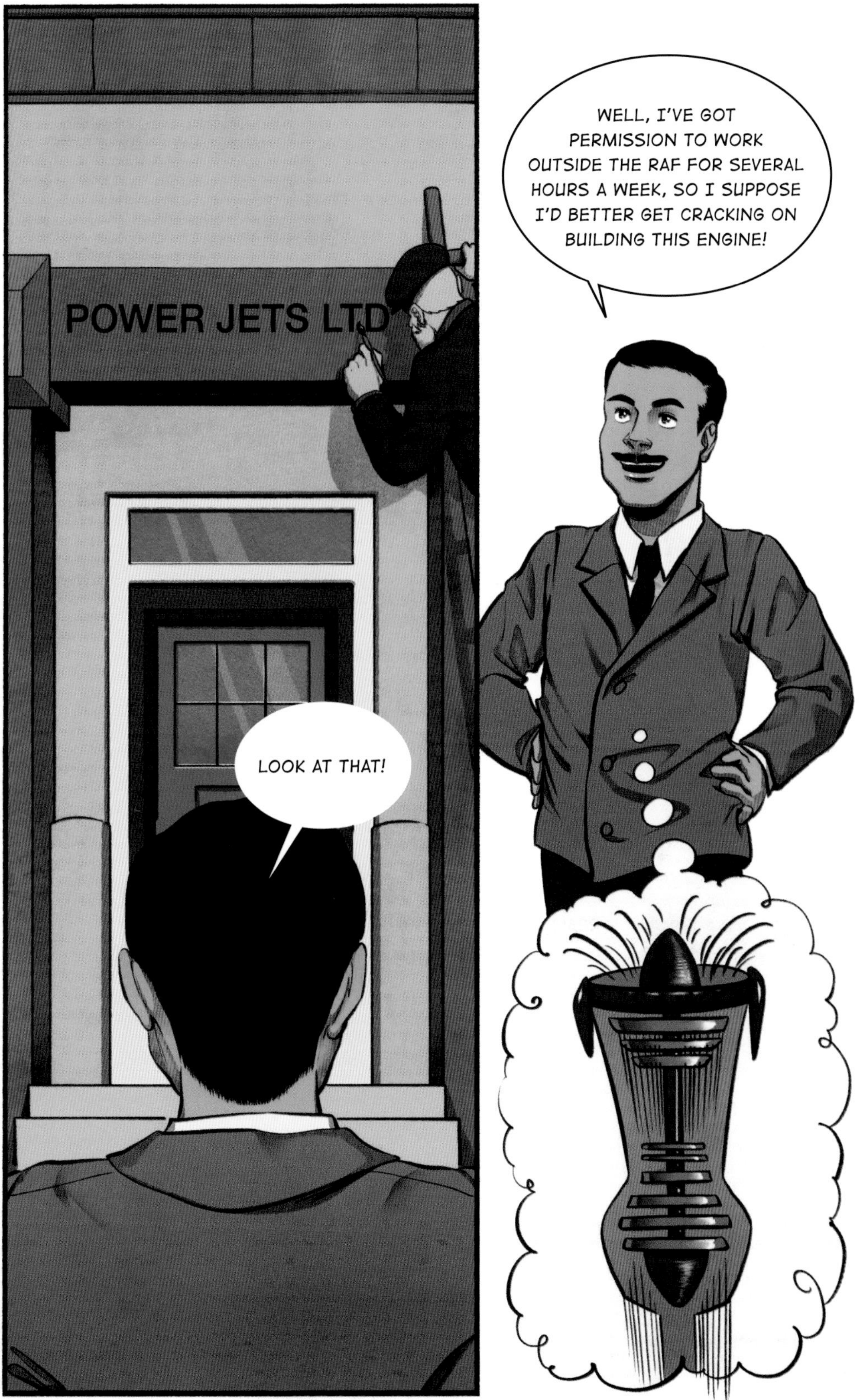
POWER JETS LTD
LOOK AT THAT!
WELL, I'VE GOT PERMISSION TO WORK OUTSIDE THE RAF FOR SEVERAL HOURS A WEEK, SO I SUPPOSE I'D BETTER GET CRACKING ON BUILDING THIS ENGINE!

WITH THE OUTBREAK OF WORLD WAR II ON SEPTEMBER, 1, 1939 AND NOW WITH MORE MONEY BEHIND THE PROJECT, FRANK'S TEAM AT POWER JETS LTD BUILT THE TURBOJET ENGINE IN LESS THAN A YEAR.

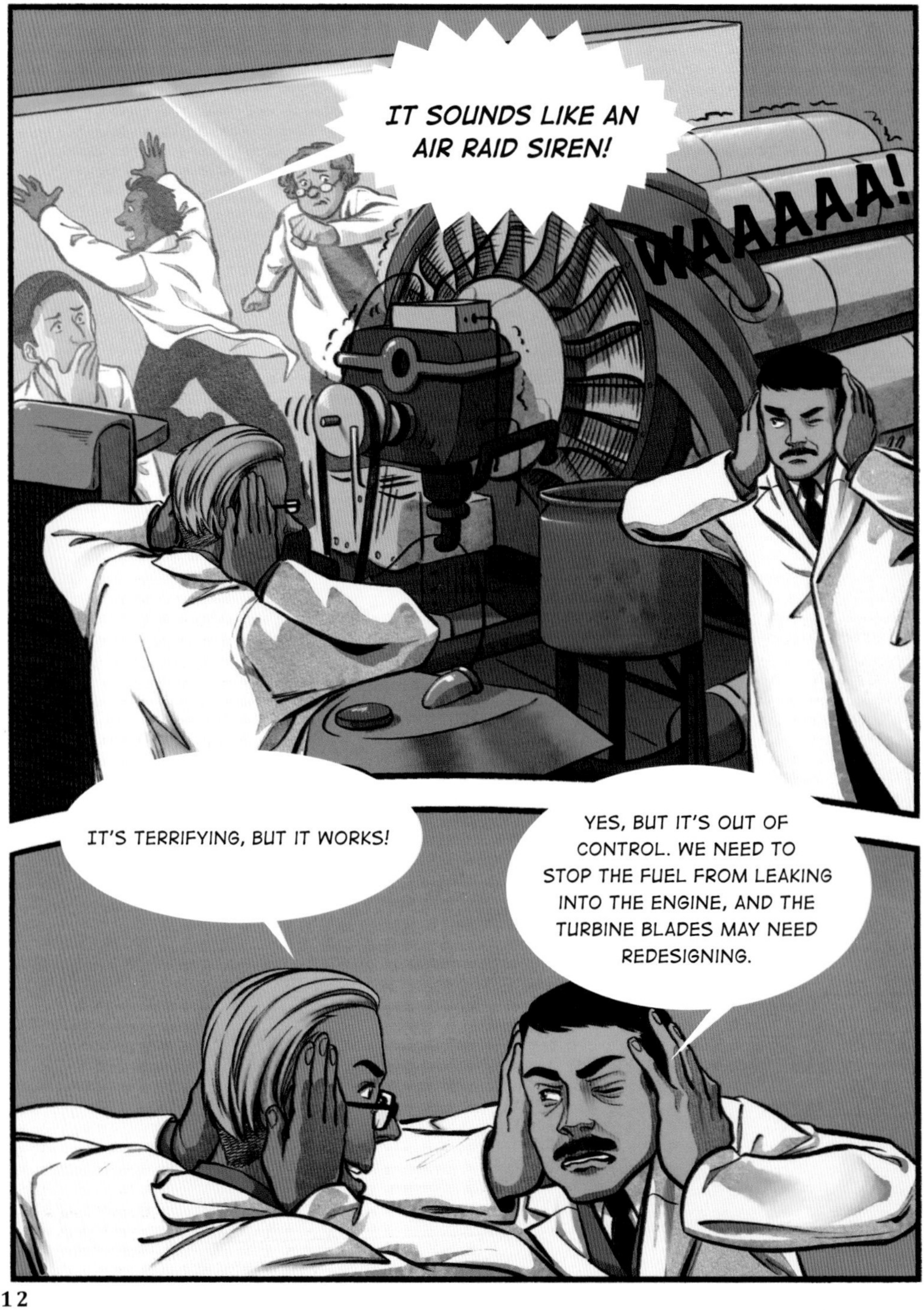

IT SOUNDS LIKE AN AIR RAID SIREN!
WAAAAAA!
IT'S TERRIFYING, BUT IT WORKS!
YES, BUT IT'S OUT OF CONTROL. WE NEED TO STOP THE FUEL FROM LEAKING INTO THE ENGINE, AND THE TURBINE BLADES MAY NEED REDESIGNING.

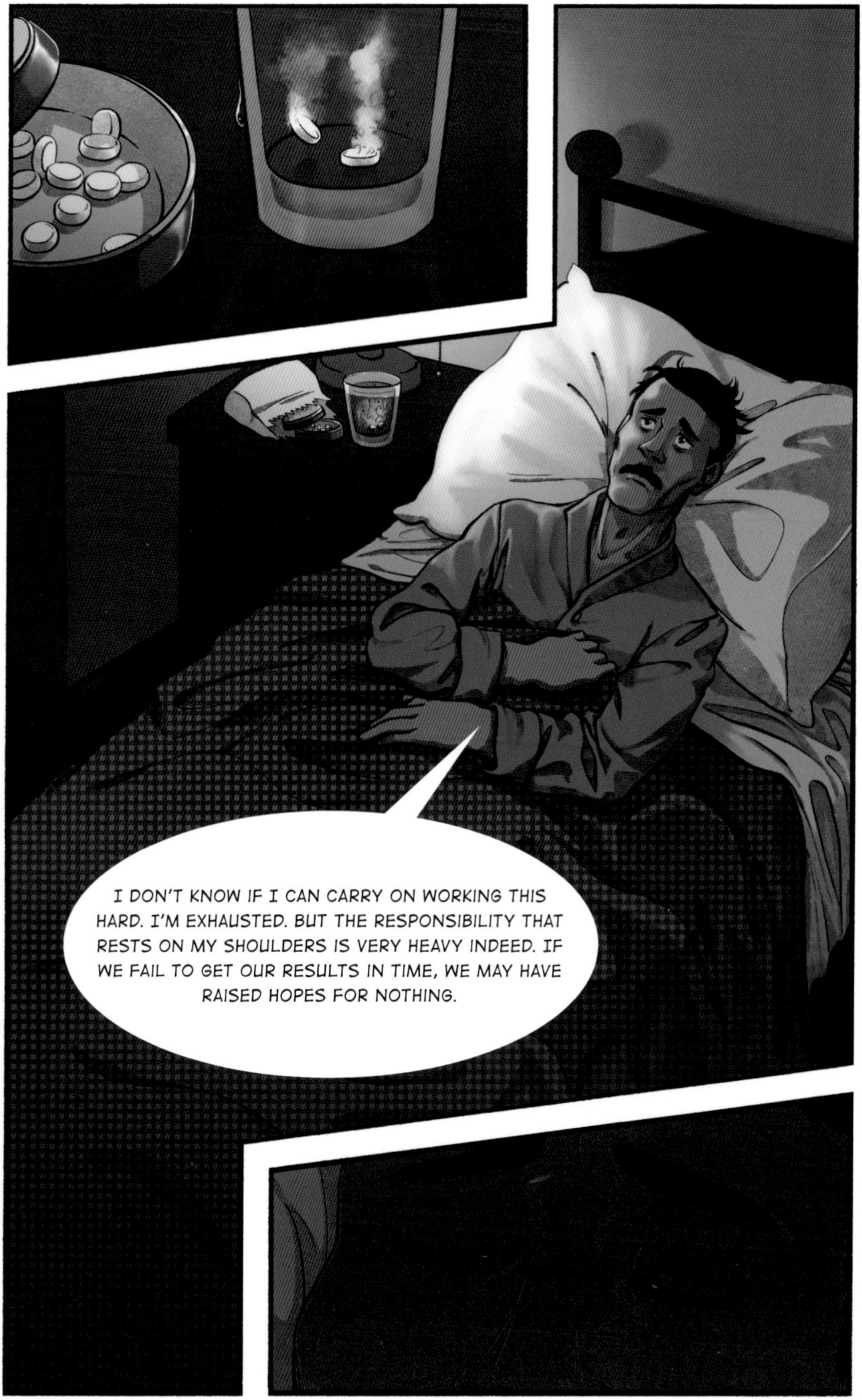
I DON'T KNOW IF I CAN CARRY ON WORKING THIS HARD. I'M EXHAUSTED. BUT THE RESPONSIBILITY THAT RESTS ON MY SHOULDERS IS VERY HEAVY INDEED. IF WE FAIL TO GET OUR RESULTS IN TIME, WE MAY HAVE RAISED HOPES FOR NOTHING.

FRANK'S JET ENGINE FIRST TOOK TO THE SKIES AT RAF CRANWELL IN LINCOLNSHIRE, UK ABOARD A GLOSTER METEOR PLANE IN 1941. IT IS SAID THAT BRITAIN'S PRIME MINISTER, WINSTON CHURCHILL, REALIZED IMMEDIATELY HOW MUCH THEY WOULD HELP THE WAR EFFORT.

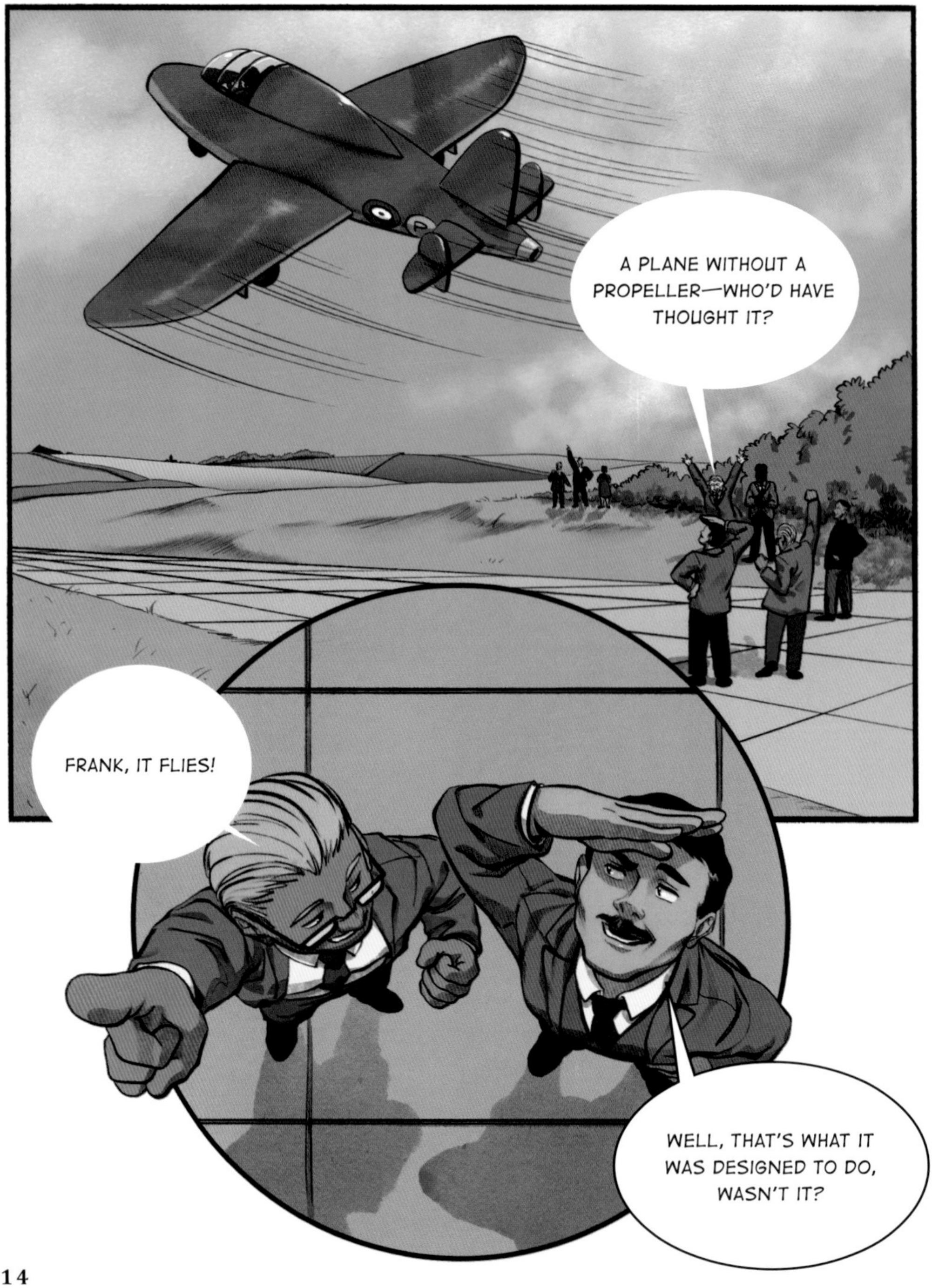
A PLANE WITHOUT A PROPELLER—WHO'D HAVE THOUGHT IT?
FRANK, IT FLIES!
WELL, THAT'S WHAT IT WAS DESIGNED TO DO, WASN'T IT?

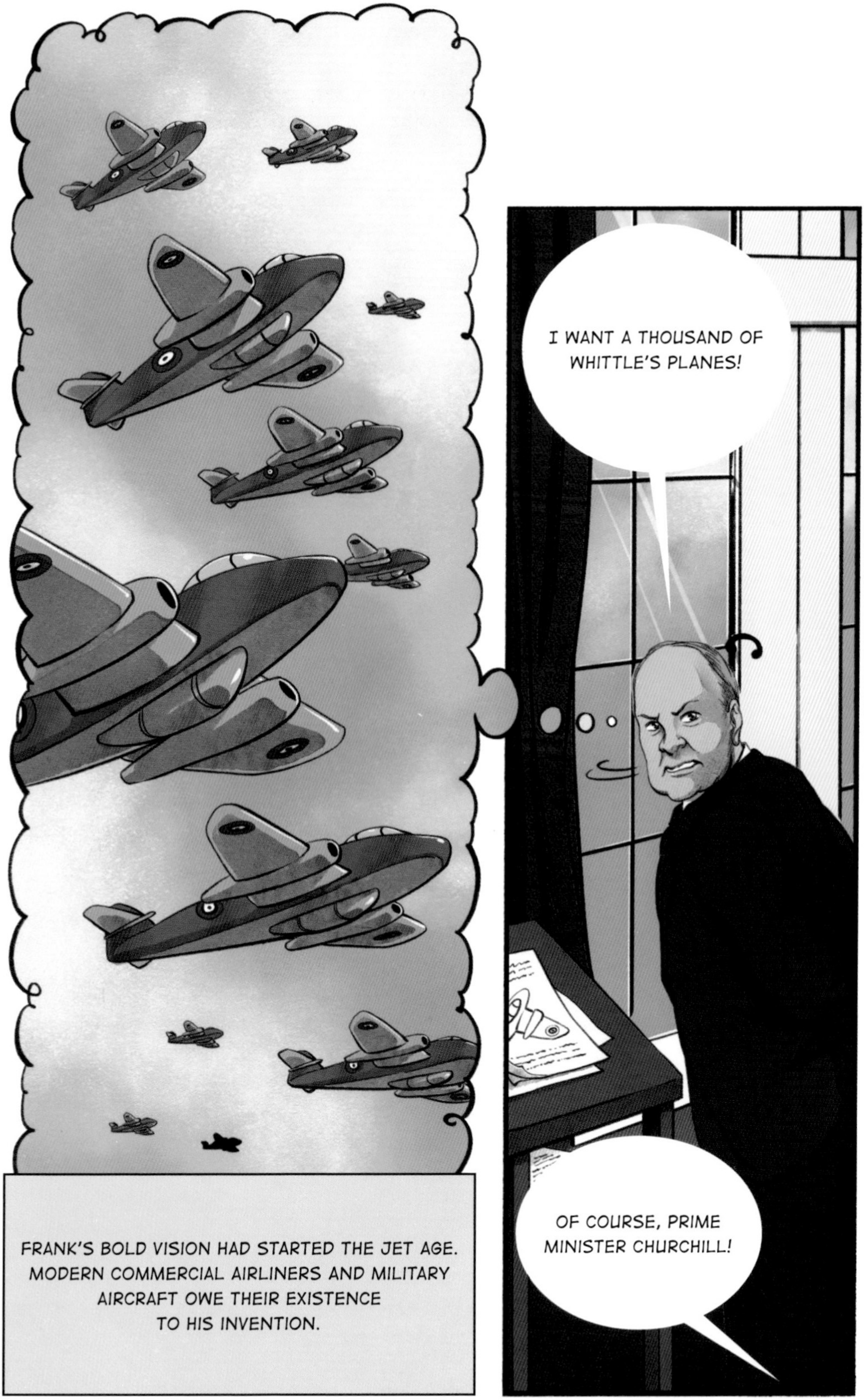
FRANK'S BOLD VISION HAD STARTED THE JET AGE. MODERN COMMERCIAL AIRLINERS AND MILITARY AIRCRAFT OWE THEIR EXISTENCE TO HIS INVENTION.
I WANT A THOUSAND OF WHITTLE'S PLANES!
OF COURSE, PRIME MINISTER CHURCHILL!

CHUCK YEAGER
(1923–present)
SUPERSONIC

CHUCK SERVED IN THE U.S. ARMY AIR CORPS, STARTING OFF AS A MECHANIC. BUT WITH A NATURAL TALENT FOR FLYING AND SUPERSHARP VISION, HE ROSE UP THROUGH THE RANKS TO BECOME A PILOT.

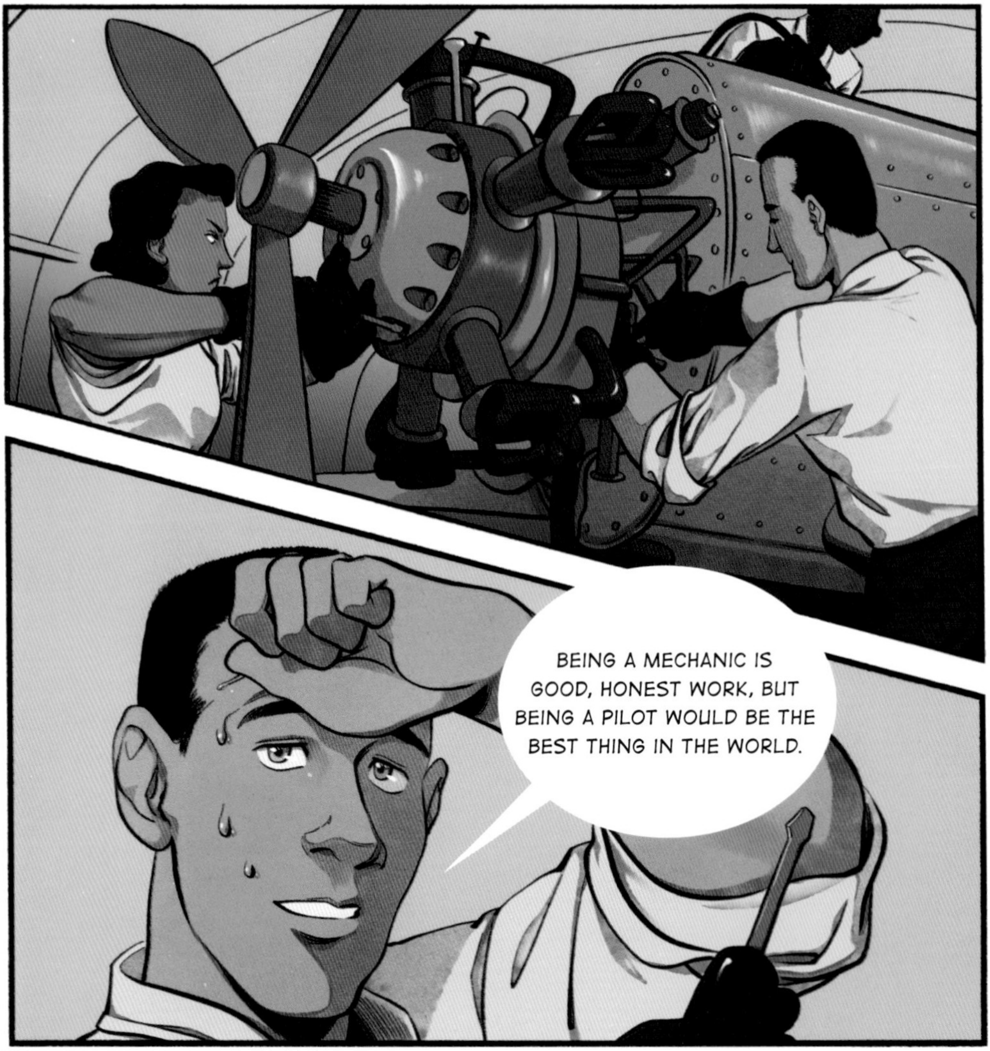
BEING A MECHANIC IS GOOD, HONEST WORK, BUT BEING A PILOT WOULD BE THE BEST THING IN THE WORLD.

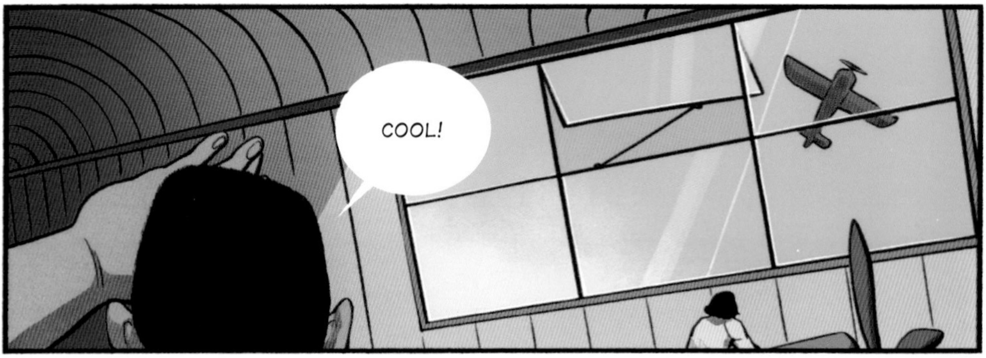
COOL!

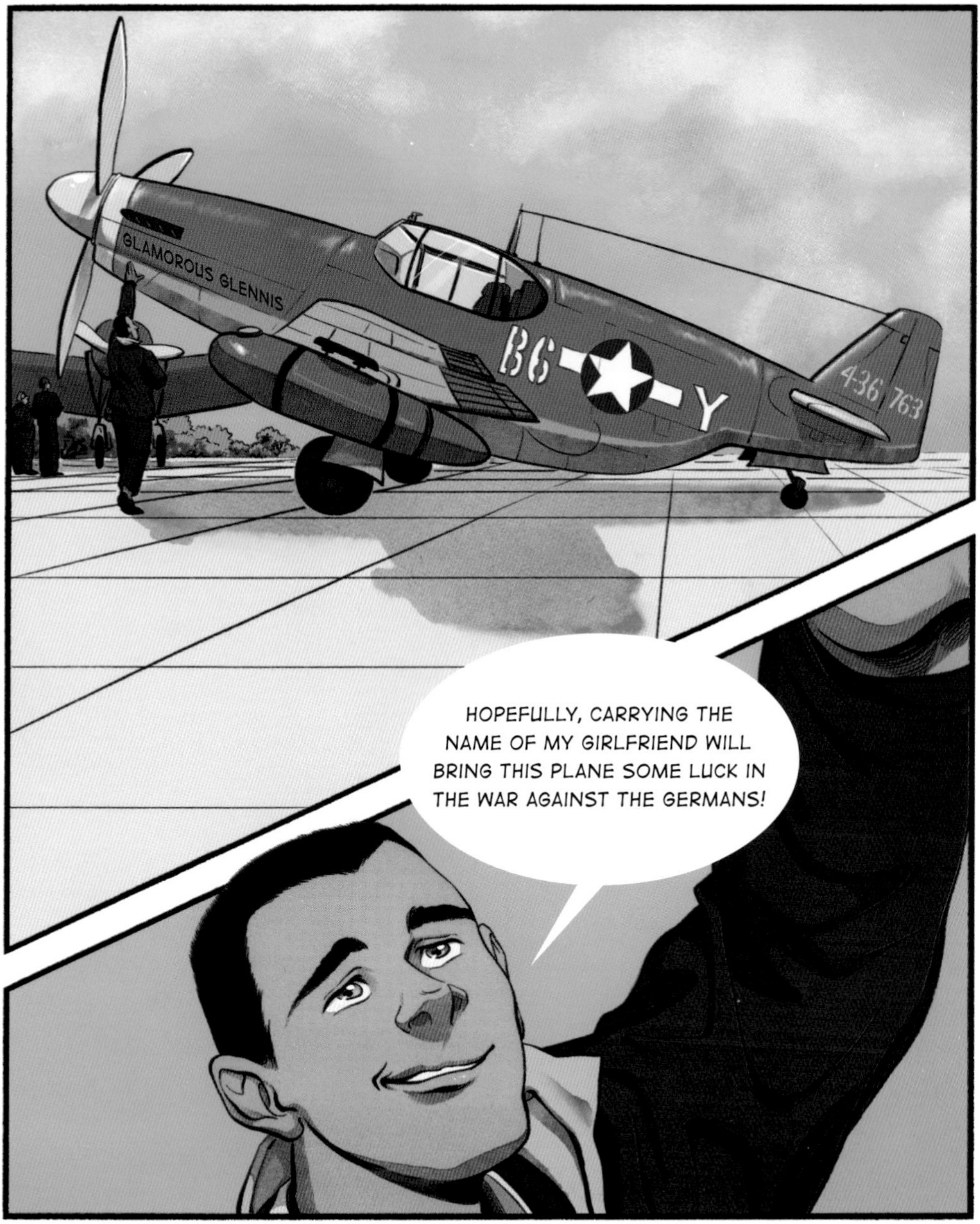
GLAMOROUS GLENNIS
B6 Y
4-36 763
HOPEFULLY, CARRYING THE NAME OF MY GIRLFRIEND WILL BRING THIS PLANE SOME LUCK IN THE WAR AGAINST THE GERMANS!

CHUCK WAS AN INCREDIBLY SKILLFUL PILOT AND IN WORLD WAR II HE BECAME ONE OF THE UNITED STATES' LEADING FIGHTER PILOTS. CHUCK WAS SHOT DOWN ON HIS EIGHTH MISSION OVER FRANCE IN MARCH 1944.

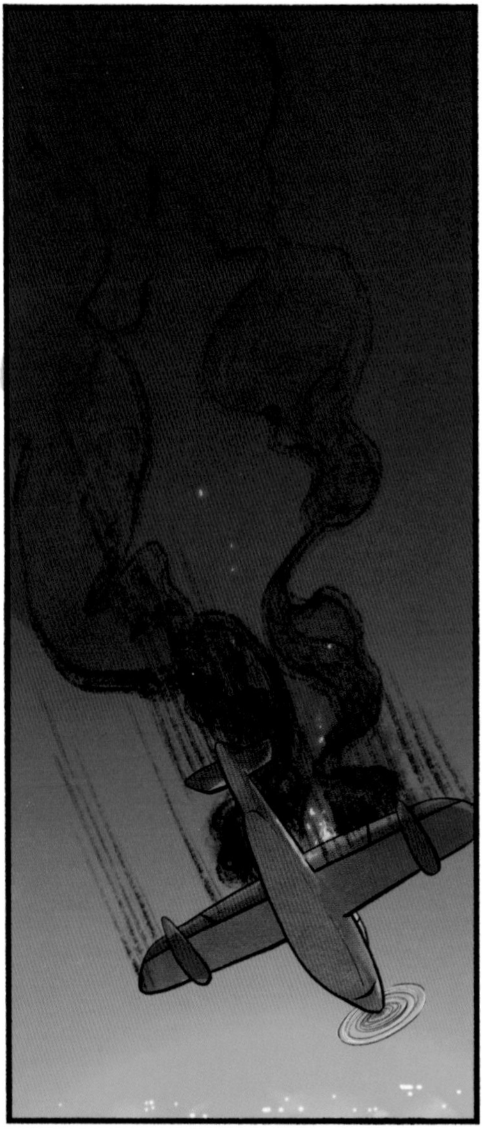

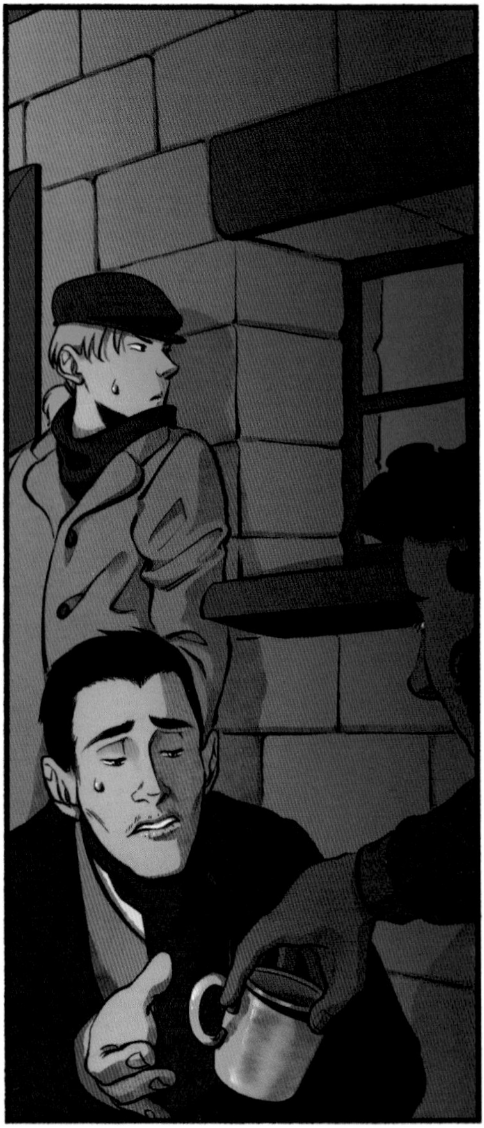

HE SPENT FOUR MONTHS EVADING CAPTURE IN FRANCE BEFORE BEING SMUGGLED TO SPAIN AND REJOINING THE BRITISH FORCES IN GIBRALTAR.

CHUCK WAS DECORATED WITH THE BRONZE STAR FOR HIS HEROIC SERVICE.

IN OCTOBER 1944, HE DOWNED FIVE ENEMY AIRCRAFT IN A SINGLE MISSION, BECOMING AN "ACE IN A DAY."

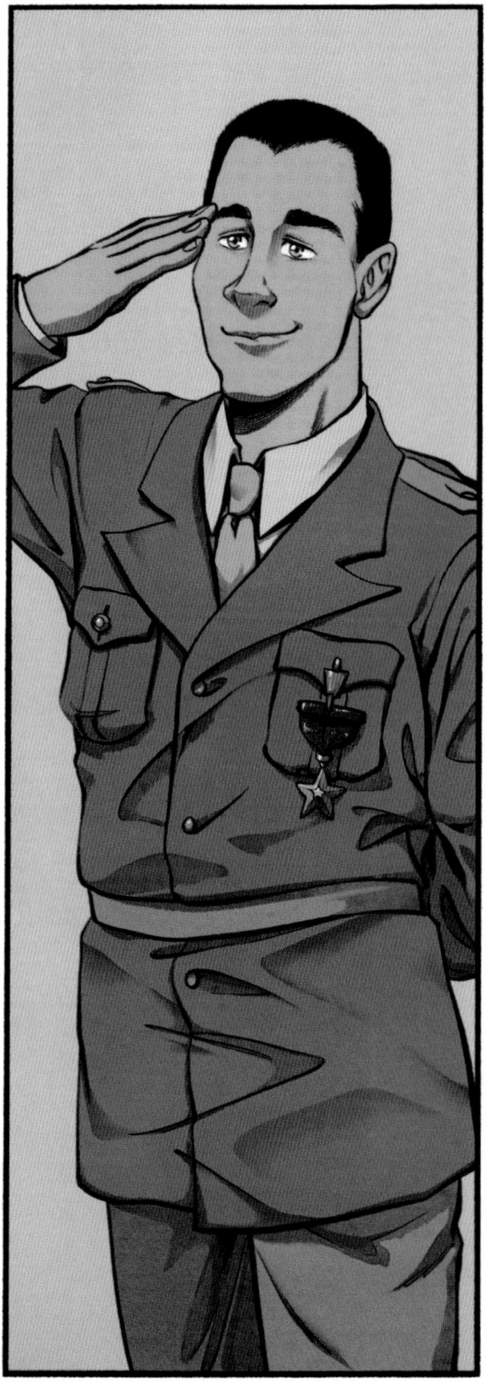

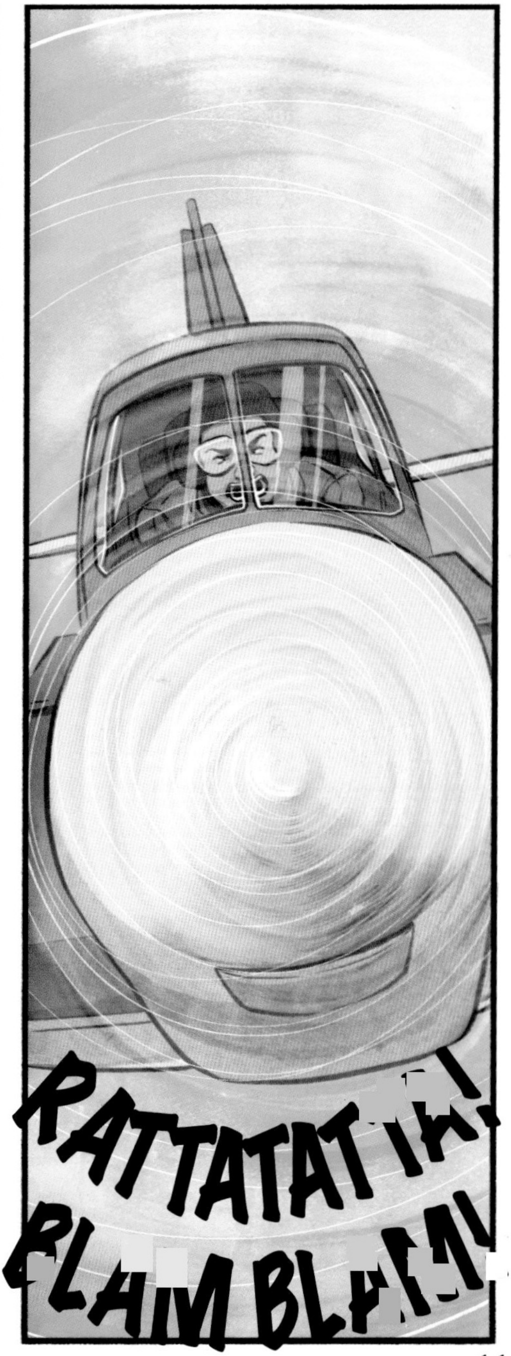
RATTATAT
BLAM

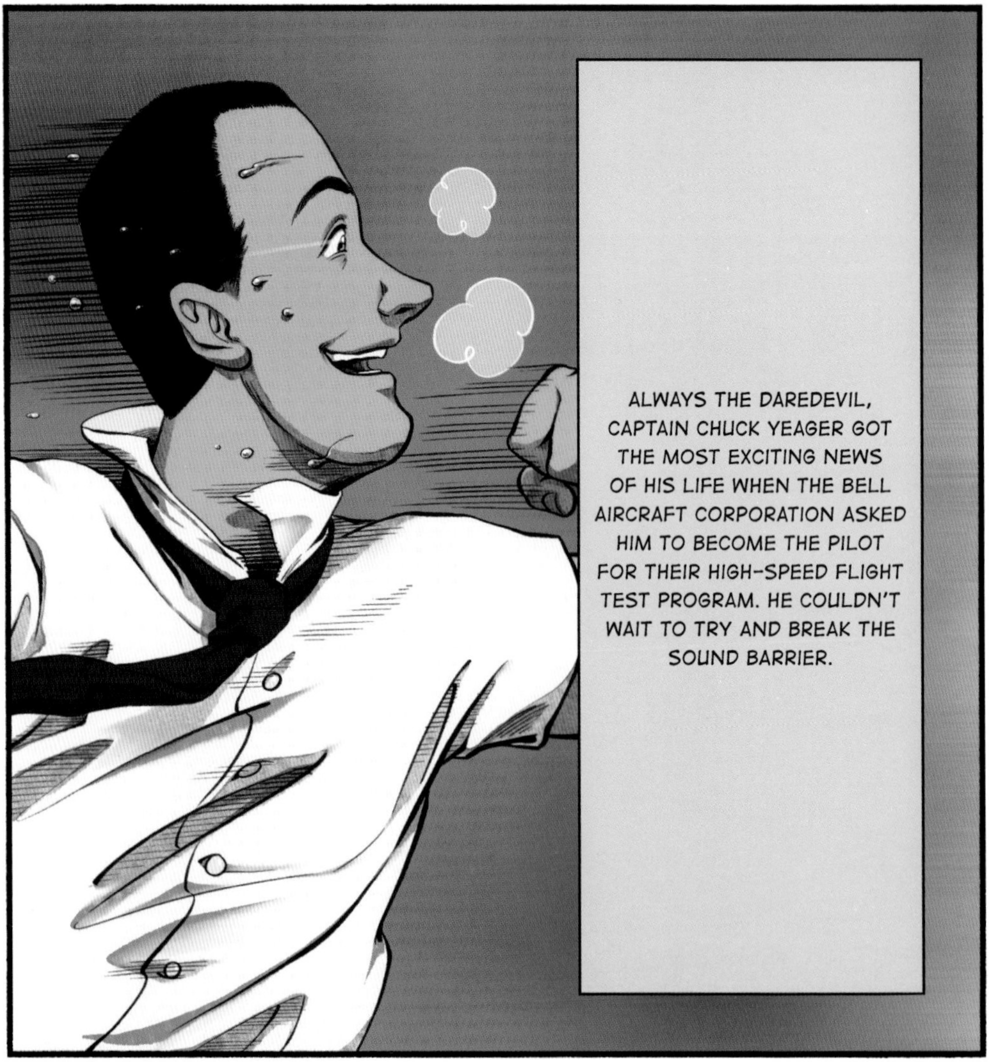
ALWAYS THE DAREDEVIL, CAPTAIN CHUCK YEAGER GOT THE MOST EXCITING NEWS OF HIS LIFE WHEN THE BELL AIRCRAFT CORPORATION ASKED HIM TO BECOME THE PILOT FOR THEIR HIGH-SPEED FLIGHT TEST PROGRAM. HE COULDN'T WAIT TO TRY AND BREAK THE SOUND BARRIER.

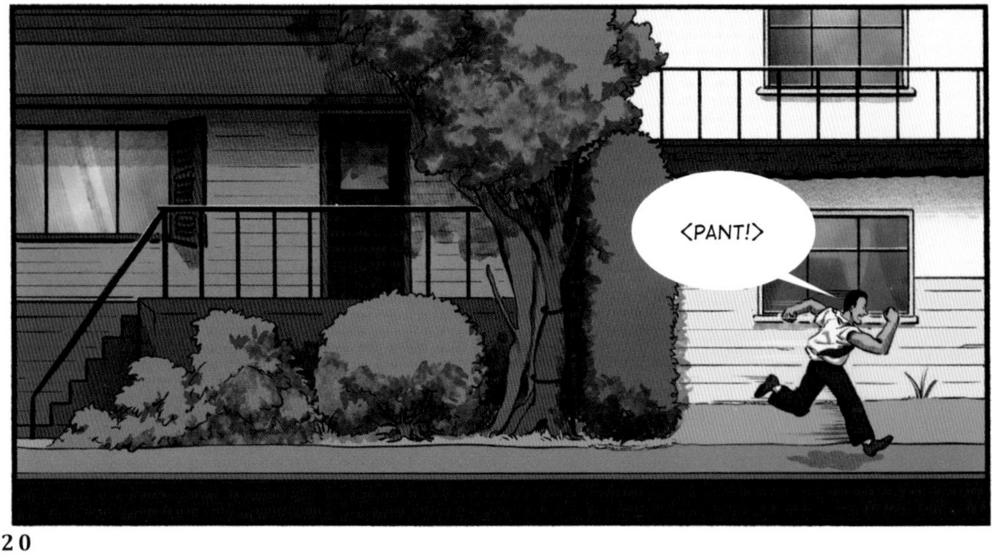
<PANT!>

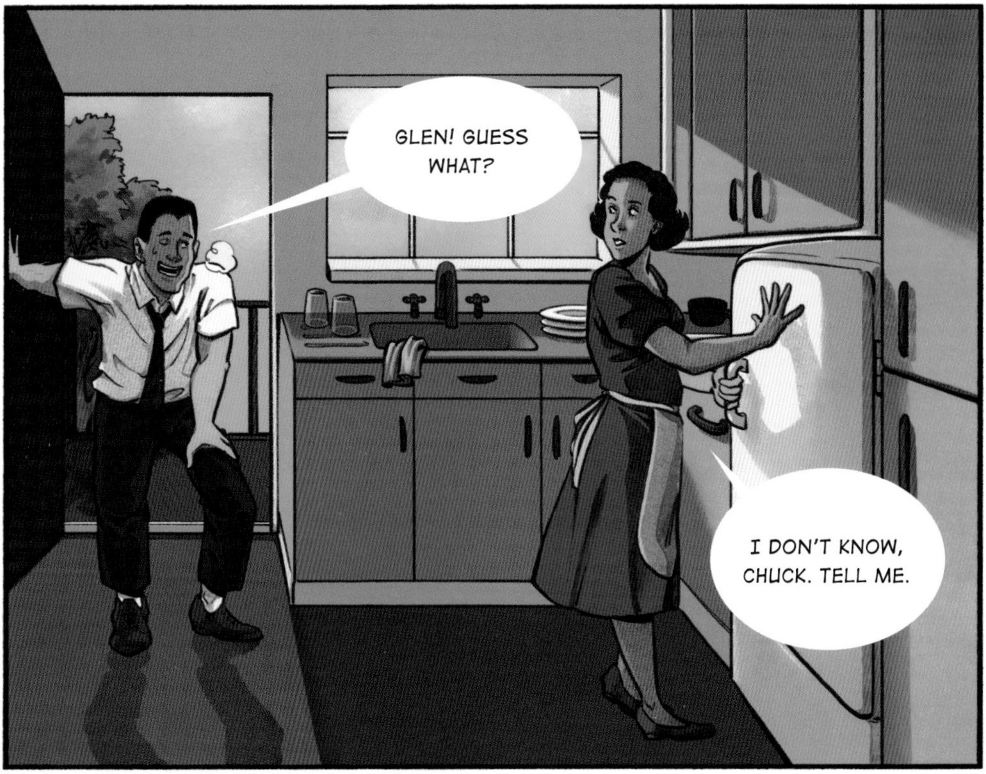
GLEN! GUESS WHAT?
I DON'T KNOW, CHUCK. TELL ME.

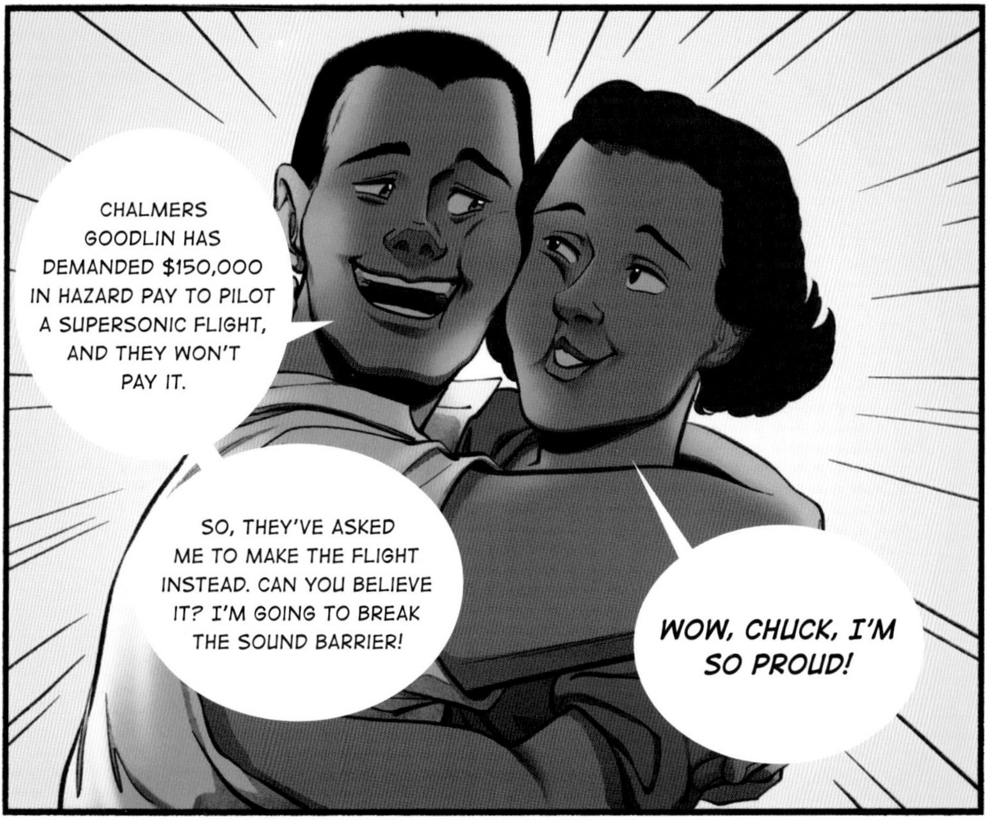
CHALMERS GOODLIN HAS DEMANDED $150,000 IN HAZARD PAY TO PILOT A SUPERSONIC FLIGHT, AND THEY WON'T PAY IT.
SO, THEY'VE ASKED ME TO MAKE THE FLIGHT INSTEAD. CAN YOU BELIEVE IT? I'M GOING TO BREAK THE SOUND BARRIER!
WOW, CHUCK, I'M SO PROUD!

TWO DAYS BEFORE THE ALL-IMPORTANT SUPERSONIC TEST FLIGHT, CHUCK HAD A HORSE RIDING ACCIDENT. HE WAS IN GREAT PAIN AND COULD HARDLY SLEEP OR WALK, LET ALONE FLY.

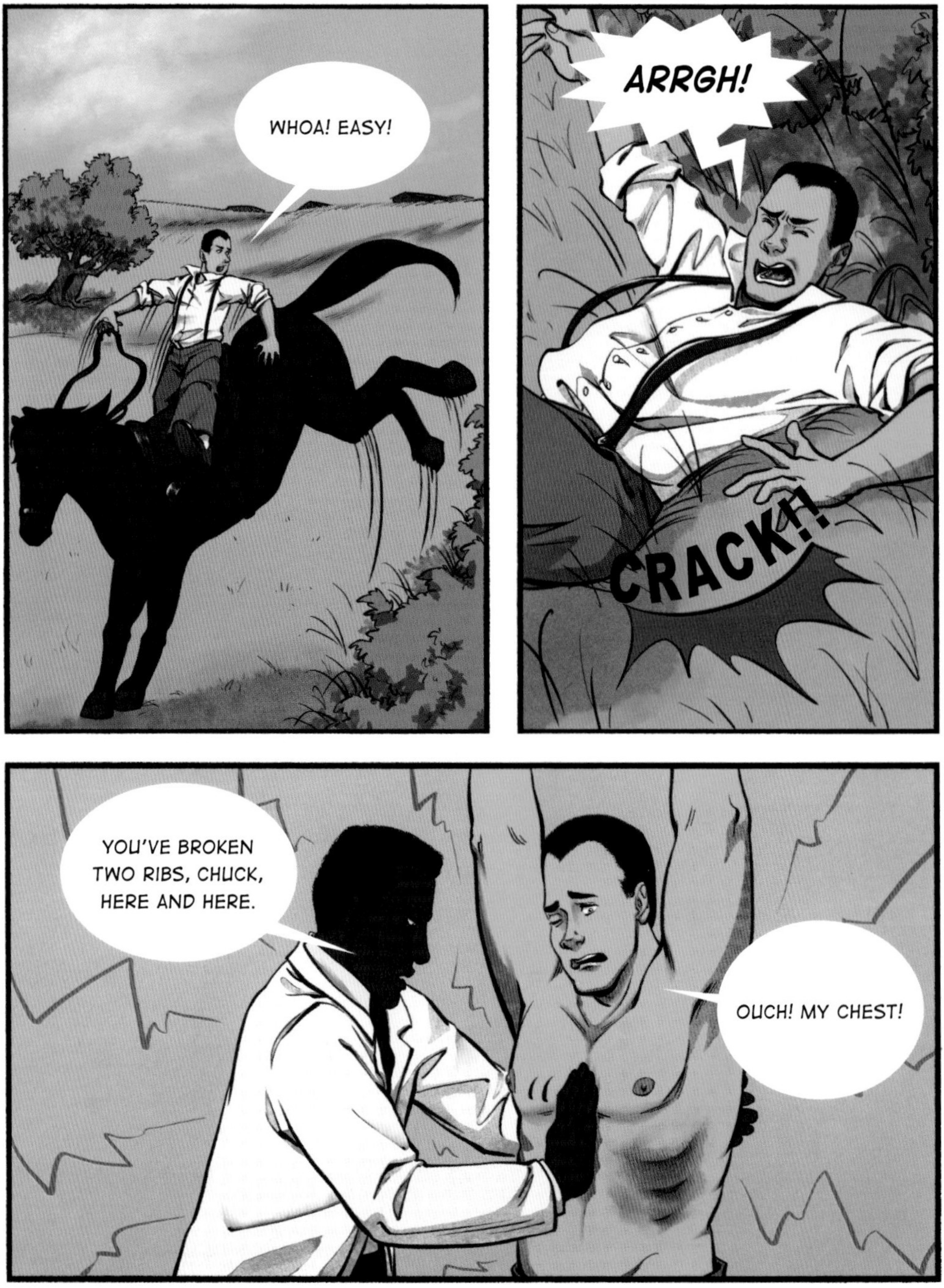
WHOA! EASY!
ARRGH!
CRACK!!
YOU'VE BROKEN TWO RIBS, CHUCK, HERE AND HERE.
OUCH! MY CHEST!

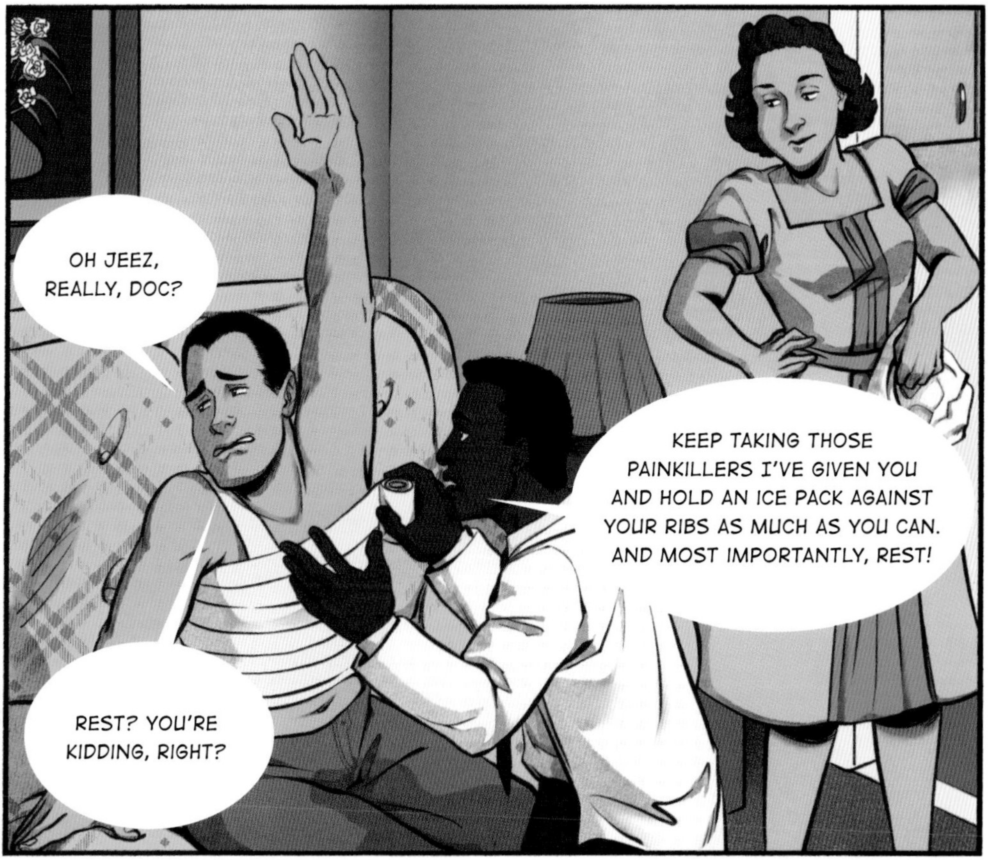
OH JEEZ, REALLY, DOC?
KEEP TAKING THOSE PAINKILLERS I'VE GIVEN YOU AND HOLD AN ICE PACK AGAINST YOUR RIBS AS MUCH AS YOU CAN. AND MOST IMPORTANTLY, REST!
REST? YOU'RE KIDDING, RIGHT?

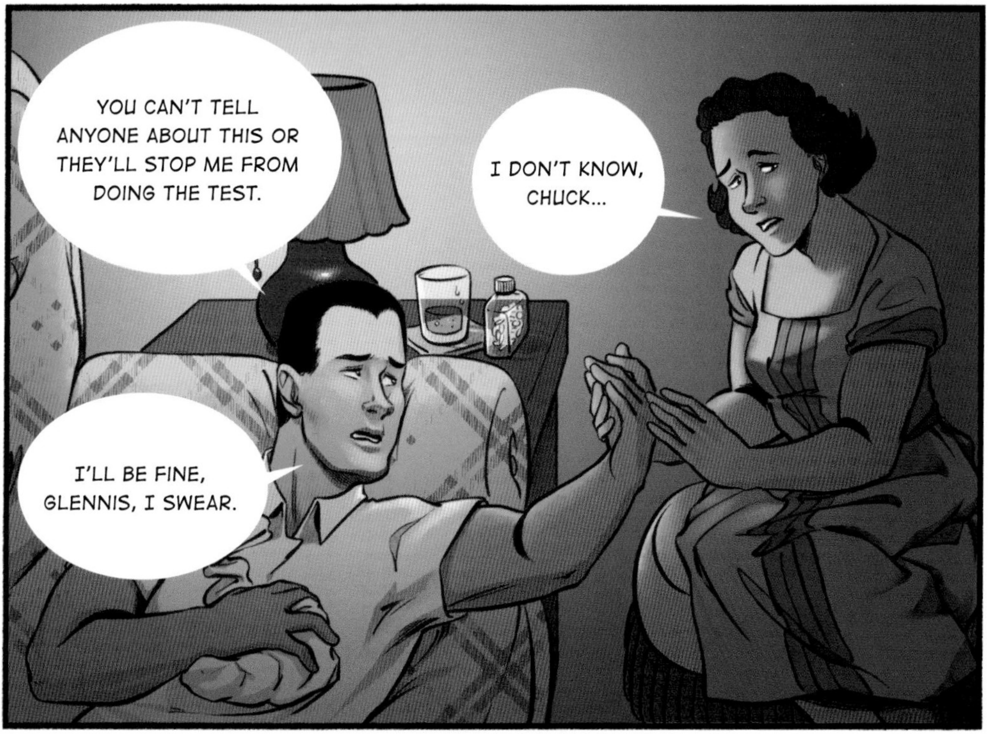
YOU CAN'T TELL ANYONE ABOUT THIS OR THEY'LL STOP ME FROM DOING THE TEST.
I DON'T KNOW, CHUCK...
I'LL BE FINE, GLENNIS, I SWEAR.

ON THE DAY OF THE TEST FLIGHT, CHUCK STRUGGLED TO GET INTO THE COCKPIT OF THE X-1 ROCKET PLANE. BUT HE WAS ABSOLUTELY DETERMINED THAT HIS INJURIES WOULDN'T HOLD HIM BACK.

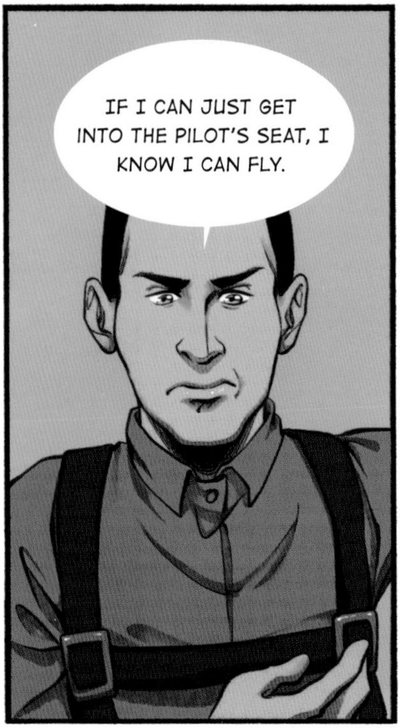
IF I CAN JUST GET INTO THE PILOT'S SEAT, I KNOW I CAN FLY.

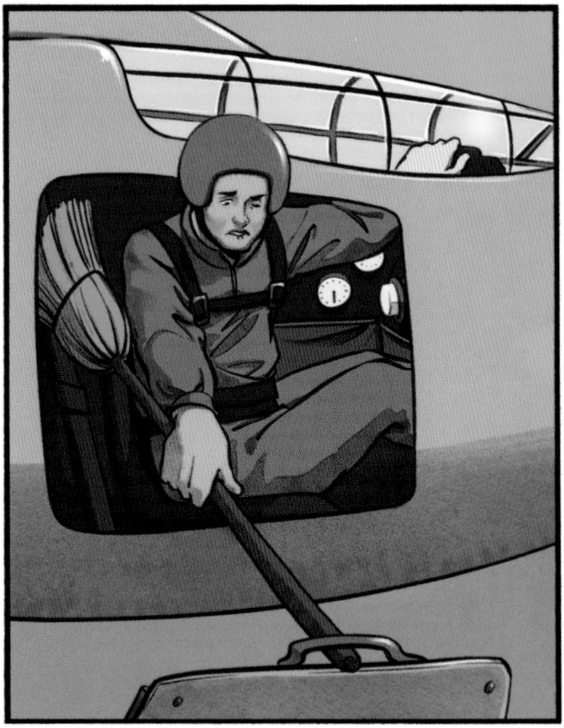

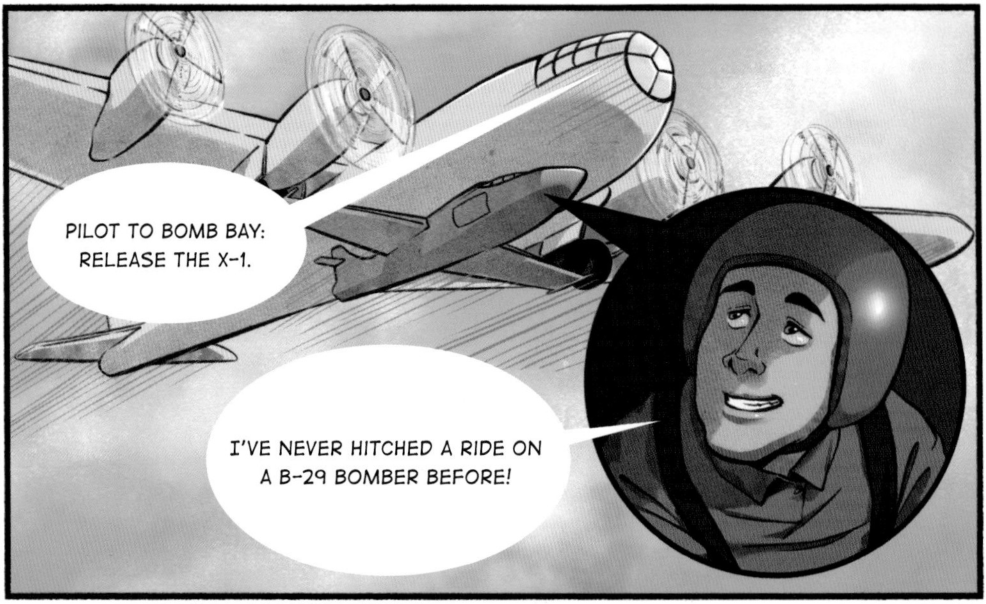
PILOT TO BOMB BAY: RELEASE THE X-1.
I'VE NEVER HITCHED A RIDE ON A B-29 BOMBER BEFORE!

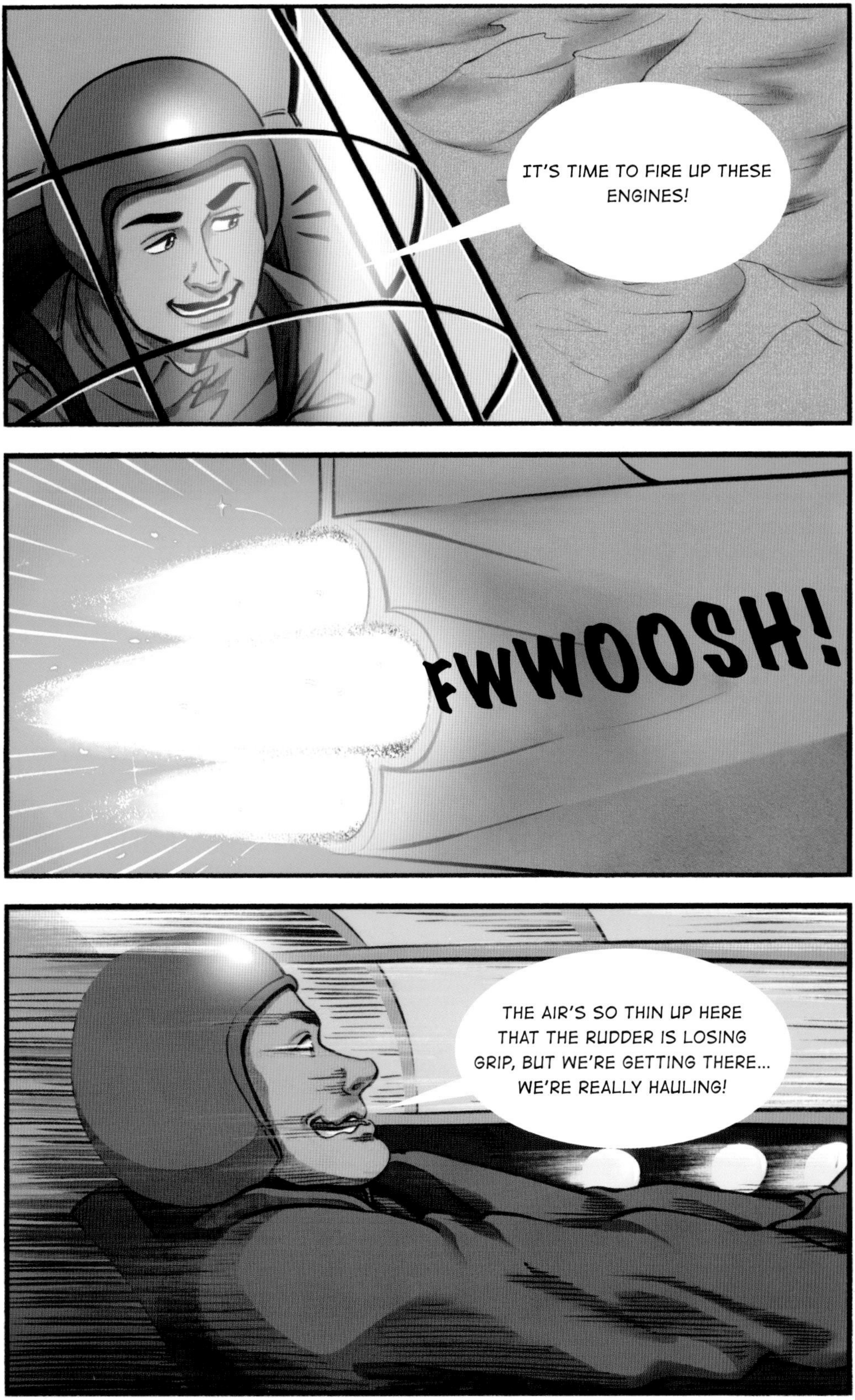
IT'S TIME TO FIRE UP THESE ENGINES!
FWWOOSH!
THE AIR'S SO THIN UP HERE THAT THE RUDDER IS LOSING GRIP, BUT WE'RE GETTING THERE... WE'RE REALLY HAULING!

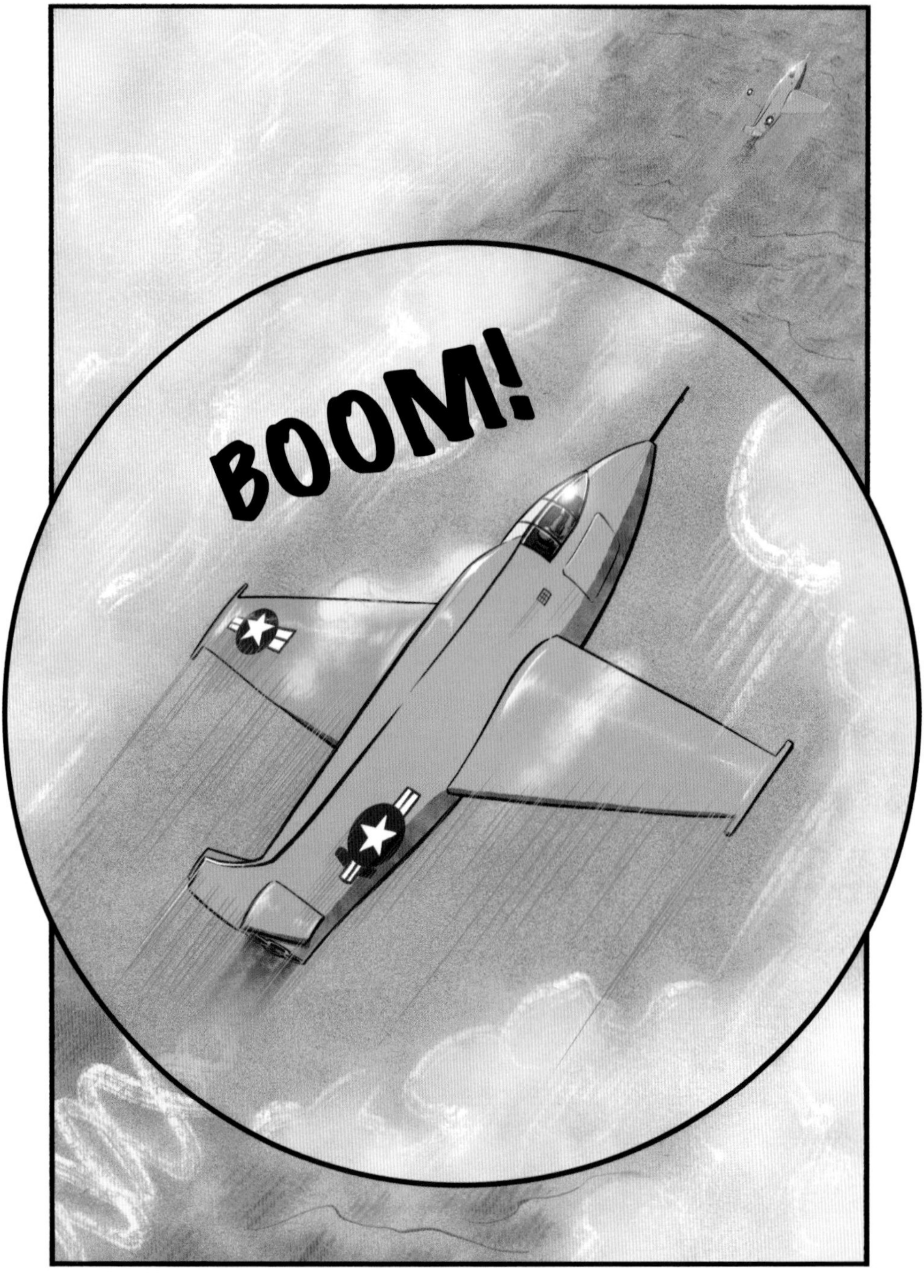
BOOM!

CHUCK FIRST BROKE THE SOUND BARRIER IN HIS BELL X-1 PLANE ON OCTOBER 14, 1947, AT AGE 24. HE FLEW 46,000 FEET ABOVE THE MOJAVE DESERT, CALIFORNIA, REACHING SPEEDS OF UP TO 800 MILES PER HOUR.

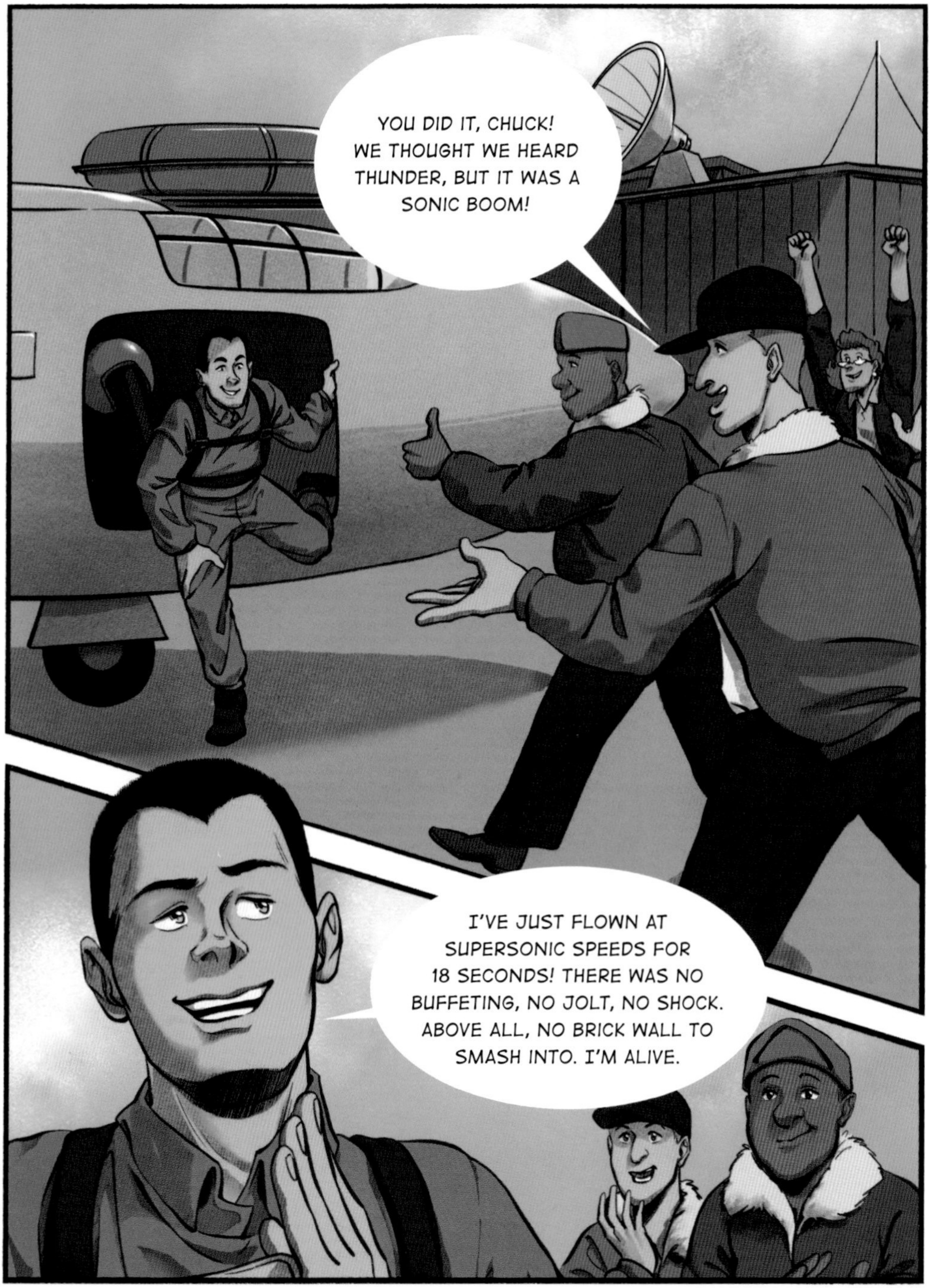
YOU DID IT, CHUCK! WE THOUGHT WE HEARD THUNDER, BUT IT WAS A SONIC BOOM!
I'VE JUST FLOWN AT SUPERSONIC SPEEDS FOR 18 SECONDS! THERE WAS NO BUFFETING, NO JOLT, NO SHOCK. ABOVE ALL, NO BRICK WALL TO SMASH INTO. I'M ALIVE.

BY GOING SUPERSONIC, CHUCK PROVED THAT HUMANS COULD CONTINUE TO BREAK RECORDS AND PUSH THE LIMITS OF FLIGHT.

INDEX